The Future
of Consumerism

The Future of Consumerism

Edited by
Paul N. Bloom
University of North Carolina

Ruth Belk Smith
University of Baltimore

Lexington Books
D.C. Heath and Company/Lexington, Massachusetts/Toronto

Library of Congress Cataloging-in-Publication Data
Main entry under title:

The Future of consumerism.

Includes index.
1. Consumers—United States—Addresses, essays, lectures. 2. Consumers—Addresses, essays, lectures.
I. Bloom, Paul N. II. Smith, Ruth Belk.
HC110.C6F87   1986   381'.3'0973   84-48450
ISBN 0-669-09428-5 (alk. paper)

Published simultaneously in Canada
Printed in the United States of America
International Standard Book Number: 0-669-09428-5
Library of Congress Catalog Card Number: 84-48450

The paper used in this publication meets the minimum requirements of American National Standard for Information Sciences—Permanence of Paper for Printed Library Materials, ANSI Z39.48-1984. ∞™

The last numbers on the right below indicate the number and date of printing.

10   9   8   7   6   5   4   3

95   94   93   92

Contents

Figures and Tables

Figures

Tables

Preface

The activities and accomplishments of the consumer movement do not receive nearly as much media coverage as they did a decade ago. Consumerism is no longer a major focal point of public interest and debate, and the movement has evolved into a quieter phase. But consumerism has not died. Considerable amounts of energy and resources are still being devoted to obtaining better deals for consumers in the marketplace. Many consumer organizations are as financially healthy as they have ever been, and they are waging spirited fights for more government consumer protection and more socially responsive behavior by major corporations. Consumerism lives—although not as visibly as it did in the recent past.

What does the future hold for consumerism? Will it slowly fade away because of lack of interest, or will it experience a huge resurgence of activity and publicity? What consumer issues are likely to come to the forefront of public discussion? How can consumer organizations and corporate consumer affairs offices function most effectively in a rapidly changing sociopolitical environment? These and other related questions are addressed in this volume by a highly diverse group of authors who provide readers with richer insights into what might happen to consumerism. Marketers, consumer psychologists, sociologists, consumer economists, lawyers, consumer affairs professionals, business and society experts, and consumer advocates present their views in these pages.

This volume grew out of a conference that took place in April 1982 at the Wye Plantation in Queenstown, Maryland. Titled the "Consumerism and Beyond" workshop, this three-day event brought together over sixty well-known observers of consumerism for an exciting set of sessions devoted to evaluating the movement's future prospects. The papers in this volume are updated versions (in 1985) of many of the ideas originally presented at this conference. Unfortunately, space limitations prevented us from including contributions from all those who participated in the conference.

We obviously feel considerable gratitude toward the authors who generously contributed to this volume. We would also like to thank Chesebrough-Pond's, Inc. for sponsoring the conference, and the Marketing Science Institute and the University of Maryland's Center for Business and Public Policy for serving as presenters of the conference. Among the many nonauthors who deserve mention for helping this project come together, we would like to thank Alden Clayton (Marketing Science Institute), Stephen A. Greyser (Harvard Business School), Kenneth Lightcap (Chesebrough-Pond's), Grace Richardson (Chesebrough-Pond's), Christine Gram (Chesebrough-Pond's), and Mary Lou Matovich (University of Maryland). Finally, we would like to thank Caroline McCarley from Lexington Books for encouraging us to put this volume together.

Introduction

Paul N. Bloom
Ruth Belk Smith.

The future of consumerism is of great relevance to consumer advocates, public policymakers, consumer affairs professionals, business managers, educators, and, of course, to individual consumers. This volume was put together to provide these people with an improved ability to understand and interpret where consumerism is headed. Many provocative and insightful predictions are offered by a distinguished group of experts.

The contributors to this volume were sought out because of their well-recognized expertise in the areas in which they write. Consumerism has become such a fragmented and wide-ranging movement that it was necessary to draw on the thinking of a varied group of experts to obtain an accurate picture of where the movement stands today and what it might become tomorrow. In spite of the diverse backgrounds of the authors—and in spite of the diversity of the movement itself—there seem to be some persistent themes running through the papers. Our reading of the papers sees the authors converging on the following notions:

1. Consumerism will endure, despite a variety of threats to its survival.

2. Better management of consumer organizations has been and will be a key ingredient in maintaining the vitality of the movement.

3. There is a shifting constituency for consumer organizations, and more support is likely to come from elderly, disadvantaged, and community-oriented consumers.

4. Consumerism faces shifting issues, and more debate is likely to occur over:
   a. how to make necessities more affordable.
   b. how to introduce new technologies in a fair, efficient, and usable manner.

   c. how to make big institutions more responsive to the needs of society.

   d. how to avoid consumer problems for Third World citizens.

5. More creative corporate responses are needed, because old ways of managing consumer affairs and corporate responsibility programs will become less effective.

We elaborate on these themes in the following paragraphs. For convenience, we only provide citations for works that do not appear in this volume.

Consumerism Will Endure

Several of the papers warn about consumerism's future prospects. For example, Gaski and Etzel point out that public attitudes toward business have grown more positive in recent years. And Warland, Herrmann, and Moore suggest that relatively few people can be characterized as consumer activists. The consumer movement has apparently not been able to sustain the fervor and commitment that Mitchell sees in the environmental movement. But in spite of these ominous signs, the consensus seems to be that consumerism will remain an important force in our society.

As Metzen puts it, "consumerism has become an element of our social fabric and is engrained in our national consciousness." Both he and Richardson stress how the movement has learned to adapt to rapidly changing political, social, and economic conditions. They predict that conditions like the "malarial economy" ("plagued by recurring fevers of inflation and chills of recession", as Metzen describes it) will create continued discontent and support for consumerism among substantial segments of the population.

Evidence that consumer discontent still runs high can be found in the Smith and Bloom paper. In fact, even Gaski and Etzel suggest that consumer attitudes toward business are, on average, slightly unfavorable—although they have improved in recent years. Moreover, Warland, Herrmann, and Moore see a possibility that a substantial group of "complete" community activists, who have focused their attention on nonconsumer community issues, could be mobilized in vocal support of consumer causes during serious crises.

Having consumer discontent and general support for consumerism is one thing; channeling these feelings into actions that will create better deals for consumers is another. The consumer movement is endowed with a huge assortment of organizations that claim to offer ways to channel consumer discontent into meaningful marketplace reforms. Many of these organizations have become much more effective at accomplishing their missions.

Better Management

The need to overcome the free-rider problem plagues most social movement organizations, and according to Mitchell, this is a substantial obstacle to the consumer movement. It is easy for consumers to accept safer products, lower prices, or other benefits won by a consumer organization without providing any support to the organization. In an earlier article, Bloom and Greyser (1981) foresaw that the free-rider problem would push consumer organizations toward more specialization and more emphasis on local issues. Consumers might be more inclined to pay their way if they could see an organization fighting for specific issues that had immediate relevance to them. This thinking has apparently taken hold in the consumer movement during the last few years, and much of the activity of the movement has been in local and/or highly specialized organizations. This phenomenon is discussed in the papers by Metzen, Richardson, Preston and Bloom, and Smith and Bloom.

Smith and Bloom also report evidence of the increased membership and financial strength of local organizations. Their findings are consistent with data supplied by Stephen Brobeck (1984), executive director of the Consumer Federation of America, who identified 393 state or local consumer organizations, sixty percent of which had been active for eight years or more. Brobeck also states that more than a dozen single-issue (e.g., nutrition) national organizations have successfully emerged in recent years.

It appears that the relaxation of federal regulation in recent years has forced consumer leaders to become better marketers and managers. They have employed a variety of strategies to keep their groups healthy, including what Richardson labels as three "essential ingredients for survival": media access, salable ideas, and believability as a consumer spokesperson. Consumer leaders are appealing to new, growing constituencies and stressing new issues.

A Shifting Constituency

Several of the authors stress that support for consumerism is less likely to come from middle-class, middle-aged consumers—as it often has in the past—and is more likely to come from the elderly, the disadvantaged, and the community-minded. Smith cites compelling statistics on the growth of the elderly segment, and predicts that the elderly will become increasingly concerned and vocal about their marketplace difficulties. Metzen also sees the elderly becoming prime constituents of consumerism, along with younger people undergoing financial hardships and declining expectations (as compared to their parents). This segment would include single mothers, minorities, and others whose disadvantaged situations are discussed by Andreasen. Many of these people, as Warland, Herrmann, and Moore point out, have been active in community politics and could naturally move into consumer activism.

Much of consumerism's future constituency could be categorized by the "rich/poor" label suggested by Preston and Bloom. These authors believe that an increasing proportion of the U.S. population feels rich and poor at the same time. People are able to buy luxuries they never dreamed of a few years ago—like headphone stereos and trips to glamorous casinos in Atlantic City—for relatively small amounts of money; yet necessities like food, housing, utilities, and health care are strapping them seriously. Preston and Bloom anticipate that attempts to serve this constituency will lead consumer leaders to stress a very different set of issues than they have in the past.

Shifting Issues

Preston and Bloom suggest that feeling rich and poor at the same time will make consumers concerned with "abundance" issues (e.g., how to allocate new technologies fairly) and "scarcity" issues (e.g., how to lower health care costs). These authors also foresee that "process" issues (e.g., how to deregulate) and "public service" issues (e.g., how to keep government monopolies fair) will become more prominent. According to Preston and Bloom, these issues could potentially replace the old, traditional agenda that came out of President Kennedy's consumers' rights speech (i.e., the rights to safety, to be informed, to be heard, and to choose).

The following categorization of future issues differs somewhat from Preston and Bloom's, but it is not inconsistent with theirs. The contributions of all the authors in the volume are reflected in this framework.

Necessities

With an aging constituency that feels more hard-pressed economically, it would be natural for consumer organizations to stress pocketbook issues. The formation of several state-level "citizen utility boards" and the emphasis many organizations are placing on telephone charges, bank charges, health care costs, energy costs, and nutrition indicates that pressure for a better deal on necessities has already materialized. This pressure can be expected to continue in the long-term, especially on the local level. Besides citizen utility boards, Metzen sees the possibility that the number of buying cooperatives, designed to help members obtain necessities for less money, will increase substantially.

But Metzen also warns against overemphasizing the attainment of short-term, pocketbook benefits for consumers. He feels that the resource needs of our society in the long run must not be overlooked and that a degree of sacrifice should be advocated by consumerists.

New Technologies

The implications for consumers of new technologies like videotext, computer shopping and banking, and cellular telephones will clearly be matters of considerable discussion. The papers by Harding and Jones review the various arguments over issues such as: Who should collect the consumer information to be stored in consumer data banks? Who should pay for it? Will only the rich be able to use it? What information display formats are most effective? Can privacy be guaranteed for users?

Big Institutions

Concern about how big institutions will treat consumers was expressed by several of the authors. For example, Enis and Yarwood discuss how government agencies often provide consumers with bad deals in the form of unsafe surplus jeeps, unsanitary public health facilities, or lottery tickets. Metzen, Fernstrom, and others express concern about how large corporations will exhibit social responsibility, particularly as huge mergers create larger and fewer companies. Although calls for actions to make big institutions more responsible (e.g., consumer representation on boards) may not occur as frequently as they have in the past, it seems likely that they will persist in the future.

Consumer Problems of Third World Citizens

The papers by Post and by Peterson stress how consumerism is gaining strength in developing nations. Multinational corporations must now be much more conscious of the health and economic consequences of their actions. Codes of conduct from bodies like the World Health Organization and the United Nations are becoming serious matters for firms to consider. As Post discusses, failure to adopt the code for marketing infant formula created considerable difficulty for Nestlé, and he sees similar problems emerging for marketers of other controversial products (e.g., cigarettes, alcohol) if firms are not careful.

More Creative Corporate Responses

Several of the papers emphasize how the business community will need to adapt to a changing consumer movement. The paper by Bloom is specifically addressed to heads of consumer affairs departments in corporations. It suggests several strategies that these people could use to improve their relationships with consumers, consumer groups, and top management. Fernstrom's paper looks at broader programs for corporate social responsibility. She presents several interesting examples of successful programs.

Organization of the Volume

The papers are divided into four parts. Part I contains papers that essentially provide broad overviews on where consumerism is headed. This is followed by a part containing papers that present empirical evidence that can be used to evaluate consumerism's health. Part III includes papers that focus on either specific constituencies or specific issues. Finally, part IV provides ideas on how business can respond most effectively to consumerism.

References

Bloom, Paul N., and Stephen A. Greyser. 1981. The maturing of consumerism. *Harvard Business Review* 59(Nov.–Dec.):130–139.
Brobeck, Stephen. 1984. The consumer movement: An assessment. *At Home with Consumers* (Dec.):2–9.

Part I
Perspectives on the Movement

1
Consumerism in the Evolving Future

Edward J. Metzen

C onsumerism has become an element of our social fabric and is engrained in our national consciousness. It seems safe to predict that it will have significant implications for consumers, producers, marketers, and government—irrespective of the direction of particular developments. The balance of efforts to improve the well-being of consumers will undoubtedly change as the future unfolds, as will other conditions in our society; such changes will, in turn, help to shape future social conditions. Economic conditions, institutional structures and policies, demographic factors, and orientations toward lifestyles and the quality of life will all affect consumer behavior and the nature of consumerism in the future. The consumer movement will adapt, will move in directions that people perceive to have the best chance of paying off under particular conditions.

It will be in the best interests of society for consumerism to be as effective as possible, for the resources allocated to improving the conditions of consumers and their environments to obtain maximum benefits; the long-run interests of consumers are consonant with the long-run interests of society. Specifically what will maximize the well-being of consumers over time may be difficult to determine, but surely the principle prevails, even though other interests may challenge it. Adam Smith (1887), in his treatise that provided the blueprint for a competitive market economy, put the matter clearly: "Consumption is the sole end and purpose of all production; and the interest of the producer ought to be attended to, only so far as it may be necessary for promoting that of the consumer. The maxim is so perfectly self-evident, that it would be absurd to attempt to prove it." But he went on to point out that, "In the mercantile system, the interest of the consumer is almost constantly sacrificed to that of the producer; and it seems to consider production, and not consumption, as the ultimate end and object of all industry and commerce." Unfortunately, many people and many elements of our social and economic policies adhere to the latter orientation today, more than two centuries after Smith, and after volumes of rhetoric about the consumer as king in our ostensibly market-oriented economic system.

What conditions will the future hold for consumers, and what will be the consumer response? The answers to those questions are very important to the economy and to society.

A Malarial Economy

Ours has become a malarial economy—plagued by recurring fevers of inflation and chills of recession. We seem hard pressed to achieve inflation accompanied by prosperity or recession accompanied by stable prices; we seem instead in conditions and policies that provide us all too regularly with only the drawbacks of inflation and recession. Such economic conditions—and the policies intended to achieve cures—create economic pressure, uncertainty, and often disaster for individuals and families. The greatest absolute hardship often falls on the poorest and most vulnerable people in society, and the greatest relative pressures affect many in the middle class who have extended themselves to the limit in an effort to achieve the material lifestyle envisioned in the American dream. A combination of inflation and recession creates vulnerability for all but the most economically powerful and secure.

The rampant inflation of the late 1970s was reduced in part by policies that created the worst recession since the Great Depression of the 1930s. This recession resulted in high levels of unemployment, a high incidence of bankruptcy among small businesses and households, and an increase in poverty to 1960s' levels. Major factors in reducing inflation were bountiful harvests and a sudden glut of oil on world markets. The economic recovery of 1983–1984, fueled by tax reduction and massive deficit spending by the federal government, has been unequally shared. Maldistribution of income and wealth has increased, the incidence of poverty remains high, social services have been reduced, and levels of inflation and unemployment that would once have been regarded as totally unacceptable have come to be considered as substantial accomplishments. The resulting gigantic federal deficit threatens to ignite a burst of inflation or to trigger policies that will lead to another serious recession. Farm families in rural America are already experiencing a financial crisis, resulting largely from monetary and tax policies. The climate is marked with uncertainty and anxiety.

There is ample reason to project that the economy will continue to suffer. The increasing pressures on the world's natural resources, combined with the large amount of market power employed by giant corporations and the natural reluctance of private investors to risk capital unless there will be a high potential rate of return on investment, combine as an excellent prescription for stagflation. And the tendency, in a private enterprise economy, to provide tax breaks and subsidies to private investors in efforts to induce investments, potentially subsidizes inefficiency, distorts markets, and creates a maldistribution of income. This income inequality is questionable from an equity standpoint, inadequate to sustain a smoothly functioning economy, and provides an increasingly fertile seedbed for social unrest.

Toward a Declining Material Level of Living?

The halcyon days when it seemed reasonable to project continued real economic growth as traditionally measured—economic stability with relatively full employment and stable prices—are apparently behind us. Of course, the growth period was never as glorious as we thought it was. Treating nonrenewable resources as though they were perpetual, relegating the environment to a giant cesspool to absorb the pollution from both industrial production and consumption, and skimping on worker and consumer health and safety are all ways to reduce the dollar costs of production of market goods and services. But these practices do violence to the quality of our lives, they fail to reflect the true economic costs of our present material well-being, and they stockpile conditions that must inevitably result in resource scarcities, increased economic costs, and upward pressure on real prices in the future. Add to this scenario the growing pressure on the world's resources from the developing and underdeveloped countries, and the implications for our society are substantial. We may very well be rounding the turn toward a revolution characterized by declining expectations. Some elements of this revolution are already in place. Most noteworthy among them is the fact that many young people are giving up on the American dream of owning their own home, and those who can buy a home are setting their sights lower than the spacious suburban ranch-style house that was once regarded almost as a right of any hardworking American. Some toning down of aspirations for material goods seems healthy, given the economic conditions projected here, because it is essential to avoid excessive discordance between people's aspirations and possibilities. We are witness to the first generation of Americans whose material lives may not be better than those of their parents.

While per capita real income rose during the 1970s, median real household income was the same in 1980 as in 1970—despite the increase in the number of multiple-earner households. And incomes were further depressed in 1981–1982, before regaining sound ground in 1983–1984. Given the increased number of single-parent and single-person households, and the number of households with two working spouses, the opportunities for increasing real household incomes in the face of rising prices have been largely exhausted. And the prospect of increasing real hourly wage rages as a formula for increasing incomes does not seem to hold much hope in the period ahead. Thus, conditions suggest a need for belt-tightening by American households. Living as a single parent or as a single-person household may contribute to the quality of the individual's life in his or her terms. However, such choices mean foregoing the economies of scale inherent in multiple person households; per capita income gains are absorbed and household incomes come under increased pressure.

The Marketplace Increases Economic Uncertainty for Consumers

At the same time that general economic conditions have been pressing consumers, the marketplace has been devising strategies for shifting more of the burden of economic uncertainty from financial institutions to consumers. Examples of this shift are the development of variable rate mortgages and creative financing of homes which contribute to mortgage foreclosures and bankruptcies among buyers who hoped that inflationary gains in house prices would absolve them from their highly vulnerable, leveraged positions), and the current advent of variable finance charges on credit card obligations for consumer purchases. Thus, both economic conditions and financial arrangements increasingly create an environment of uncertainty for consumers. Uncertainty tends to result in cautious behavior; and given the degree to which our economic system hinges upon the behavior of consumers, such a development has substantial implications. The ready optimism that accompanies predictions of unceasing economic growth has faded, and for good reason. To the extent that sophisticated mass promotion of market goods and services entices consumers and stimulates their material aspirations, there will be intensified frustrations and increased likelihood that households will get into financial difficulty.

Consumer Response to Projected Conditions

Toward Increased Consumer Effectiveness in the Marketplace

Irrespective of the exact details of future conditions, their general direction, combined with current trends in consumer orientation, provide a basis for predicting that consumers will be more insistent upon quality, will seek functional value from purchases, will keep and use things longer, and will be increasingly conscious of repair and operating costs of purchases. Consumers are likely to be more sophisticated in their purchasing behavior, making better use of available information and making more deliberate purchasing decisions. Consumers will probably be more insistent on receiving satisfaction

for their expenditures, and more willing to take necessary steps to attain satisfaction if it is not readily forthcoming. The rights of consumers have been
engrained to a substantial degree in people's expectations. In addition, the
pressure people feel on their time and other resources makes them impatient
with spending hours seeking redress of grievances, so the future is likely to
witness consumers who increasingly insist upon quality of goods and services,
and upon satisfaction with each transaction without follow-up effort.

Consumers who require quality and satisfaction from purchases will increasingly insist that the market environment provide them with the tools for
making efficient consumption decisions, rather than forcing them to rely on
guesswork or the enticements and assurances of the product/service promotion fraternity. Improved consumer information on goods and services will
be demanded; consumers will push for conditions in which they can act more
like the textbook version of the perfectly rational, informed consumer—that
heroic myth upon which the effective functioning of a market economy
depends.

Along with increased insistence upon firm bases for decision making, and
upon satisfaction with purchases, it is likely that the future will witness no
abatement in the willingness—perhaps even eagerness—of consumers to
bring product liability suits as a result of injury from faulty products. In an
era of liberally strewn superlatives about even the most innocuous products,
and of prices implying good reason to expect satisfaction, consumers will
surely be impatient, resentful, and demanding in cases where anticipated satisfaction becomes injury.

There is also likely to be increased emphasis on consumer education,
through formal programs in the schools—with more parental support, as the
need to be an effective consumer is more clearly recognized—and through
adult education programs via university extension, local consumer groups,
and mass media. And as people cope with constraints on attaining "the good
life" and become more aware of economic problems and the limitations of
policies to solve those problems, there will be increasing disenchantment with
educational programs and materials that purport to serve the interests of consumers but that too often serve as thinly veiled propaganda for vested interests, or as a facade for commercialism under the guise of education.

Toward Local Organization Activity

Consumers will be more likely to respond to problems in the local marketplace through local organizations, many of which will probably address a
narrow range of concerns. Large, national, multi-issue consumer organizations may have more difficulty attracting and retaining members, a challenge

that is common to all large organizations during times of economic malaise. This development would have unfortunate aspects, because the national consumer organizations have done much to promote and support consumer interests, and will continue to have an essential role, particularly in affecting national legislation and policy. On the other hand, if more groups and leaders are vying for the support of consumers, perhaps they will also serve consumers more effectively, in selected domains and with more specific results.

Consumers may also seek purchasing economies by forming cooperatives and buying clubs, and perhaps by multiple-household ownership of expensive goods that are infrequently used.

Impact of Demographic Factors

Among demographic factors that will affect consumer markets and consumerism are changes in household composition, which will lead to greater diversity in lifestyles and consumer needs, and the projected growth of the elderly population. The greater number of elderly consumers will not only mean an increased need for certain types of goods and services, but will also result in a force of more experienced consumers, people less likely to be swayed by sales pitches and glamorous appeals, people likely to be more conservative in their spending habits and willing to insist upon full returns for their dollars. And while they will influence market conditions as individual consumers, the elderly will also be a prime population for active involvement in consumer organizations and collective efforts to achieve reforms in the marketplace.

As the average household size declines and the size of household living units shrinks, each household will contain fewer things than has been the case. On the other hand, because each household is likely to have a basic stock of certain things—selected appliances, for example—may become more goods-intensive per person. Two factors that might affect this situation could be a trend toward shared ownership of housing and certain consumer goods by multiple household units, or an increase in the incidence of extended families, as a result of young people's inability to afford satisfactory living arrangements and of the enormous cost of maintaining the ever-increasing elderly population in independent quarters or special care facilities.

Either or both developments, while creating costs in terms of privacy and independence, provide economies of scale and the potential for sharing not only financial costs, but tasks as well—an economic consideration of substantial consequence. In my view, one of the more interesting developments in the future will be the price—in terms of both dollar costs and loss of economies from shared effort—that people in this society will be willing to pay for the niceties of privacy and independence. Economic realities may force us to change our orientations and preferences—or at least to compromise them.

Toward Decreased Reliance on Commercial Markets?

The future is likely to witness more reliance on household production (production within the home), inter- and intra-family grants and assistance, and a search for satisfaction that does not come from consumer goods and services. There are several reasons for predicting this. If market goods and services are increasingly costly to attain, people may quite logically turn more of their attention elsewhere in the search for an improved quality of life. Indeed, as people become increasingly satiated with consumer goods, it is reasonable to speculate that some change of this type is inevitable. Surely the harried lifestyles of so many people and increasing social maladies provide cause for questioning whether the good life lies in the quest for an ever-higher material level of living, or whether diverting of some time and energy to introspection, leisure, interpersonal relationships, and creative nonmarket endeavors would contribute more to self-fulfillment and satisfaction.

Along this same vein, financial pressure on households tends to result in personal and interpersonal stress, which in turn may be reflected in the breakdown of personal relationships, divorce, spouse- and child-beating, depression, drug and alcohol use, suicide and homicide, desertion of spouse and children, and antisocial behavior directed at the larger society. Stress that results in the deterioration of family relationships and functioning creates conflict in the aspect of life that research has consistently shown to be most important to people. If human behavior is basically rational, then people may be expected to reduce the stress that is causing family problems by eliminating the factors that cause the stress. To the extent that they perceive the stress as a result of their pursuit of market goods and services, they may be expected to become less enthusiastic about the pursuit of the "good life"; and more cautious about extending themselves to earn money, and more reluctant to put themselves in a vulnerable financial position through the acquisition of market goods and services. Additionally, people may recognize and increasingly appreciate the satisfaction that comes from their own creativity in household production and the intrinsic qualities of home-produced products—the human interactions and values expressed in their production that cannot be purchased in the market at any price.

Another possibility is whether, as energy and other resources become more scarce and high-priced and as the real earned incomes are squeezed, the market might lose enough of its advantage over the household as a production unit (by virtue of specialization and economies of scale) to cause some shift from market to household production. As with other tools, the market must have some advantage over its alternatives if it is to be used; if people perceive, when all factors are taken into account, that the market has lost some of its relative advantage for them, we may well witness a future shift to more home production. A step in this direction, in the form of an increase in organizations like cooperatives that share the production and distribution of goods and services, can be predicted with some assurance in the economic climate that is projected in this paper.

It seems likely, too, that when the current wave of antigovernment and antitax sentiment is over, an assessment of social needs and the best means for satisfying them may well lead citizens to renew demands for the services provided by the public sector. Certainly, in the long term, the public is not going to forgo adequate education, health care, police and fire protection, and other essential and highly desirable services, and opt instead for more baubles, bangles, and beads from private markets.

None of this is meant to suggest that markets in the traditional sense are going to dry up; only that, on balance, the significance of market activity is likely to be somewhat less in the future than a linear projection of the past might suggest. Beyond that, it seems likely that within the market sector there will be relatively less emphasis on the quest for goods, and relatively more on services, as consumers become increasingly satiated with goods and begin to search for alternatives that will make life both manageable and interesting.

Increased Focus on Incomes and Public Policies

Irrespective of the details of economic developments, consumerism will have to compete for people's attention as their restiveness increases over their decreasing incomes. Consumer issues have commanded a substantial amount of the spotlight in recent decades because many of the issues have a direct, visible impact on people. Consumer issues are understandable; some are matters over which people feel they can have a degree of direct control—and incomes were rising. As the economy has faltered, as incomes have failed to make their anticipated smooth journeys to new heights, and as income-earning opportunities have been eroded, people's attention has naturally been drawn to their incomes.

Attention will not be focused on local job markets and pay scales alone. People are becoming increasingly aware of the fact that in the modern United States it is not the "invisible hand" of Adam Smith, but the visible hands of the President, the Chairman of the Federal Reserve Board, the special-interest-serving legislators, the legislation-buying lobbyists, and the members of corporate boards that to a large extent control economic destiny. Increasingly, citizens are demanding greater equity in income distribution; a voice in the policies and performance of corporations, particularly as relates to job security; and reform of the tax system, which is pockmarked with so many loopholes and so much favoritism toward special interests that nominal rates are a mockery. Otherwise honest citizens are increasingly taking to the underground economy in an effort to create what they perceive to be the equity of establishing their own tax shelters.

I project that public concern over the tax system will lead to a reform movement that will command at least as much public attention and support as consumerism had during the past two decades. And I fully expect that unless corporate management and organized labor can establish a continuing accord that helps reduce inflation, the clamor that will arise for a national income policy will make the battle over truth in packaging seem like a Sunday school picnic. Yet such matters will not relegate more traditional consumer concerns to the back burner; the latter have become too deeply embedded in the American consciousness to slip out of sight and mind.

Consumers and consumer organizations are casting skeptical glances not only at slack-filled packages and the hollow superlatives of advertising messages, but also at:

policies that preserve and nurture market power;

trade barriers, subsidies, and market regulations that result in higher prices, higher taxes, or both;

the impact on government policy of political action committees and lobbyists for economically powerful special interests, who benefit from regulations that give deductions to lobby organizations, but not to individual consumers for similar actions;

the mix of economic conditions, government policy, and business behavior that regularly confronts the nation with grinding inflation (except when we are in the grips of a wrenching recession) and with the attendant waste of productive resources, unemployment, and underemployment.

Can anyone doubt that pressure for national policies to mitigate these circumstances will increase as long as such conditions continue to prevail and recur, or that the public will grow increasingly impatient with the rhetoric of deregulation, trickle-down economic policies, and the increased maldistribution of income and opportunity? Surely a civilized society expects its government to do more than to sit idly while unbridled economic forces work their effects on the powerful and the weak alike. And, at a minimum, citizens should expect their government not to aid and abet the cause and the condition of the already powerful. Societies function with policies and conditions that are established by someone; they affect everyone. Surely citizens in a supposedly democratic society will increasingly insist that the representatives of all the people will take responsibility for establishing policies and conditions that will benefit all the people equitably. While economic conditions are likely to make consumers increasingly concerned about matters that affect their pocketbooks directly, concern for the environment, for consumer and worker safety, and for the broader factors that influence consumer interests—

such as market structure and economic policy—is not likely to recede from their consciousnesses. Rather, it seems that the public has become somewhat more sophisticated and sensitive to these matters, and that a much higher degree of concern is likely to exist in the future as a matter of course.

The Dilemma of Present–Future Trade-Offs

A development of particular importance will be the degree to which consumers will be willing to trade off some immediate satisfaction of their wants, comfort, and convenience in the interests of preserving resources and the environment for the benefit of future generations and their needs. This issue is the potential Achilles' heel of the consumer movement—the one instance in which the current interests of people as consumers do not coincide with the long-run interests of society as a whole. The stimulus for this conflict is the same one that causes producers to create—but not cover—social costs in the form of environmental degradation and to use up nonrenewable resources if those practices increase profits above what they would be with a conservation strategy. Keeping the long-term future in mind when making decisions, whether privately or in the market, is difficult at best. Given the uncertainties of the future, the fact that pleasures forgone today may or may not accrue to the benefit of someone in the future, people tend to follow the impulse to maximize present benefits. When it comes to the pursuit of our interests, mankind finds it easy to respond in keeping with Keynes' reminder that "in the long run we are all dead." The tendency is compounded enormously in a society in which the marketing community has done its best to inculcate a materialistic philosophy as the only way to live, in which the future is discounted at a very high rate, and in which the economy requires a high level of consumption to provide the rates of return essential to create and use private economic capital.

I have written elsewhere that, "Perhaps the fundamental responsibility of each generation in the long history of mankind is to conduct its affairs in a manner which will assure that that generation is prologue to the future, not epilogue to the past" (Metzen 1976). It is time that we become sophisticatd enough to see that it will be to the long-run benefit of mankind if people can attain a high degree of personal satisfaction while using resources efficiently in both production and consumption. There do seem to be signs that conservation of nonrenewable resources is becoming an element in the national consciousness, along with maintaining a wholesome and aesthetically appealing environment. Whether people in a consumption-oriented society can bring themselves to whole-heartedly adopt that consciousness is a significant question for the future. If people do—whether as a response to crunching economic pressure or out of a sense of responsibility to future generations—there will be important implications for production, marketing, and economic policy. These elements of society too, will need to be oriented toward the long-run good of the society, rather than toward maximizing current benefits to the private industrial and commercial sectors of our economy.

Consumer Response Under a More Favorable Economic Scenario

At least some of the preceding projections are based on the expectation that the U.S. economy will not produce strong, regular gains in real income for Americans in the period ahead—rather, that substantial stagflation will plague us regularly, and that, at best, gains in real income will be modest, if there are any at all. But suppose that we experience technological breakthroughs that resolve some of our real economic problems, and that we develop policies that enable the economy to prosper, with growth and stability; what will be the face of consumerism under those conditions? There will probably be less intense focus on consumer issues and problems, less effort devoted to "making do" activities, less involvement in local consumer groups, somewhat casual support for consumer interests through nominal membership in national consumer organizations. But the basic public sensitivity to consumer interests that flowered during a period of increasing material prosperity will not wither in a healthy economic climate.

If material abundance in the marketplace is achieved, not by fundamental improvements in our production processes, but by continuing to pollute the environment, waste nonrenewable natural resources, despoil our natural heritage, and harm the health and safety of consumers and workers, then consumerists, along with environmentalists, conservationists, and organized labor will burst forth with renewed vigor onto the national scene. If these several interests act in concert, with a balance of shared objectives, they can do much to foster optimum outcomes from our economic system and to weave a strong social fabric. If these movements are played off against each other in order to render them impotent, to the extent that such efforts are successful, the social fabric will be rent and the result will be an unhealthy climate in which neither business—nor government—can expect to flourish or function effectively.

In any event, the interests of American corporations will not be left unchallenged: consumers, workers, and the public have come to view themselves—along with stockholders—as stakeholders in the productive enterprise of the United States. The producers and sellers of goods and services will increasingly be held accountable to that balance of stakeholders.

Business Response: Projection and Recommendation

Past experience suggests that, as consumer issues arise, the short-run response of business is likely to be somewhat negligent, even hostile, somewhat insensitive to fundamental consumer interests. This is particularly likely to be the case as long as the current government's philosophy prevails, with its pro-wealthy, trickle-down, ostensibly pro-business economic policies, its relative disregard for the interests of consumers and workers, and its relative insensitivity to the social and real economic costs of our industrial activity. But in the longer run, a more responsive attitude toward consumer interests—and toward the long-term well-being of the society—must prevail. The gains that have been made in business awareness of, and responsiveness to, consumer concerns and welfare will not—must not—be lost. Maintaining a healthy climate for consumer interests will benefit business in the long run, as well; in the long run our economic system will function effectively—and therefore somewhat preserve its present form—only if the consuming public is reasonably well served. And people's standards for being well served are rising. So it would behoove the business community to remember that the end purpose of economic activity is to satisfy the needs and wants of consumers, not to create profit; the latter is the means for encouraging efficient, innovative production and distribution—the carrot luring the donkey into pulling the cart—but not an end from a *social* point of view. It is time for the business community to put aside the vision-obscuring slogan that "the business of business is to make profits" and to recognize that from society's standpoint a more appropriate statement is that "the business of profits is to stimulate business into performing as effectively as possible." To consumers, profits are just another cost, and they will continue to be increasingly insistent upon getting their money's worth. This is a legitimate posture, one that is consonant with—indeed, essential to—the best interests of our economic system. Business needs to recognize consumers' interests as the bottom line, rather than trying to win hearts and minds with public relations gimmicks, apologies for high prices and poor quality of services, polemics aimed at conscientious critics, and glowing praise for "our system." No amount of so-called free enterprise education, currently so heavily promoted by the business community, will provide an effective facade for enterprise's failure to serve people effectively, or for behavior that is the antithesis of a true competitive market system. Consumers are becoming too skeptical and sophisticated to focus on posturing rather than results, on rhetoric rather than reality.

The business community would do well also to adopt a reasonable, public interest response to legislation and regulations designed to assure consumer rights. Such an admonition is likely to fall on relatively deaf ears in the current climate, and in the short-term future. But in the long run, conditions in the marketplace must be consonant with the true purpose of economic activity. Business postures that frustrate legitimate consumer expectations will be met with increasing hostility and will erode confidence in the ability of our economic institutions to serve society effectively.

Conclusion

Consumerism has a long way to go before it comes into full fruition. When it does, it will have fostered a marketplace that functions effectively, government policies that are responsive to the needs of all citizens and to the long-term future of our society, and equity between and among producers and consumers, and will thereby have enriched the human condition.

References

Metzen, Edward J. 1976. *Family Life Styles and Resources for the Future.* 1st Annual North Carolina Family Living Seminar, North Carolina State University, p. 16.
Smith, Adam. 1887. *An Inquiry into the Nature and Causes of the Wealth of Nations.* (3rd ed. London: George Bell and Sons.) II:177.

2
The Evolving Consumer Movement: Predictions for the 1990s

Stewart Lee Richardson, Jr.

T he consumer movement is a creature of its environment. It has flourished under the right conditions, yet it has been nearly invisible when out of vogue. Its current structure and recent history show again that its effectiveness and strength are beyond its own control.

Ask a consumerist to predict the future of consumerism and you will get an optimistic forecast. Of course, the movement's opponents are equally likely to predict a shipwreck to end its journey through the seas of recent American political history.

Clearly, the late 1970s were a time when the consumer movement began to decline in influence, particularly at the national level. The consumer leadership and the movement in general were more prominent and influential than in the previous several decades. Forces were turning the tide against it, however, in a manner that should dispel the notion that the movement's leaders shape its form.

The Carter administration's inaction contributed to the decline of the national consumer movement. The Carter White House could not pass legislation to create any structure or agency lasting beyond 1981. This administration campaigned as the consumers' friend and even had a game of baseball with Ralph Nader in Georgia during the 1976 campaign. Carter said of himself that he was the number one consumerist in the nation—not Ralph Nader. Although public opinion polls overwhelmingly favoring a federal consumer agency, it took only a year in office for the Carter administration to lose in its effort to create even a watered-down, understaffed, toothless consumer protection agency. The White House hardly made a worthy lobbying effort on the consumers' behalf. The consumerists appointed throughout the Carter administration, ironically, were the last to see the immensity of their own Waterloo.

During its last three years, the Carter White House devoted its effort on consumer issues to a well-meant, but hopeless, internal restructuring of existing consumer activities within the bureaucracy. The world outside Washington was not aware of the task forces and massive paper output of the

Carter consumerists. The Washington consumer establishment saw little benefit resulting from the administration's effort, but did not openly criticize. The bureaucracy committed few resources to help develop the consumer plans. The U.S. Office of Consumer Affairs, the White House consumer unit, nonetheless, put nearly everything else aside for three years to try to create a consumer-input system for the federal government. All for nought. Seen today, the only result is a historical footnote to the period ending January 19, 1981.

The lesson of this history is not in a critique of the strategies followed by the consumer interests, but in the study of the larger political and social forces that doomed those strategies. Marketing myopia, perhaps, on the part of consumer forces, but instructive in the sense that consumer organizations and leaders did not understand the uncontrollable forces that worked on their destiny.

Historical Relativism

The origins of social movements are many, but such movements tend to be the products of their times more than the creatures of their leaders. Consumer activism has arisen several times during this century in the United States and has lain dormant more than it has been in bloom. The documentation of these active periods is well known and accepted, but it may be instructive to summarize certain forces that seem to allow consumer movements to flourish.

The years 1900 to 1914, the 1930s, and the period since the early 1960s were times of domestic reform, and the nation's attention for the most part was turned inward rather than on war or foreign crises. These three time periods also saw the growth of consumerism at government levels as well as in the private sector. Consumer groups appeared and grew at these times; the business community showed the greatest response or reaction to consumer problems. The federal government's attention to consumer legislation or regulation peaked at these same times. Media coverage of consumer issues was at its highest levels, too.

The private consumer organizations that have appeared at any time in the United States have been small and have lacked financial resources. They have never found the right formula for membership or money to carry them through hard times with appreciable political clout. Comparable social and economic organizations of business, labor, and other interests typically dwarf consumer groups, even when consumerists are riding high on their cycle.

Much attention has been devoted to the credibility of consumer groups in recent years. The discussion of legitimacy centers on the size of organization budgets or the numbers of members more than on any other factors. The consumer leadership has had to resort to obfuscation of substance and power. When asked to provide the actual number of members, the right of privacy took precedence over the public's right to information about the groups. The wrong facts are being sought, however, if influence is to be properly gauged.

Whether the Maryland Citizens Consumer Council, for example, has 5 or 50,000 members is not that important. It is perceived today as the voice of the general consumer interest in Maryland—perhaps. Its credibility stems from its ability to speak forcefully and to elicit some feedback that verifies to many people that the council is indeed the consumer's voice in Maryland. If the media believes and quotes the group, it adds power to the voice. On the other hand, the press could and likely would destroy groups that were illogical, untruthful, or that had no support for their views from others. But the process is not perfect. One-person organizations occasionally get into print. Consumer groups have been exposed from time to time as fronts for corporate sponsors or others clearly not operating in the consumer interest by any definition. One national group, the Conference of Consumer Organizations, has been criticized as being too heavily dependent on funding from the telephone industry throughout most of its ten year history.

Lacking resources, consumer organizations do not control their destinies. They do not set policy. They adapt to their environments. Thus an analysis of the future of the consumer movement must begin with a study of the environment of consumerism. The conditions that control the movement's success—for example, press interest—are so dominant that at times the consumer movement does not exist in the public policy arena for all intents and purposes. At least, it is not relevant to the debates on certain issues. The market for consumerism sometimes lies dormant, and those who produce for this market (i.e., consumer groups) cannot develop and flourish under such uncontrollable adverse conditions.

Consumerism's Environment

If the consumer movement can succeed in the future, it will have to come to grips with its environment. The leadership will have to be realistic as well as opportunistic. Leading a successful organization is more art than science; it is a little like marketing, but the marketing mix is unconventional because of the unusual environment.

It is necessary to separate the factors that underlie long-term trends and conditions from those that produce the cycles. There has undoubtedly been a long-term increase in the complexity of the marketplace, which in turn has created opportunities for mistakes, deceptions, and problems. Perhaps this trend contributes to the degree of activity of the consumer movement, but it does little to explain the cycles. Essentially, the role of the media in popularizing consumer issues is cyclical. The media may not lead or cause the movement to burst forth, but books by muckrakers, exposés by the print media, and investigative reporting by the broadcast media parallel the success of consumer groups. It is useful to note that there were numerous articles about the demise of consumerism in 1978, after the House defeated the Consumer Protection Agency legislation.

Analyses of the rise and fall of other social movements would prove relevant to evaluating the cyclical nature of consumer activism. Undoubtedly, the rise of the civil rights, environmental, and women's movements in recent years resulted from some of the same forces that encouraged consumerism. These movements also have cyclical histories. The political changes in Washington, in the last few years in particular, seem to have seriously slowed the progress of reformers in many fields. The parallel trends are noteworthy, but alone do not offer much understanding of root causes and effects of the cycles.

Consumerism's Marketing Mix

Because consumer organizations do not have many members or much wealth, they have to exploit the resources they can muster. Looking at the day-to-day activities of leading groups, the essential controllable variables are:

1. Media access.
2. Salable ideas in the public policy arena.
3. A believable claim to consumer authenticity.

Numerous varieties of consumer groups produce consumerism in varying forms: some produce a crowd for the cameras; some muster coalitions of supporters on any issue; some generate direct pressure on legislators (but this is rather rare). Others feature expertise—often one person with special talent. There are specialty sellers and general merchandisers of many issues. No mere listing does justice to the rich variety of consumer groups and other organizations that sometimes deal with consumer issues.

A consumer movement with a set of variables as intangible as this marketing mix has a limited ability to manipulate its market. The products—essentially concepts and ideas—often cannot be sold at all. There is little control of the product life cycle of such ideas by particular organizations. The National Consumers League, founded in 1899, still emphasizes labor-related issues (e.g., workplace safety) as it always has.

There is distinct confusion about the product being sold by consumer groups. The conventional wisdom is that consumerism is a political movement trying to tie business in knots of regulation in order to reduce business's abuse of customers. Consumer groups, notwithstanding such a perception, favor economic deregulation in many of the transportation and communications sectors. They almost universally oppose state laws that limit business competition under the guise of consumer protection. The actual product is subject to change as conditions change, and it does not clearly favor government control. Consumerists do not subscribe to ideology in the religious sense and thus the movement may change its priorities and directions more easily than might be expected.

Looking to the 1990s

Projections about consumerism are hazardous. The most influential factors appear to be social and political trends. The control of Congress by one group or another will influence consumer affairs, and the occupant of the White House will be a vital ingredient of the environment for consumerism.

The successful marketer in the "consumerism industry" will have to look at emerging marketplace conditions to see which ones are creating problems. The creative marketer will have to develop programs or sets of solutions and approaches to these problems that are salable in the public policy marketplace.

The most likely areas of increased consumer movement activity in the 1990s are those with most unsolved problems today. The underlying causes in part can be measured with safety statistics or dollar losses. Which issues emerge at a particular date will depend on many factors, as well as on public and institutional perceptions of the seriousness of the problems. Some likely areas of future concern are presented in the following paragraphs.

1. *Food safety and health.* The role of many natural (cholesterol, caffeine, salt) and added (preservatives, coloring, extra salt, sugar, caffeine) ingredients in causing major diseases is becoming clearer. The public has so far made few overall adjustments in basic diet. Food interests (agriculture, manufacturing, and retailers) and public health concerns are following a collision course.

2. *Product safety.* No consumer organization dares to condemn the Consumer Product Safety Commission (CPSC) in the 1980s, lest the criticism be manipulated into an excuse to dismantle the agency. Critics who point out that several hundred million dollars have produced few results in bottom-line safety and death statistics are right, of course, but the CPSC is a victim of its badly selected chairman and overall poor management. Needless deaths and injuries persist in many areas where the CPSC has not even begun to investigate.

3. *Sinful products.* Certain drugs, tobacco products, and alcoholic beverages are viewed by many as morally wrong, for reasons historically rooted in their alleged harm to health. The allegations are being increasingly ac-

cepted by a wider spectrum of persons, especially in the health fields. Most consumer organizations have remained apart from expanding efforts to control smokers and smoking, to penalize drunken drivers, and to stop drug abuse. Consumer organizations are not essential to the growing movement against these products, but consumerists could change their priorities.

4. *Advertising and deception.* The new leadership of the Federal Trade Commission under the Reagan administration has been universally perceived by critics and friends as less aggressive in consumer protection. The results are easiy predicted: an increase in deceptive practices and an eventual public demand for reform. While state, local, and self-regulatory mechanisms do remain, the Federal Trade Commission has been the ultimate resource for them all. They cannot do their work as effectively without the threat of the FTC's "big stick".

5. *Insurance.* This industry is on almost all consumer reformers' lists of major problems, but it has not yet been a priority project. Worst of all is life insurance—in many cases an unwanted good that people often buy for the wrong reasons and in the wrong form and amounts. It is a national industry hopelessly regulated by underfunded state agencies that lack the jurisdiction and political support to protect consumers. The consumer interest has been failed by the marketplace, but reform awaits public recognition of that fact.

6. *Cable television.* Few are aware of the total economic deregulation of cable television in an unheralded act of Congress in 1984. Because local franchises are, by nature, natural monopolies, this law defies the realities of local government. As the industry continues its rapid growth and initial low-bidder cable subscription rates rise dramatically, the debate will become heated. Ironically, the Washington, D.C., area had very little cable television in 1984, and neither consumer groups nor Congress had much hands-on experience with a monopoly service that is soon destined to become a necessity.

There are many issues of the 1970s and 1980s that are not on this agenda. Some, no doubt, will persist as problems. The deregulation of financial institutions, telecommunications, and transportation industries will produce repercussions for many years to come. It appears, though, that the major issues will have been decided by 1990, and no really new issues will emerge to dominate the decade.

3

Consumerism and Environmentalism in the 1980s: Competitive or Companionable Social Movements?

Robert Cameron Mitchell

Ralph Nader's father once told him that, no movement in history could ever succeed unless it was described in one word. Environmentalism and consumerism certainly share this trait, and other commonalities between the two groups far outweigh any inherent conflict between consumerism's emphasis upon prices and consumption and environmentalism's emphasis upon protection and conservation. These commonalities include: a shared ideology, a common constituency, broad public support, a common enemy, and policy middle grounds. Looking to the future, I believe that both movements will persist, but that environmentalism will continue to be the stronger of the two movements in the 1980s, as it has been in the 1970s. Companionability rather than competition will characterize the relations between the two movements.

The Environmental Movement

Before comparing and contrasting the two movements, it is necessary to briefly describe the environmental movement. The most visible and best known of the contemporary environmental organizations in the United States are the national membership groups, of which the largest are the National Wildlife Federation, the National Audubon Society, and the Sierra Club. These three groups and several others that were founded before 1965, such as the Isaac Walton League, had their origins in the conservation movement of the nineteenth century, which came of age in the early years of the twentieth. The conservationists were deeply concerned by the mounting evidence that America's natural resources were in danger of exhaustion, that various wildlife species would soon be extinct because of indiscriminate and unregulated hunting, and that the nation's heritage of magnificent wilderness areas and wild rivers was fast being lost to the public because of private development.

Some, such as John Muir, the founding father of the Sierra Club in California, emphasized the preservation of land in its natural state; others, such as Gifford Pinchot, America's first professional forester and the founder of the U.S. Forest Service, promoted the utilitarian idea of wise and careful use of natural resources and areas by the government. By the 1920s, thanks in good part to the efforts of both the preservationists and conservationists, a series of important laws were passed which produced many new national parks, protected wildlife, and created government agencies to manage Western water resources (Bureau of Reclamation), national forests (U.S. Forest Service), and national parks (National Park Service). The Depression, World War II, and perhaps these victories, temporarily caused conservationism to lose its momentum as a popular movement.

The modern environmental movement emerged in the 1960s. It was a product of several forces, one of which was the return to activism of the older conservation groups. The first display of their new spirit was the successful series of well-publicized battles they fought against projects that threatened Dinosaur National Park, the Redwoods in California, the Cascades in Washington, and the Grand Canyon. These efforts mobilized a new generation of activists. The conservation groups also turned their attention to new types of threats (Sills 1975:4)—such as the dangers posed to wildlife by pesticides and the degredation of air and water from pollution—and to Washington, where they began to concentrate on lobbying for protective federal legislation—such as the Wilderness Act, which was passed in 1964.

The conservationists' efforts to publicize the seriousness of environmental problems were assisted in the 1960s by books such as Rachael Carson's best-selling work on the environmental impact of DDT, *The Silent Spring* (1962); the legislative efforts of several key Congresspeople such as John Dingell, Henry Reuss, Henry Jackson, and Edmund Muskie; the climate for reform created by the efforts of Ralph Nader, John Gardner (founder of Common Cause), and other public interest advocates; highly publicized environmental insults like the Santa Barbara oil spill in 1969; and the ever-increasing amount of attention given to environmental problems by the news media.

In 1970, the campus-based but national celebration of "Earth Day" mobilized hundreds of thousands of Americans, who attended rallies and participated in numerous local environmental cleanups and demonstrations. "Ecology" suddenly entered the American vocabulary. About this time, the two environmental law organizations, the Environmental Defense Fund and the Natural Resources Defense Council were begun; Friends of the Earth was founded by David Brower, the former executive director of the Sierra Club; and Environmental Action emerged as an organizational continuation of the Earth Day student movement.

One of the outstanding characteristics of the environmental movement is its mass membership base. During the 1960s, skillful use of direct mail appeals by the national groups yielded an ever-increasing membership. By 1970, the 10 national environmental membership groups had a combined membership of about one million people. A decade later that membership had doubled to two million[1] for the now 13 groups.[2] Several of the national groups organize their members into local chapters; in 1978, the Sierra Club had 250 local groups and National Audubon's chapters numbered 385. The United States environmental movement also includes an array of regional and local organizations, national nonmembership organizations, and allied citizen's groups who have environmental issues as part of their wider social reform agenda, such as Common Cause and the League of Women Voters. According to some estimates, there were about 20,000 environmental/conservation groups in the United States (counting each chapter of a national organization as a separate group).

The Two Movements

Those familiar with the history of the consumer movement (Nadel 1971) will detect more than a few similarities between the consumer and environmental movements.[3] Both emerged in their present form in the late 1960s and both trace their lineage back to the Progressive Era. In the 1960s, both developed new issues and both have come to regard national legislation, federal regulatory bodies, and federal courts as crucial arenas of action. For both, the amorphous but real entity known as "the movement" consists of a variety of groups, both national and local, although among the consumer groups only Ralph Nader's Public Citizen organization has obtained significant public support for consumer lobbying through the use of direct mail.

The environment–consumer similarity extends to substance as well. The two movements, along with the governmental reform movement whose principal organization is Common Cause, together constitute what is known as the public interest movement. The common feature of this larger movement is that it lobbies on behalf of issues that involve "public goods." These goods, such as less polluted air, greater product safety, and more accountability by public bodies to their constituents, are similar in that:

1. no one can be excluded from receiving the benefits of these goods, even if they never contributed to the groups that lobbied for them;

2. because of the free-rider effect outlined in item 1, the interests of the many citizens who wish to expand public goods are diffuse and hard to mobilize;

3. those who oppose the expansion of public goods, such as corporations that would have to comply with stricter clean air regulations, are strongly motivated to lobby against their provision.

Since the political system gives special weight to organized groups that practice issue politics, the public interest movement seeks to counterbalance what it calls the special interests by representing the hitherto-underrepresented citizens' interests in the provision of these public goods.

Potential for Conflict

Thus far the environmental and consumer movements have enjoyed an amiable association. Each has its unique agenda of concerns that it pursues independently of the other. For example, many environmentalists are particularly interested in wilderness and wildlife issues, while consumer advocates worry about children's advertising and passenger restraints in motor vehicles. But each has shown sympathy toward the concerns of the other—two environmental groups, Friends of the Earth and the Sierra Club, joined the coalition that lobbied for the Consumer Protection Agency (Vogel and Nadel 1977:36). Where they share a common interest, the two movements have been able to cooperate without undue strain. These common interests have included procedural reforms such as intervenor funding, regulatory reform, energy conservation, and food safety.

But this collegiality should not to be taken for granted, because not every public good can be maximized simultaneously. The public goods sought by environmentalists and consumerists appear to involve potential conflicts over such things as economic growth, consumption, and the appropriate way to relate to nature. Consumerism's aims—to help people consume products that are safe and low in cost—are congruent with the prevailing values of a growth-oriented industrialized society. Consumer advocates are not given to philosophical proclamations, but rest their cause on the practicalities of an everyday utilitarianism, which takes for granted that the furtherance of unfettered consumer preferences constitutes the common interest. One consumerist defines the consumer interest simply as: "the interest in a free market economy characterized by rigorous competition and consumer's information" (Schuck, in Vogel and Nadel 1977:33). Environmentalism, on the other hand, seeks to preserve natural resources and settings, to protect wildlife, and to prevent damage to the environment by human activities. It views the maintenance of natural stability, which many environmentalists believe to be seriously threatened by modern industrial activity, as a guiding principle for human social life. Although its legislative agenda is well within the conventional bounds of American politics, environmental arguments are based in part on values that transcend the utilitarian calculus and involve aesthetic, intergenerational, and survivalist considerations.

Many environmentalists lay the blame for environmental problems on society's emphasis on progress and growth, materialism, technological development, and property rights—dominant American values (Dunlap 1976) that are seemingly promoted by consumerism. In his influential work, *The Closing Circle,* Barry Commoner attributes the "environmental crisis" to:

> the faults in productive technology—and in its scientific background—that generate these stresses, and finally to the economic, social, and political forces which have driven us down this self-destructive course. (Commoner 1971:10–11)

David Brower scorns "our anxiously acquisitive consumer society" and argues for a "more serenely thrifty conserver society" where "growthmania will yield to the realization that physical growth is wholesome only during immaturity." He feels that continuing growth beyond that point will lead to malignancy or other "grim devices" that keep the planet from "being suffocated with a surfeit" (Brower 1977).

The difference in the two movements' concerns is captured in an imaginary conversation that Robert Holsworth has constructed between a factory worker who drives an air-conditioned Chevrolet Impala with a 427-cubic-inch engine, an environmentalist, and a consumerist. According to Holsworth:

> The consumerist would center his queries on the performance of the car. He might want to discover if any injuries occurred because of faulty internal design when the car was involved in a minor accident and he might be interested in hearing about the quality of service in the dealership. . . . The ecologist would . . . test his persuasive capacities. He might attempt to convince the owner that it would be in his long-term interest to trade in the Impala for a compact. . . . Failing all, our ecologist might abruptly terminate the conversation by remarking that he hopes the price of gas doubles in the next year. (Holsworth 1980:66–67)

Holsworth's book, *Public Interest Liberalism and the Crisis of Affluence* (1980), is a critique of Ralph Nader's consumerist philosophy from the point of view of radical environmentalism. Holsworth duly notes Nader's concern about environmental issues and his personally ascetic lifestyle, but charges that Nader ignores the contradiction between his consumerism, which enshrines economic self-interest and consumer wants as the touchstone of politics, and the ecological destruction wrought by the production of these very same consumer goods. By building a social movement on people's economic self-interest Nader implies, according to Holsworth, "that our strivings and efforts should be directed toward acquiring more of these satisfactions" (Holsworth 1980:58). In contrast, "political ecologists" like E.F. Schumacher equate the practice of a moral life with restraint in the consumption of goods.

It is not hard to move from these philosophical contradictions to the practical world of Washington lobbying and to postulate potential conflicts between consumerists and environmentalists on such issues as bottle bills and energy policy. Dedication to lower prices and the interests of low-income consumers might lead a consumerist to oppose a bottle bill if it could be shown to result in higher prices and some job losses. Even if these effects were certain (which is debatable), environmentalists would still argue that the benefits of resource conservation and litter reduction are worth the cost.

With regard to energy policy, the potential contradictions are particularly apparent. Environmentalists believe that lower energy prices promote wasteful short-term energy use in a world of long-term scarcity. They view the problem as one of too much consumption, rather than one of a scarcity of energy supply. A single-issue consumerist approach, however, would place greater emphasis on lower prices and sufficient production, since without the latter, economic growth and affluence are threatened.

Why No Conflict Is Expected

What I have just described is the underlying ideological cleavage that seems to be inherent in the philosophies of consumerism and environmentalism. The views which I have juxtaposed represent both philosophies taken to their extreme. The fact that views as extreme as these do not presently dominate the two movements' lobbying does not preclude them from affecting their movements' agendas in the future. After all, a trend toward greater extremism characterized the civil rights and antiwar movements as the 1960s wore on. What, then, are the prospects for a growth in extremism that might create conflict between environmental and consumer goals in the 1980s? In my view the prospects are very small. There are five important factors that promote cooperation between the two movements, and I do not foresee any change in these factors.[4]

Shared Ideology

The first reason why I believe the movements will continue to cooperate is that most of the activists appear to share a basic public interest ideology that mitigates against the kind of extremist single-issue approach that would set one movement off against the other.[5] Included in this nonexplicit but nonetheless real set of views is an environmental sensitivity, a concern about hidden health hazards, a distrust of corporate power and of bigness generally, a preference for community autonomy, liberal concerns about equity, and belief in the worth of government regulation to protect the diffuse interests of the public. This shared view allows the activists in one movement to view their counterparts in the other movement as fellow reformers with whom they share important interests.

A crucial ideological similarity is that the environmental and consumer movements are both quality-of-life movements rather than movements for social justice. While both are sensitive to equity issues—the distributional effects of the policies they advocate on the poor and minorities—neither movement is dedicated to promoting redistribution of wealth. Instead they seek to enhance the well-being of all citizens who are victims of overcharging for goods and services, of products that are unsafe, of foods that are contaminated, of air and water that are polluted. Both movements believe that their efforts will enhance the well-being of the poor as well as the middle class. In 1968, at the height of urban social unrest, Ralph Nader was asked: "Don't the problems of the black ghetto—which are at the root of the explosive racial situation in this country today—seem to you more urgent than earthquakes and auto safety?" He replied in part:

> The problems I deal with intimately affect most Negroes, as well as the rest of the population. . . product safety, reasonable prices, quality merchandising and environmental purity—are related as much to the quality of life in the ghetto as to the quality of life in Scarsdale or Grosse Pointe. . . . I have not addressed myself to specific areas of the civil rights struggle, because there are many people working in this area already. . . . My prime abilities are . . . discovering new facts in areas in which no action is being taken. (Playboy c.1968:218–19)

Another important aspect of this common worldview is that many consumer activists share the environmentalists' belief that consumer sovereignty needs to be tempered by an environmental imperative. If consumerists doubted the seriousness of environmental problems and believed that the environmentalist concern for preserving nature was an expensive luxury that unnecessarily threatened consumer well-being, the prospects for future conflict between the movements might be quite different. But this does not seem to be the case. Consider Ralph Nader, whose importance in the consumer movement stems from his national prominence (Handler 1978:73) and the fact that his organization (Congress Watch) alone has mobilized a significant number of individuals to support lobbying on consumer issues. Earlier I mentioned Nader's personal lifestyle which, in its frugality, is almost a paradigm of the ecologically sensitive way of life. His environmental concern is also longstanding; in the late 1960s he included air and water pollution among the issues he planned to work on (Playboy c.1968:218). That these particular issues have not been priorities for him in recent years is due to his desire to avoid duplicating the efforts of the environmental groups rather than to a lessening concern about environmental problems.

For their part, environmentalists' concerns are not restricted to the rights of baby seals, whales, snail darters, and trees. Most environmentalists are as deeply concerned as consumerists about the human health effects of substances introduced into the environment by modern technology, such asbestos, red dye no. 2, and PCBs (Environmental Defense Fund and Boyle 1979). Environmentalists were key proponents of such consumer-oriented health measures as the Safe Drinking Water Act and the Federal Insecticide, Fungicide and Rodenticide Act.

Common Constituencies

A second reason why I do not expect future conflict between the two movements is that their constituencies also share the same ideology. The environmental and consumer groups that rely on direct mail to recruit supporters both draw on the pool of approximately five million "liberal givers" who contribute to public interest causes.[6] These givers consist for the most part of well-educated, middle-class people, many of whom are self-described liberals and who share the same cross-cutting concerns that I described above for the activists.

I surveyed the members of five national environmental groups 1978.[7] The findings of this survey illustrate the compatibility between the environmentalist and consumerist constituencies. Fifteen percent of the 3,000 environmentalists said they belong to Ralph Nader's Public Citizen group and an additional six percent claimed to be active in the consumer movement. Thus one out of five environmentalists might be regarded as consumerists. As for their attitudes toward the consumer movement, the environmentalist sample as a whole expressed a great deal of sympathy for consumerism. One out of three said they were "very sympathetic" to the consumer movement, while only seven percent said they were either "unsympathetic" or "very unsympathetic" to it. Multivariate analysis of the differences between those environmentalists who are consumerists and those who are not shows no strong value differences.[8]

Broad Public Support

A third unifying factor is the strong support given to both movements by the general public. The environmental movement has frequently been attacked (Neuhaus 1971; Horowitz 1972; Epstein 1973; Udall 1974; Tucker 1977) as elitist, as representing the interests of a privileged upper-middle class group that is antithetical to the interests of blue collar workers (among others). To quote William Tucker (1982:45): "At heart, environmentalism favors the affluent over the poor, the haves over the have-nots." If this view were shared by the public at large or by groups such as minorities and workers that are identified as harmed by environmental programs, consumer advocates might feel constrained to press for changes in environmental regulations in order to bring savings to consumers. Public opinion polls, however, consistently show that this view is not shared by the less-affluent public (Mitchell 1979, 1980 a, b; Ladd 1982). Public concern about environmental problems, willingness to continue or increase environmental regulation, and support for the environmental movement all remain high in the 1980s. According to Everett Carll Ladd, "One of the most striking features of public opinion on environmental questions is the evenness of support across various groups in the population." (Ladd 1982:18). Polls on consumer issues show similar findings (Bloom and Greyser 1981).

Common Enemy

Fourth, the presence of a common enemy serves to unify the public interest movement. Activists in both the consumer and the environmental movements have always regarded the business community as their chief adversary. Carol Tucker Foreman, when she was the executive director of the Consumer's Federation, described the narrow margin of victory in the House for the bill to establish the Agency for Consumer Protection in 1976 as a victory.

> People say that wasn't much of a margin. But we were up against the National Association of Manufacturers, the Business Round Table, the National Association of Independent Businesses, and the White House and we still got it passed. (Cerra 1976)

Environmentalists condemn the "filthy five" corporations and decry the efforts "by 25 of the biggest corporations in America—chemical, steel, energy, paper—to gut the Clean Air Act" (Brown 1981). Now that the Reagan administration, with its markedly probusiness orientation, has placed both movements on the defensive, they are too busy fighting to preserve their earlier gains to find fault with each other, even if they were inclined to do so.

Policy Middle Ground

Finally, the issues on which the two movements might disagree the most— simpler lifestyles and energy—are issues on which the two movements have a large middle ground of agreement. Although some radical environmentalists advocate deindustrialization (Devall 1980), which would entail the imposition of simpler lifestyles on the publics in the West, this view is held by only a small minority of environmentalists. The environmentalist mainstream appears to accept the level of present lifestyles as a given (Morrison 1976:294) and prefers to speak of balanced growth and to advocate policies like the bottle bill that will reduce wasteful consumption.[9] The anticonsumer rhetoric which characterized much of environmentalist discourse around the time of Earth Day in 1970, has given way to a more sophisticated advocacy of simpler lifestyles and to the exigencies of lobbying in Washington. Instead of buying new cars and burying them, as student activists did on Earth Day in 1970, the Clean Air Coalition is currently working to maintain reasonable auto emission standards. Environmentalists argue that these and the other controls they advocate are technically feasible and add only modest amounts to the cost of new cars, arguments that parallel those of the consumer movement when it advocates requiring safety features such as the air bag.

As for national energy policy, environmentalists believe the so-called soft energy path (Morrison 1980), which relies on energy conservation and on decentralized, renewable energy sources, is far superior to the "hard," or high-technology, centralized sources of which nuclear power is the epitome. The environmentalist wish list on energy policy includes the following components:

1. Low energy growth in order to minimize national dependence on foreign sources and the environmental effects of energy production.

2. Government subsidies for research and development of solar technologies and for the promotion of energy conservation.

3. A moratorium on nuclear power and an end to the breeder reactor program.

4. The pricing of energy at its long-run incremental cost, taking into account as fully as possible all environmental and social costs.

5. Elimination of government subsidies for synthetic fuel commercialization.

6. Subsidies for low-income consumers to improve the energy efficiency of their houses and fuel grants for poor people.

7. Smaller, more efficient automobiles.

8. Government subsidies for mass transportation.

Consumerists, with the exception of the Consumer Federation of America, support every item on this agenda but item number 4.[10] This is shown in documents such as the *Citizen's Energy Platform* (National Consumers Congress 1975), which ten national environmental, consumer, and antipoverty groups published in 1975; the Center for Science in the Public Interest's critique of President Carter's National Energy Plan (1977); the DC Public Interest Research Group's *National Energy Policy Recommendations* (1977); and the report, *Warning: Reaganomics is Harmful to Consumers* (National Consumers League 1982), issued last January. Ralph Nader is a long-time critic of nuclear energy and his Critical Mass organization is one of the major antinuclear organizations. More recently, consumer groups supported the environmentalists' Energy Coalition's fight against President Carter's proposed Energy Mobilization Board (Coan and Pope 1980:47). Consumers Union recently joined with the Natural Resources Defense Council, Solar Lobby, and the National Wildlife Federation (among others) to file an *amicus curiae* brief relating to a federal statute promoting energy conservation by public utilities and production of energy by small, private producers (Silbergeld 1981).

The middle ground on which this consensus is based is that the soft path promises lower energy prices and a better quality of life.[11] Environmentalists argue that their proposals will not require a lower standard of living because the greater efficiency (rather than sacrifice) will be sufficient to avoid the construction of costly new energy production facilites (Habicht 1977:674). Moreover, their program seeks to remove energy decisions from the powerful oil companies, which both they and the consumerists distrust, and to decentralize such decisions by placing them in the hands of consumers.

This broad area of agreement, and the fact that environmentalists support mechanisms to compensate the low income and poor people who are particularly disadvantaged by increasing energy prices, make it possible for environmentalists and consumerists to agree to disagree on energy pricing issues such as natural gas decontrol.

Conclusion

I have argued that we can expect continued cooperation and mutual support between the environmental and the consumer movements in the 1980s. If the potential cleavages have not generated conflict by now, despite the energy shocks of the 1970s, the tax rebellion, stagflation, and now a recession, I find it hard to believe that they will in the next decade.

Let me end on a more controversial note. In the course of my research for this paper I came to realize how relatively thin the mobilized popular support for the consumer movement is. By mobilized I mean the number of individual consumers who directly contribute to the consumer lobbies. Consumers Union is, of course, an enormous group, but at the present time its two million members are motivated to contribute primarily because of the private good that they obtain, *Consumer Reports,* and the organization is suffering from such severe financial problems that it can no longer support its lobbying efforts. Only Public Citizen, to my knowledge, has a successful direct mail program. This stands in sharp contrast to the environmental groups, whose mobilized constituency is large and enduring. Thus another factor promoting harmony between the two movements in the 1980s may be that in order to maintain their past successes consumerists will have to enlist the support of the environmentalists in the future.

Notes

1. The number of separate individuals is fewer in each case, since many people belong to more than one environmental group. However, these figures include only the associate members of the National Wildlife Federation. The federation's affiliate membership comprises more than 1.5 million people who belong to local sports clubs that belong to a state NWF affiliate.

2. In addition to the groups mentioned, I include the Cousteau Society, Defenders of Wildlife, The National Parks and Conservation Society, the Wilderness Society, and Solar Lobby in this count.

3. I should point out that my knowledge of the environmental movement stems from my current research on this topic, whereas my knowledge of the consumer movement is derived principally from the literature cited in this paper and a few interviews with Washington-based consumer activists.

4. When I refer to the consumer movement and the environmental movement in what follows, my referent is the major national groups. These groups constitute the two movements' principal Washington lobbyists and include those who have the widest and most effective access to the press as spokespeople for these causes. I have already identified the major national environmental groups. One list of their consumer counterparts is the seven groups that endorsed the recent consumer review of the Reagan administration (National Consumers League 1982). These are: the National Consumers League, the Center for Science in the Public Interest, the Community Nutrition Institute, Congress Watch, the Consumer Federation of America, Consumers Union, and the National Council of Senior Citizens.

5. By activists I mean the volunteer leaders and, especially, the paid staff of the national groups.

6. I realize that this observation pertains primarily to Public Citizen, although Consumers Union will soon begin to use direct mail to solicit support for its lobbying activities. The constituency of the Consumer Federation of America is notably electric cooperatives and labor unions, whose interests are more narrowly economic (Handler 1978:75) than the public interest ideology I describe here.

7. These groups are the Environmental Defense Fund, Environmental Action, the National Wildlife Federation, the Sierra Club, and the Wilderness Society. A random sample of the members were sent mail questionnaires. The response rate was approximately sixty-five percent.

8. For example, in an ordinary least squares regression, the only value differences that are statistically significant show environmentalists who belong to Public Citizen to be slightly more liberal, somewhat less interested in wilderness issues, and slightly more likely to blame environmental problems on industry than those environmentalists who do not belong to Public Citizen.

9. Far from opposing such bills, consumerists, such as several state PIRG

groups, have taken the lead in advocating bottle bills (Estep 1977); Barbanel 1982) despite the opposition to the bills by labor (Cannon 1977).

10. According to McFarland (1976), the Consumer Federation of America's energy position is more favorable to nuclear and less favorable toward strict environmental standards for coal-fired power plants than the other public interest groups, owing to the membership of public power companies and rural electric cooperatives in the organization.

11. In the prose of Amory Lovins, the soft path assumes a distinctly utopian cast: "a soft path simultaneously offers jobs for the unemployed, capital for business people, environmental protection for conservationists, enhanced national security for the military . . . a rebirth of spiritual values for the religious . . . energy independence for isolationists" and more (Lovins 1977:23).

References

Barbanel, Josh. 1982. Deposit bill to be given vote on assembly floor. *New York Times* (Feb. 25).

Bloom, Paul N., and Stephen A. Greyser. 1981. The maturing of consumerism. *Harvard Business Review* 59 (Nov.–Dec.):130–139.

Brower, David R. 1977. Foreword. *Progress as if Survival Mattered*. San Francisco, Calif.: Friends of the Earth, 7–13.

Brown, Janet Welsh. 1981. *Fund Raising Letter*. Environmental Defense Fund.

Cannon, Lou. 1977. A dream turning dust. *The Washington Post* (July 17):

Carson, Rachael. 1962. *Silent Spring*. Boston, Mass.: Houghton Mifflin Co.

Center for Science in the Public Interest. *Critique of the National Energy Plan*. Washington, D.C.: Center for Science in the Public Interest.

Cerra, Frances. 1976. A lobbyist for consumers. *New York Times* (Oct. 31).

Coan, Gene, and Carl Pope. 1980. Energy 1979—what happened and why. *Sierra* 65 (Jan.–Feb.):11–13, 47.

Commoner, Barry. 1972. *The Closing Circle*. New York: Alfred A. Knopf.

DC Public Interest Research Group. 1977. *National Energy Policy Recommendations* Washington, D.C.: DC Public Interest Research Group.

Devall, Bill. 1980. The deep ecology movement. *Natural Resources Journal* 20 (April):299–322.

Dunlap, Riley E. 1976. *Understanding Opposition to the Environmental Movement: The Importance of Dominant American Values*. Unpublished paper, available from the Department of Rural Sociology, Washington State University, Pullman.

Environmental Defense Fund, and Robert H. Boyle. 1979. *Malignant Neglect*. New York: Alfred A. Knopf.

Epstein, J. 1973. Can we afford sliced eggplant? *The New York Review* April 5:13–16.

Estep, Rhoda J. 1977. Legislative reform as a social movement strategy: The deposit bill and the environmental movement. *Western Sociological Review* 8:48–60.

Habicht, Ernst R., Jr. 1976. Testimony on February 24, 1976. *Hearings Before the Subcommittee on Energy Research, Development and Demonstration (Fossil*

Fuels). House Committee on Science and Technology, vol. II. Washington, D.C.: Committee Print.

Handler, Joel F. 1978. *Social Movements and the Legal System.* New York: Academic Press.

Holsworth, Robert D. 1980. *Public Interest Liberalism and the Crisis of Affluence— Reflections on Nader, Environmentalism, and the Politics of Sustainable Society.* (Cambridge: Mass.: Schenkman Publishing Company.

Horowitz, Irving L. 1972. "The environmental cleavage: social ecology versus political economy. *Social Theory and Practice* 2:125–134.

Ladd, Everett Carll. 1982. Clearing the air: public opinion and public policy on the environment. *Public Opinion* 5 (Feb.–March):16–20.

Lovins, Amory B. 1977. *Soft Energy Paths: Toward a Durable Peace.* San Francisco, Calif.: Friends of the Earth.

McFarland, Andrew S. 1976. *Public Interest Lobbies—Decision Making on Energy.* Washington, D.C.: American Enterprise Institute for Public Policy Research.

Mitchell, Robert C. 1979. Silent spring/solid majorities. *Public Opinion* 2 (Aug–Sept.):16–20, 55.

———. 1980a. How "soft," "deep," or "left?" Present constituencies in the environmental movement for certain world views. *Natural Resources Journal* 20 (April):345–358.

———. 1980b. *Public Opinion on Environmental Issues: Results of a National Opinion Survey.* Washington, D.C.: President's Council on Environmental Quality.

Morrison, Denton E. 1976. Growth, environment, equity and scarcity. *Social Science Quarterly* 57 (Sept.):292–306.

———. 1980. The soft, cutting edge of environmentalism: why and how the appropriate technology notion is changing the movement. *National Resources Journal* 20 (April):275–298.

National Consumers Congress. 1975. *Citizen's Energy Platform.* Washington, D.C.: National Consumers Congress.

National Consumers League. 1982. *Warning: Reaganomics is Harmful to Consumers.* Washington, D.C.: National Consumers League.

Neuhaus, R. 1971. *In Defense of People: Ecology and the Seduction of Radicalism.* New York: Macmillan.

[Playboy Interview]. c.1968. Ralph Nader. *Playboy Magazine.*

Silbergeld, Mark. 1981. *Washington Office Activities Since May 21, 1981.* (Memo to Consumer's Union Board of Directors, September 25, 1981.)

Sills, David L. 1975. The environmental movement and its critics. *Human Ecology* 3:1–36.

Tucker, William. 1977. Environmentalism and the leisure class. *Harper's* 255 (Dec.):49–80.

———. 1982. The environmental era. *Public Opinion* 5 (Feb.–March): 41–48.

Udall, Morris K. 1974. The environment at valley forge. *Congressional Record* 120 (April 4):

Vogel, David, and Mark Nadel. 1977. Who is a consumer? An analysis of the politics of the consumer movement. *American Political Quarterly* 5 (June):27–56.

4

The Concerns of the Rich/Poor Consumer

Lee E. Preston
Paul N. Bloom

T he contemporary consumer environment is turbulent. Familiar necessities like heating fuel, food, and medical care have risen dramatically in price, while unfamiliar luxuries like video games, portable headphone stereos, and designer clothing have suddenly become commonplace. Middle income families, stunned by inflation and an abrupt reduction in lifestyle expectations, have become intensely concerned with pocketbook issues, while young up-scale professionals plunge into condominium ownership and health-club contracts without reading the fine print. The structure of consumer interests and issues that evolved over the past two decades has become fragmented and diffused, and established approaches and programs in both government and business are being reviewed, revised, or abandoned.

There is, however, no indication that either the number or the urgency of consumer concerns has declined. Quite the contrary, persistent stagflation and sudden changes in relative prices and incomes have intensified some old problems and also given rise to new ones. Even while the Reagan administration attempts to implement its claimed mandate to deregulate the economy, polls continue to show a clear majority of the general public is concerned about "business exploitation of consumers" and in favor of strong consumer protection regulation.[1] The agenda of consumer policy issues confronting business and government—and the consumer organizations as well—remains long and compelling. This agenda is, however, different—both in overall structure and in specific detail—from what it has been in the past, and both the appropriate modes of policy formation and the content of effective policy responses will prove to be different as well.

This essay seeks to review and formulate the consumer policy agenda as a guide to policymaking, both private and public, in the light of the changed environment of the 1980s and the likely outlook for the rest of the century. This new formulation is based upon our own observations and on the proceedings of two conferences involving some 200 leading analysts, executives, policymakers, and consumer advocates.[2] We have drawn freely upon the viewpoints expressed at these sessions, synthesizing and interpreting them in ways that may not be clearly recognizable to their original authors.

We focus here on policy issues—that is, matters that responsible persons may reasonably be expected to do something about—rather than simply on trends, basic social conflicts or continuing differences of opinion. Neither trends (the aging population, the communications revolution) nor attitudinal differences (hedonism vs. asceticism; individualism vs. communitarianism) are policy issues in themselves, although they may give rise to issues and may have impact on the range and effectiveness of possible policy responses. Our focus here is on consumer policy—that is, policy issues associated with the consumption of goods and services by domestic households, and defined and viewed from their perspective.

The Old Agenda: Rights through Regulation

Consumer policy from 1960 to 1980 centered on the achievement of the four elements of the Consumer Bill of Rights outlined initially by President John F. Kennedy in his Message to Congress of March 15, 1962:

> The right to safety.
>
> The right to be informed.
>
> The right to choose.
>
> The right to be heard.

These general objectives were more or less endorsed by both Presidents Johnson and Nixon. President Gerald Ford added a fifth:

> The right to consumer education.

Professor E. Scott Maynes has more recently distilled from the literature two more:

> The right to representation and participation in policy-making bodies (as distinct from the "right to be heard" in private sector decision-making).
>
> The right to recourse and redress.[3]

An underlying right to consume was apparently taken for granted in all of these formulations, leaving unaddressed the possibility that this more fundamental "right" might be abridged by inadequate purchasing power and/or by measures taken in pursuit of some of the other rights themselves.[4]

Consumer policy in the 1960s was intended to achieve these proclaimed rights primarily through regulation, and with the principal initiative coming from the federal government. Two different regulatory approaches were utilized. In some instances, business was required to perform specified functions directly for consumers (as in Truth-in-Lending and Truth-in-Packaging) or to modify its behavior in other ways (e.g., Federal Trade Commission affirmative disclosure requirements). In other instances, business was required to conform to specific government-set standards and reporting requirements (as in auto safety and emissions standards). The latter approach involved considerably more initiative and activity by government and made use of the power of large government purchases to influence compliance. Both approaches required extensive compliance effort and expense on the part of business.

The pursuit of rights through regulation was not without its successes. Product safety and health protections were improved in a number of specific instances (lawnmowers, toys, water and air pollution), and the general emphasis on safety probably had economy-wide effects. On the other hand, prescribed product quality standards in many instances increased costs and eliminated alternatives preferred by some buyers. New procedural safeguards were alleged to discourage new product development (as in the case of prescription drugs). In case after case, an operational definition of safety eluded common sense. The Delaney amendment banned cancer-causing food additives, not cancer-causing foods or tobacco. An appropriate trade-off between the hazards, costs, and benefits of new versus old technologies and products proved difficult to make. Indeed, attempts to introduce economic rationality into such decisions ran up against the realities of political rationality (as in the case of seat-belt interlocks), and cost–benefit methodology generated its own cadre of disillusioned, and highly sophisticated, critics.[5]

The related rights to be informed and to consumer education generated noticeable amounts of activity, but the results were even less clear. Drug package inserts, Truth-in-Lending documents, and product warning labels littered the landscape, but much of the information contained in these materials did not appear to be used, or even useable, by consumers.

The right to be heard has probably been most importantly expanded by a voluntary increase in complaint-handling efforts (consumer hot lines and other quick-response techniques) on the part of business. Consumer affairs offices, both public and private, have made the stimulation of these services one of their principal activities. Some businesses have also given their consumer offices a role to play in the design of products and services, the review of advertising claims, and the provision of marketing research data. However, the influence of most offices in these areas has been limited.

All of these informational and service efforts for consumers undoubtedly expand their right to choose in the sense that choices may be better informed and dependable. In addition, some deregulatory initiatives, antitrust enforcement, and support of specific competition-expanding policies (such as generic drug identification) have clearly contributed to some widening of the range of consumer choice in the marketplace.

In spite of the adversary atmosphere that the regulatory approach generated, one surviving theme from the 1960s era is a widespread recognition of the mutual interest of business, government, and consumers in the identification of consumer concerns and the development of appropriate responses. Denial ("There isn't any jug, and anyway it isn't broken.") is no longer a viable business response to widespread consumer dissatisfaction. Nor is easy resolution through government directive ("We'll make them do it.") an effective response for bureaucrats. Both a long-run marketing perspective and a self-serving desire to attract customers while avoiding product liability suits account for the widespread perception that "consumer protection is business protection."[6] The stage may be set for the development of new modes of consumer policy formation, as well as new substantive responses, to the problems and challenges posed by a new environment.

The New Environment: Scarcity and Abundance

> We are gathered here today not merely to dedicate a shopping mall but to rededicate ourselves, mind and body, to the spirit of consumerism, and to seek an ever more deeply indebted relationship to the process of purchasing merchandise.
>
> —"Congressman Bob Forehead"
> in "Washingtoon," *The Village Voice*

The world-wide consumer movement of the 1960s and early 1970s took place primarily within an environment of increasing production and productivity. Consumerism was a "baby of prosperity."[7] However, as Scherf has noted, consumerism "was not born out of the gratitude of consumers for their good fortune . . . but out of a desire for 'more.'"[8] And, even more surprisingly, the demands for more focused not on continued increases in the quantity of goods and services available (indeed, a counter-trend toward voluntary simplicity emerged in some quarters), but on more satisfaction through a reduction in hazards and problems and an improvement in the overall quality of life. Consumer policy in the sense of collective action that might affect general consumer interests, became a topic of widespread discussion, and not only in the United States. The Organization for Economic Cooperation and Development's Committee on Consumer Policy issued a major factual compendium on member countries in 1972, and annual reports from 1974 onward. In 1977, the *Journal of Consumer Policy* was established in Germany with an international list of editors and contributors, and the material appearing there attested clearly to the substance and seriousness of world-wide interest in the subject.

In all of this activity, it was implicitly assumed that increased consumer well-being, along with environmental protection and an improved quality of working life, were among the social benefits made possible by continuing prosperity and productivity gains. However, by the mid-1970s it began to become apparent—at least in the United States—that this assumption was no longer valid. Instead, critical shortages and rapidly increasing prices occurred in one sector of the economy after another, and instability in major industries undermined established patterns of income and employment. At the same time—while cheap energy became a thing of the past and the cost of a single-family dwelling rose beyond the reach of a major share of households—startling new products otherwise associated with affluence became commonplace and the demand for more from the entertainment industry—including professional sports—increased enormously.

This turbulent environment is the habitat of the rich/poor consumer. Economy-wide inflation is an important part of the picture, but the more significant phenomena are the changes in relative prices and incomes, and the consequent shifts in status and lifestyle, that occur within the great secular inflation wave. This turbulence will probably continue, perhaps even increase, during the transitional years of the 1980s and when (and if) it subsides, the shape of the economic landscape will be quite different from what it was before.

Several different, but closely related, processes are going on at once. The permanent underclass of the disadvantaged is growing with the addition of an aging population and the casualties of economic decline in the older industrial sectors and regions. External forces (e.g., changes in job locations and skill requirements), the growing mass of the underclass, and cutbacks in government assistance programs increase the difficulty of returning to the economic and social mainstream. Distinctions between lifestyles and expectations associated with comfort and need have become sharpened and entrenched. And, as a result of changing relative prices and incomes, households well above the poverty line are beginning to feel and act poor, even while they are constantly confronted with, and occasionally adopt, the consumption opportunities of contemporary affluence. Indeed, since all but the direst poverty is clearly relative, even families in very low economic brackets occasionally sample the smorgasbords of the rich. Thus, the great mass of U.S. consumers are both rich and poor at once, and policies for dealing with their problems need to reflect this new complexity.

Dealing with Scarcity

> Sometimes I have to shoplift packages of beef stew for my son and me. You
> just pray you're not going to get caught.
> —Divorced mother with a $230 part-time job, whose
> welfare payments were reduced to $172 a month.
> The Wall Street Journal

Contemporary consumers are affected by three distinct forms of scarcity. One
is traditional scarcity associated with inadequate levels of household income.
This familiar condition has been aggravated both by economy-wide inflation
and recession and by industrial change. These have increased substantially
the number of vulnerable households and significantly altered their consumption patterns, even though many of the new have nots remain well above the
poverty level. The second contemporary form of scarcity is associated with
periodic specific shortages of critical basic commodities—gasoline, sugar, and
so on. These shortages have been largely due to external developments, although the extent to which they have been or could be affected by domestic
policies and actions is debatable. Finally, there is the problem of induced
scarcity: those shortages and price increases that result from deliberate policies of government, often with the strong collaboration of affected business
and labor. These three types of scarcity require different kinds of policy
responses.

Traditional Scarcity

Consumer goods and services are always scarce in households with inadequate income. The development of an underclass consisting of such households has been a well-observed phenomenon of the postwar decades. In spite
of the inflationary boom of the late 1960s, massive expenditures for maintaining subsistence, and the War on Poverty, this persisting underclass has
been a major domestic policy disappointment. There is, unfortunately, nothing new about the existence of this other America, nor is there any sign that
its situation will be significantly altered in the near future. What is new at
the present time, however, is the massive shift of formerly middle class families from have into have-not status as a result of the loss of purchasing power
due to general inflation and loss of income and employment caused by recession and industrial change.[9] These families are distinguished from the hard-
core underclass by their accumulated assets (and debts) and their established
consumption patterns and lifestyles. They are not acclimated to the culture
of poverty, but they are in straitened circumstances. With reduced incomes
and the need to consume out of savings, they are prime targets for low-price
merchandising in all its forms. In particular, they are willing to substitute time

and inconvenience for money by pumping their own gas, bagging their own groceries, performing do-it-yourself repairs and services, and searching for basic bargain models of household durables.

From the business perspective, the important point is that these families constitute a substantial and growing market. Effective business response involves an emphasis on pocketbook consumerism—discount pricing, providing no-frills versions of products and services, and offering information clearly designed to guide consumers toward best buys. Special efforts to meet the needs of highly vulnerable consumers—such as Giant Food's recent program to give the poor edible but unsaleable items like dented cans and wilted produce—may also yield substantial public relations benefits.

On the government and philanthropic side, a wide assortment of actions can help alleviate the plight of the have not consumers. Continued or increased subsidization—in the form of food stamps, free cheese, health insurance, discounted mass transit, and low-interest mortgages and loans—can help many people. Innovative approaches—such as schemes that enable older people to extract a portion of the equity of their homes for living expenses, while continuing to live in them as long as they are able to do so—can respond to problems of imbalance between assets and income. Consumer education and direct assistance (e.g., the meals on wheels program) make an important contribution, and broader initiatives such as the establishment of weekly farmers markets in urban neighborhoods can widen the range of choice for both producers and consumers. All responsible groups can be vigilant in monitoring bargain offers aimed at vulnerable groups, so as to assure their legitimacy and appropriateness.

Specific Shortages

Periodic shortages and associated rapid price increases for individual products pose quite different problems. Although, like most other social ills, these developments usually have their gretest impact on low income groups, policy response to the shortage of individual products necessarily involves the consuming public as a whole. Assuming that the shortage itself cannot be forestalled or rapidly eliminated, the policy response has two main dimensions: anticipation and adjustment. Responses in both dimensions were conspicuously inadequate during the commodities shocks of the 1970s.

A major problem with devising better responses to this type of scarcity is that many of the superficially appealing schemes—those involving rationing, taxes, and subsidies—are immensely complicated and costly. They inevitably generate negative side effects, such as black markets, that may simply worsen the situation. Therefore, a preferable policy response from both business and government involves developing alternatives wherever possible and facilitating reductions in consumption. Examples of this are the carpooling programs generated by employers, unions, and local governments during the gasoline shortage and the energy-saving practices being urged more recently by electric power companies. The coming environment will probably provide many more opportunities for various forms of demarketing, either market-wide or for specific types of users. To some extent, the use of demarketing strategies is a complement to an emphasis on best buy products. The elimination of products or product attributes not offering favorable values may become an innovative, although perhaps dangerous, marketing strategy for the 1980s. Such a strategy might involve removal of nonnutritious foods or potentially hazardous products from the market, or a reduction in color, style, or performance options on durable goods.

Induced Scarcities

With respect to induced scarcities, the obvious proposal that they should not be induced in the first place is, unfortunately, wrong. The fact is that deliberate business and government policies to induce scarcity and increase prices are adopted for clear and compelling reasons; and the mere allegation that these will result in harm to consumers is unlikely to cause them to be reversed. However, it is important that the consumer impact of deliberate scarcity policies be recognized and taken into account in public discussion. The Russian Wheat Deal of 1973, although not specifically designed to have domestic market impact, resulted in a doubling of wheat prices and transferred $1 billion from consumers to farmers.[10] Current voluntary quotas on imports of Japanese automobiles have already raised domestic auto prices by almost $2,000 per car, and proposed "local content" legislation would result in even greater increases.[11]

Dealing with Abundance

> Fifty thousand dollars a year. What can you do with it really? Just eat and sleep and make a down payment on a home. These days it's just a decent wage.
>
> —$12,000-a-year security guard, father of eight,
> winner of $1 million lottery ($50,000-a-year for 20 years)
> *The Washington Post*

The classic focus of the contemporary consumer movement has been on dealing with abundance. Making wise choices among a wide range of products, evaluating individual product features, and understanding the trade-offs among performance alternatives have been conventional goals. The proclaimed rights to be informed and to choose are essential in our rich and varied market environment.

Paradoxically, the goals of adequate information and wise choice are made more difficult, not easier, by the contemporary explosion of new technologies and products. As Daniel Bell has pointed out, the very wealth of the postindustrial environment has created new kinds of scarcities, particularly of information and of time:

> When there's so much [knowledge] we have to have better judgment . . . and more guides to tell us what's relevant and what's not. . . . The growth of knowledge means . . . we have more problems in dealing with it. . . . Time is an absolute standard. . . . You can't build a stock of time the way you can build a stock of capital. . . . In an industrial society the producer was basically the economist. . . . [But] in a post-industrial era, it's the consumer who becomes the economist, calculating cost-benefit opportunity cost and trade-offs, in his allocation of time, information and money.[12]

It has been widely believed, or at least been desired, that the contemporary innovations in communications and electronics would greatly increase the amount of consumer information available and decrease search costs. Experience to date suggests precisely the opposite. Consumers are confronted with a mystifying array of new product and service alternatives—home computers, video games, health maintenance plans, telephone contact systems, energy-conservation devices, money market funds, etc.—many of which have totally unfamiliar performance features. The costs (including installation and routine operation) and benefits of many of these items are genuinely difficult to understand and estimate. Maintenance and enhancement features are not readily comprehended by the inexperienced. (Consider the state of common knowledge of the automobile, after half a century of widespread use.) It is no exaggeration to say that the communications revolution and its related technologies have, at least to date, exacerbated rather than mitigated the informational and choice problems of consumers.

The two areas of consumption currently presenting the greatest dilemmas of abundance are financial services and health care. The media are filled with advertisements featuring interest-bearing bank accounts, twenty-four hour teller locations, new insurance protections (and limitations), and personal financial services. Many of these offerings are genuinely new. Some are competitive alternatives made possible by changing government regulations; others are new options created in response to changing financial needs and lifestyles. Similarly, increasing health care costs and expenditures have spawned an incredible array of service alternatives and prepayment plans. Major employers are now sponsoring a range of options with a wide variety of contributory, deduction, and service features. Consumers are genuinely baffled by the range of choice available in both of these areas. Unlike the equally perplexing range of computer options, both financial services and health care are purchased as necessities by the great mass of consumers. The two areas share many common features: both are services rather than goods, and hence involve some descriptive ambiguity as well as considerable case-by-case variability; both involve complex combinations of features, for which trade-offs are hard to analyze and evaluate; and finally, criteria for good value and the best buy vary greatly depending upon the particular characteristics of the consuming household and on future developments that cannot be anticipated.

Policy proposals for dealing with this new abundance move in two different directions. One is an informational approach that attempts to develop sets of performance criteria for new and unfamiliar products and devise means for describing and rating them for convenient reference and comparison by both producers and consumers. This could be done by government agencies, trade associations, individual companies, or other organizations. The various energy-conservation ratings now in use (e.g., Environmental Protection Agency mileage ratings) are examples. Unfortunately, conscientious attempts to provide more comprehensive information in complex product/service areas—such as the large matrixes of data provided by *Washington Checkbook*—often convey little more to the consumer than the fact that "this is even more complicated than I thought."

The other and more controversial policy approach involves organizing and channeling the flow of consumer information already passing, or available for transmission, through new communications systems. The new communications environment is incredibly noisy. Relevant pieces of data are fluid and fugitive within an electronic system subject to abuse through manipulation and drown-out. (How many commercials did you see during the last television station break? What products do you remember? Why?) Although any restriction or selectivity in the information flow (e.g., Sears' proposal to transmit information over its own cable TV channel) raises issues of both monopoly and free speech. The notion that all additions to the number and volume of signals being sent constitute increasing information is clearly preposterous; in fact, they are more nearly the opposite. Some combination of reducing the communications noise and organizing the large volume of data (as, for example, in classified advertising) could clearly increase the amount of useable information available.

Process Issues and Responses

In twenty years of political brawling, I have from time to time been disconcerted to recognize decent (though benighted) impulses lurking in adversary's breast. And a small voice occasionally breaks through the rhetoric of combat to urge that true problem solving means bridging controversy, achieving empathy with adversaries, seeking common ground, compromise and accommodation, not polarization.

—Michael Pertschuk
Revolt Against Regulation

Up to this point we have focused primarily on the substance of consumer policy issues. Now we turn attention to the processes that might be used to achieve various objectives and to issues involving consumption-related processes themselves, without regard to specific application. Process issues will become increasingly prominent and controversial over the coming decade, largely because the tendency of both government and business to fall back on inappropriate but conventional processes (regulation, advertising) to deal with new and emerging situations will prove increasingly unsatisfactory.

The processes used by governments to respond to consumer concerns fall into four categories:

1. formal regulation, in which government is primarily responsible both for articulating specific goals and bringing about corrective actions;
2. private litigation within a framework established by government authority;
3. subsidization, both to needy individuals and needy business;
4. facilitation, including education and information, but with a new emphasis on participative and conciliatory activity among groups with diverse interests.

Although these four policy alternatives appear quite distinct in principle, in practice they tend to overlap and intertwine. They also involve a variety of responses and initiatives from the private sector.

Regulation

We noted earlier that the main thrust of the consumer movement for the past two decades was the achievement of rights through regulation.[13] As compared to prior eras, policy shifted first toward greater reliance on formal governmental authority and second—within the regulatory process itself—toward primary reliance on federal, rather than state and local, responsibility. Many factors account for this direction of development and some of them continue to have considerable validity even in the greatly changed regulatory environment of the eighties.

Two fundamental considerations underlie the support for government regulation. One is that, since at least some consumer damage is very difficult

to correct or recompense, regulatory action that prevents damage from occurring in the first place is desirable and very probably cost effective. The
entire history of health and safety regulation in both the workplace and the
consumption environment is predicated on this proposition. The other consideration favoring a regulatory approach is the imbalance of resources and
power between individual consumers and consumer groups, on the one hand,
and individual producers and producer groups, on the other. Even if consumers suffer merely economic harm—so that financial restitution could in
principle make the damaged party whole again—the time and expense involved in pursuing solutions through private action suggests an unequal
battle.

Forces underlying the emphasis on federal, rather than state and local,
authority were similar. Consumer problems were rarely differentiated by state
boundaries, and producers and merchants were typically multistate in their
operations. Consumer groups were better organized and probably had
greater clout at the national level, and national policy action assured that
malefactors did not escape behind the walls of state authority.

Given the continuing validity of these considerations and the considerable structure of regulatory activity that has been erected upon them, the
current antiregulatory climate may seem hard to understand. Yet, as part of
the general disillusionment with activist government, there is widespread dissatisfaction with the federal regulatory approach to many consumer problems. The contrast with environmental protection, which apparently is receiving increasing public support and business acceptance, is instructive. The
environmental protection movement can point to some notable successes,
which were achieved primarily through rule-making and enforcement proceedings (continuous regulation). Case-by-case compliance procedures have
actually involved only a small number of firms, local governments and other
sources of environmental impact. By contrast, the successes of consumer protection are harder to identify when even the most conspicuous (drug safety,
flammable fabrics) seem to involve only small fractions of the population and
isolated items in the giant consumption cornucopia. Moreover, the bulk of
consumer protection activity has been ad hoc and complaint-focused. Re-
medial actions are not confined to remote sources but affect the mass of consumers in ways that often seem costly, intrusive, and conducive to new dis-
satisfactions. The saga of auto safety devices provides the classic illustration.

Perceived dissatisfaction with federal regulation has generated two policy
adjustments: deregulation and devolution (i.e., the return of regulatory control to the states). Deregulation activity has already brought about major
changes in particular industries (e.g., transportation, banking, and communications). A significant rollback in federal regulatory control over advertising and product safety seems to be in the offing. The issue of where and how
much to deregulate—and where to *re*-regulate—will remain the focus of con-

siderable debate. Dissatisfaction with the results of deregulation (from communities that have lost all airline service, for example) will inevitably emerge, just as complaints about regulation itself did in the past. Calls for continued or renewed regulatory activity will become more frequent. The confusion many consumers experience in dealing with the new abundance of specialized airline fares, financial services, and communications devices may spur demand for the creation of a simpler, if less exciting, regulated environment. Cases like the Tylenol poisonings highlight the security promised by a stricter regulatory regime.

Calls for maintaining or increasing federal regulatory activity could also emerge from those members of the business community who are concerned about the problems created by devolution and the growth of state and local regulatory activity. Deregulation has not, as yet, taken hold on the state and local level. Between 1980 and 1981, the number of proposed state regulations actually doubled, rising to a total of 50,000. Within the business community this activity created concern about regulatory Balkanization and stimulated interest in new federal preemptive legislation. State level bottle bills, franchise-protection laws, deceptive advertising rules, and the like are proving to be thorns in the sides of many businesses. This situation seems likely to continue, since consumer activism apparently maintains its greatest strength at the grassroots level. While national consumer groups struggle for dollars and attention, many grassroots organizations are able to maintain their funding and activity levels, which then allows them to continue to pressure legislatures, attorney generals, and consumer policy officials for more vigorous consumer protection action. For example, the New York State Public Interest Research Group (a Ralph Nader affiliate) now has a $2.5 million budget and 180 full-time staff members.[15]

Private Litigation

Private litigation of consumer issues has increased dramatically in recent years. The huge number of product liability suits—and the large awards and settlements that have resulted from them—have probably helped to accelerate the recall or removal of products after defects are discovered (as in the case of Procter and Gamble's Rely tampon) and may have deterred marketing of many unsafe and hazardous products. To a much lesser extent, private antitrust actions have helped consumers by increasing freedom of choice in certain markets (e.g., *Berkey Photo v. Kodak;* MCI's challenge to AT&T before the FCC).

Increased reliance on private litigation as a consumer protection process seems more likely in the future, particularly if formal regulation continues to be reduced. However, private litigation has at least two features that limit its effectiveness for policy-development. One is the problem of nuisance suits. Laws and rules of procedure may have to be modified to avoid clogging the courts with suits filed by eager lawyers willing to take on almost anything on a contingency fee basis. The second, and far more serious, problem associated with private litigation has to do with the imbalance of financial resources that typically exists between the defending business firms and the complaining parties. Class-action suits in which numerous less well-off parties band together against wealthier defendants create the possibility of enormous judgments and may generate corrective behavior or restitution as well as deter anticonsumer behavior. Although consumer class actions have not had great success in the past, recent proceedings in Cleveland led to a settlement in which three supermarkets will distribute more than $20 million in merchandise to citizens over a five year period.

Subsidization

Governments do not treat all individuals and organizations equally. Some individuals are entitled to food stamps, cheaper mortgages, or free health care, while some businesses are entitled to cheaper loans, special tax breaks, or tariff protection. While the consequences of these various forms of subsidy for the general consumer have typically been overlooked—both in discussion of the subsidies themselves and in consideration of consumer policy issues—we anticipate growing concern about the economy-wide effects of the great number and variety of current subsidy programs. This concern will increase, in part, because processes of economic change now underway are rapidly expanding the number of people and firms entitled to receive subsidies.

Facilitation and Conciliation

Many consumer problems can be made less severe without the use of regulations, lawsuits, or subsidies, and thus without the conflict and controversy often associated with these techniques. Governments can employ processes that rely less on coercion and confrontation, and more on cooperation and hard work. The establishment of an Office of Consumer Affairs in the White House—and now in hundreds of local and state governments—is an obvious example. Another example is found in the consumer advocacy programs of the Federal Trade Commission (FTC), in which the entire commission, or a single commissioner and/or staff unit, can intervene in federal regulatory processes on behalf of competitive and consumer considerations.[16] Consumer education and information programs would also fall under this rubric, as would programs designed to bring potentially hostile parties together to propose voluntary actions that might be taken to deal with consumer problems. A recent Consumer Product Safety Commission initiative to develop new voluntary safety standards for electric blankets provides an example, as does the U.S. Office of Consumer Affairs' effort to set up consumer mediation panels designed to settle consumer-seller disputes in certain industries (e.g., automobiles). Most of these new types of initiatives are still in the very early stages and both their costs and effectiveness are difficult to predict. Experimentation with such policy processes is a priority item on the current consumer agenda for both business and government.

Private Sector Initiatives

All of the government policy regimes mentioned imply, of course, a corresponding response from the private sector. Active compliance can make regulation less burdensome and more effective; recalcitrance can make it both costly and useless. Litigation opportunities and subsidy programs can be either appropriately pursued or abused. Nonadversarial initiatives are made fruitful by cooperation, useless by its opposite.

In addition to these responses to government initiatives, the private sector also has displayed significant process initiatives of its own. A major development of the past couple of decades has been the growth of the corporate consumer affairs function and the establishment of formal consumer affairs offices within major business firms.[17] The number of such offices now exceeds 600; and membership in the Society of Consumer Affairs Professionals, which provides a meeting ground for both government and business personnel working in this area, has grown to 1,200. Under the stimulus of these professionals, consumer advisory boards have been established in some firms—most conspicuously the consumer boards connected with local public utilities—and other new avenues for the expression of consumer concerns, including more broadly focused consumer market surveys, have been developed. A related trend has been the publication by many firms of formal codes of conduct, which include standards for dealing with consumers as well as with employees and others. This approach has been strongly emphasized in Great Britain, where it is particularly encouraged by trade associations under the sponsorship of the Office of Fair Trading.[18] The most notable example of industry self-regulation in the United States is the nationwide advertising review procedure operated by the Council of Better Business Bureaus. Finally, there are a few other examples of nonadversarial and conciliatory approaches to common problems arising entirely from the private sector and modeled on the joint business–environmental effort that became the National Coal Policy Project.[19]

The Special Problem of Public Services

The annual expenditures of all levels of government are more than half as great as total consumer expenditures for goods and services ($1.1 trillion and $2 trillion respectively, in 1982). Although about fifteen percent of total government spending is for defense, the remainder—consisting primarily of transfer payments, costs of government programs, and direct provision of goods and services—has a wide range of direct and indirect impacts on consumers. An international forecast of consumer issues conducted for Nestlé notes the widespread perception that the state is the biggest firm with which consumers deal and anticipates increasing consumer pressure in this area.[20]

Contemporary attention to the consumer impact of government activity as a general matter (not simply with respect to isolated issues) was initially raised in Roland McKean's presidential address to the Southern Economic Association in 1973, and has now become a well-recognized topic in the literature.[21] Although McKean's initial coverage was very broad indeed, Dennis R. Young has emphasized the need to separate macrosocietal policies and those with only indirect impact from policies involving direct government contact with individual consumers and households.[22] Even with respect to the latter, there is a great difference between contacts involving access to income maintenance programs, at one extreme, and those involving individual use of specific services (transport, postal) on the other; somewhere in between are the basic services of fire and police protection. Public education seems to raise the complete range of public service consumption issues.

Young notes that the individual consumer faces four kinds of problems in dealing with this whole range of offerings:

1. Disappointing goods and services—those that fail to meet consumer expectations;

2. Awareness and coping—knowledge of the availability of public services and the means of obtaining them;

3. Preference-matching—inability to get less, more, or different quality services than those provided by a particular political jurisdiction;

4. Access and location—availability of and access to specific service within a jurisdiction (e.g., the need to move to obtain better public schools, or to purchase transportation in order to use public health care).

Although all of these kinds of problems have their parallels in the private marketplace, their importance in the public sector is heightened by the monopoly position of government (either *de jure* or *de facto*) in many types of services and locations and by the weak connection between the tax-price (tax charge per unit of service rendered) and actual costs, benefits, or consumption decisions.

Consumption of public services in all forms raises complex issues of scarcity, abundance, and process. Leaving aside the problems of adequacy and access to income maintenance programs, and the indirect effects of McKean's list of "anti-consumer public goods (and bads)" such as tariffs, price supports, subsidies and perverse regulations, many direct consumption concerns remain. Increased demand for public payment for medical care, intense pressures on public transportation systems, and so on, reflect the scarcity impacts of rising costs and falling incomes. Simultaneously, increasing needs for conventional services—police and fire protection, refuse collection, civic facilities—and interest in increased public support for education. The arts, and cultural activities reflect increasing affluence. The Tiebout hypothesis holds that individuals will locate so as to create homogeneous clusters, in each of which an optimal (for its residents) array of public services will be offered.[23] Complete reliance on this process to balance the supply and demand for public services neglects the fact that such moves are often costly (and involve many considerations other than public service availability) and also overlooks the impact of the clustering itself on the cost and availability of local amenities. Moreover, in the larger environment where services are globally public, there may be no way to escape or exit, and therefore individual voice and public protest become the only real alternative. For example, the Center for Auto Safety, an organization originally established by Ralph Nader but now independent, has recently brought suit against the Federal Highway Administration, charging that the highway system is not being maintained and that the routes have become killers from end to end because of inadequate repair.[24]

The fact that the citizen consumer is himself a part of the government machinery may make process issues even more complex and difficult in the public sector than in the private market. The government as watchdog is, of course, entirely missing (except, of course, for the state surveillance of municipalities, federal of states, etc.) The overt political character of public service production decisions would seem to increase the openness and participative character of the decision process. However, the large scope of the issues, the remoteness of the ballot box from the committee room, and the gap between the tax payment and the receipt of services all result in powerlessness and anonymity. An informal survey of public agencies by Enis and Yarwood "indicated that dissatisfied consumers of public services had no recourse."[25]

Increased attention to the consumer perspective on public services should be a high-priority concern at every level of government. It seems likely that there will be lessons to be learned from the private sector about the technical efficiency of customer service operations; as well as about the provision of appropriate levels of variety; and about the adaptation of both quality and quantity offerings over time. The use of voucher systems to allocate both students and funds among alternative public schools is a process experiment with wide implications and potential.

Concluding Remarks

Consumer policy in both business and government has come a long way since President Kennedy proclaimed his Consumer Bill of Rights in 1962. Indeed, one might say that it has come full circle. The consumer affairs function is now well established in leading corporations. Ralph Nader has declared the U.S. Office of Consumer Affairs to be a fraud and asked that it be abolished.[26] It seems clear that the era of rights through regulation has come to an end, and that a new environment has come into being which gives rise to new issues and requires new types of policy responses. Consumer policy must shift from an *ex post* orientation focused on complaints and preexisting problems to an *ex ante* and anticipatory approach focused on the distinctive attributes of different types of consumption situations.[27]

This new environment is the world of the rich/poor consumer. Although highly vulnerable economic and social groups continue to require special consideration, the great mass of American consumers are both rich and poor at the same time. They encounter different kinds of problems, which in turn give rise to different kinds of policy needs in different consumption situations. The distinction between the problems arising from scarcity (particularly in conventional consumption areas) and those arising from abundance (particularly with respect to new technologies, products, and services) offers a basis for reformulating the consumer policy agenda. (See table 4–1). Process issues take on a new importance in the new high-communication, antiregulation environment. Concerns involving the quality, availability, and cost of public services become more and more pressing as consumers come to rely increasingly on the public sector for essential daily needs (e.g., transportation).

Will consumer policy remain a significant agenda item for both business and government over the coming decade? It is clear that consumerism as a social movement is in, at the very least, what former FTC Chairman Michael Pertschuk has called a "pause."[28] Like most social movements, consumerism arose from a widespread public discontent—in this case discontent with the commercial product environment and a perception of corrupting and exploitative behavior on the part of business. The fact that this discontent developed in a setting of unprecedented affluence may appear paradoxical, but that does not reduce its reality. And as with other social movements, consumer concerns became focused through organizations, principally the Nader groups and their local and specialized variants.

Table 4–1
Consumer Policy Agenda

Scarcity Issues

Meeting the basic needs of the poor.

Responding to emerging needs of the new poor.

Identifying economy values and best buys.

Protecting vulnerable consumers against scams and deceptions.

Using self-service and limited selection to hold down costs.

Allocating short supplies among uses and users.

Developing reserve stocks and potential substitution possibilities in advance.

Bringing the consumer impact of supply-limiting policies into explicit consideration in the policy process.

Abundance Issues

Developing appropriate product/service descriptors and corresponding information in areas of important innovation and change—particularly: communications and electronics, financial services, and health care.

Helping consumers to cut through the volume and variety of available information (and misinformation) to isolate relevant alternatives.

Highlighting the long-term cost implications of new product/service offerings and lifestyles

Process Issues

Monitoring the cost and effectiveness of regulation; minimizing its restrictive impact on both business and consumers.

Seeking optimal combinations of state/federal authority and responsibility.

Assessing the need and impact of subsidies for both production and consumption.

Reducing the unnecessary use, length and cost of private litigation of consumer problems.

Seeking nonadversarial methods of identifying and resolving consumer issues.

Encouraging more business initiative in developing innovative responses to consumer concerns.

Making more effective use of consumer education and information programs.

Increasing two-way communication and participation in consumer policy decisions in both business and government.

Public Services Issues

Mitigating effects of government monopoly on service provision and pricing.

Maintaining and/or improving service quality, controlling cost, and adapting activity to community needs.

Experimenting with innovative approaches and consumer-oriented operating modes.

Both the underlying sense of consumer unease and the organizations built upon it are still largely present. Indeed, both have become increasingly institutionalized within both business and government. Thus, it would appear that the basic theme of consumerism—and hence a continuing search for appropriate consumer policies—will continue, even if the strident rhetoric and activist flavor of the movement vanishes entirely. Moreover, as Pertschuk has emphasized, many consumer concerns are "unifying issues among disparate groups . . . [and] tend not to be broadly divisive."[29] It seems entirely possible that business, government, and consumers themselves will come to see consumer policy issues less as major sources of conflict than as opportunities for consensus-seeking and socially constructive innovation.

Notes

1. Louis Harris et al., *Consumerism in the Eighties* (Study No. 822047, conducted for Atlantic Richfield Company, February 1983); see also, Paul N. Bloom and Stephen A. Greyser, "Exploring the Future of Consumerism" (Marketing Science Institute, 1981).

2. Frank E. McLaughlin, ed., *The Future of Consumerism,* (Center for Business and Public Policy, University of Maryland, 1981); Paul N. Bloom, ed., *Consumerism and Beyond* (Marketing Science Institute, 1982). See also: H.B. Thorelli, "Consumer Rights and Consumer Policy: Setting the Stage," *Journal of Contemporary Business* 7(1979):3–16; E. Scott Maynes, "Consumer Protection: The Issues" and "Consumer Protection: Corrective Measures," *Zeitschrift Für Verbraucherpolitik* [Journal of Consumer Policy] 3 (1979):97–109, 191–212; and R. Rock, B. Biervert, and W.F. Fischer-Winklemann, "A Critique of Some Fundamental Theoretical and Practical Tenets of Present Consumer Policy," ibid., 4(1980):93–101.

3. Maynes, "Consumer Protection," p. 99.

4. The logical priority of freedom to consume is stressed by H.B. Thorelli and S.V. Thorelli, *Consumer Information Systems and Consumer Policy* (Ballinger, 1977), p. 35. These authors formulate a three-fold consumer policy agenda: education, information, and protection.

5. Steven Kelman, "Cost-Benefit Analysis, an Ethical Critique," *Regulation* (January/February, 1981):33–40; Lester B. Lave, *The Strategy of Social Regulation,* (Brookings, 1981).

6. Lee H. Bloom, "Corporations and Consumerism: Compatible Goals?" in Frank McLaughlin, *The Future of Consumerism,* p. 24.

7. Business International, *Europe's Consumer Movement, Key Issues and Corporate Responses* (1980), p.2.

8. G.W.H. Scherf, "Consumer Dissatisfaction—Search for Causes and Alleviation Outside the Marketplace," *Zeitschrift Für Verbraucherpolitik* [Journal of Consumer Policy] 1(1977):101–108.

9. For a comprehensive update on relevant data, see "Sharing the Wealth: The

Gap Between Rich and Poor Grows Wider," *National Journal* (23 October 1982):1,788–95.

10. David L.Blond, "External Effects and United States Wheat Prices," *Business Economics* (September 1976):70–80.

11. *Domestic Content Legislation,* (Harbridge House, 1982).

12. Daniel Bell, "The Frameworks of the Future," *Proceedings of the MSI 20th Anniversary Conference* (May 1982):41–42.

13. For an excellent review of major regulatory issues and a report on recent Canadian experience, see D.T. Scheffman and E. Appelbaum, *Social Regulation in Markets for Consumer Goods and Services* (Ontario Economic Council, 1982).

14. "Business Mobilizes as States Begin to Move into the Regulatory Vacuum," *National Journal* (31 July 1982):1340.

15. Juan Williams, "Return from the Nadir," *The Washington Post Magazine* (23 May 1982):6–15.

16. U.S. Federal Trade Commission, "Competition and Consumer Advocacy Policy Review Session" (24 May 1982).

17. Claes Fornell, *Consumer Input for Marketing Decisions* (Praeger, 1976).

18. Jeremy Mitchell, "Government-Approved Codes of Practice: A New Approach to Reducing Friction Between Business and Consumers," *Zeitschrift Für Verbraucherpolitik* [Journal of Consumer Policy] 2(1978):144–58.

19. "Doing It Without the Government," *National Journal* (25 October 1980):1806.

20. Business International, *Europe's Consumer Movement,* p. III–34.

21. Roland N. McKean, "Government and the Consumer," *Southern Economic Journal* 39 (1973):481–89.

22. Dennis R. Young, "Consumer Problems in the Public Sector: A Framework for Research," *Zeitschrift Für Verbraucherpolitik* [Journal of Consumer Policy] 1(1977):205–206, with subsequent comments and a reply by Young, ibid, 2(1978):265–77.

23. C. Tiebout, "A Pure Theory of Local Expenditures," *Journal of Political Economy* 64 (1956):416–24.

24. *Washington Post,* (5 October 1982).

25. Ben M. Enis and Dean L. Yarwood, "Governments as Marketers: Consumerism Issues," in McLaughlin, *The Future of Consumerism,* pp.104–107.

26. Letter, Ralph Nader to President Ronald Reagan, 6 August, 1982: *Washington Post,* (7 August 1982).

27. Rock et al., "A Critique of Some Fundamental and Practical Tenents of Present Consumer Policy."

28. Michael Pertschuk, *Revolt Against Regulation, The Rise and Pause of the Consumer Movement* (University of California Press, 1982); see also, "The Consumer Movement in the 80s—A Sleeping Giant Stirs," Keynote Address to the 1983 CFA Consumer Assembly. For an analysis of the current status of the consumer movement, see Paul N.Bloom and Stephen A. Greyser, "The Maturing of Consumerism," *Harvard Business Review* 59 (November–December 1981):130–39.

29. Pertschuk, *Revolt Against Regulation,* p. 134–35.

Part II
Relevant Empirical Findings

5
Is Consumerism Dead or Alive? Some Empirical Evidence

Darlene Brannigan Smith
Paul N. Bloom

The drastic cutback in federal consumer protection activity that has taken place in the last few years might suggest to some observers that consumerism is dead. The organized consumer movement's inability to reverse this trend can certainly be viewed as a signal that the movement's days are numbered. However, there are those who argue that, in spite of what has been happening in Washington, the consumer movement remains alive and healthy. For instance, Bloom and Greyser (1981) have proposed that consumerism has entered a mature stage of its life cycle and now consists of a highly fragmented "consumerism industry" with numerous organizations and institutions selling consumerist "products." They foresee the demand for the products of this industry remaining strong and the competition for this demand remaining heated. They predict that certain trends will favor the fortunes of local and grassroots consumer organizations over national organizations in the competition for gaining public approval and assistance. Their views have received support in the work of several individuals, including Herrmann and Warland (1981), Peterson (in Cohen 1981), Metzen (1982), Molitor (1982), and Greyser, Bloom, and Diamond (1982).

This paper presents some new evidence that can be used to evaluate Bloom and Greyser's ideas and to provide other insights into the current and future status of consumerism. Four different research studies are examined in an attempt to answer the following questions:

1. What is the current status of public attitudes toward consumerism?
2. Are people engaging in behaviors (e.g., joining consumer groups) that are consistent with their attitudes?
3. Are there specific subsegments of the population that possess more favorable attitudes and behaviors toward consumerism?
4. Are policymakers in Washington accurately assessing the public's attitudes and behaviors toward consumerism?
5. How well are various consumer groups competing in the consumerism industry?

Probing the first three questions will help reveal information about the intensity and dimensions of the demand for consumerism. Addressing the fourth question will reveal whether there is potential for the demand for consumerism to be intensified because of neglect or misunderstanding of consumerism by Washington policymakers. Finally, examining the last question will suggest which types of consumer groups might become the strongest in the coming years.

The four studies examined are:

1. *Consumerism in the Eighties,* the study conducted by Louis Harris and Associates (1983) under the sponsorship of the Atlantic Richfield Company. Although the authors of this paper were not involved with this study (as they were with the other three), its currency and size make it an important work to review in developing answers to the above questions.
2. A poll of residents of a Middle Atlantic state, conducted in the fall of 1982.
3. A survey of Washington policymakers, conducted in the summer of 1982.
4. A survey of activist organizations, conducted in the fall of 1982.

Findings

Louis Harris Survey

Data for the *Consumerism in the Eighties* study were based on responses from 1,252 randomly selected adults nationwide. The subjects were telephoned during the period October 15 through October 26, 1982, using a modified random-digit dialing procedure. The results suggest many answers to the research questions addressed above.

The public appeared more concerned about many consumer problems in 1982 than they did in a 1976 Harris study. According to Harris, forty-one percent of the total sample cited "a great deal of worry" over a majority (six or more) of eleven consumer concerns (Harris 1983). Four of the concerns showed at least a ten percent increase, three showed a slight increase, and only two showed improvement since 1976. In addition, when consumers were asked to assess how things have changed in the last ten years, several areas were thought to have gotten worse. Seventy-six percent of all respondents perceived that the value obtained for money spent on most goods and services had gotten worse. And fifty-nine percent said that the quality of most products and services had grown worse. Overall, fifty-four percent of the public felt the deal consumers got in the marketplace was worse, as opposed to thirty-one percent who felt it was better than ten years ago. Thus, there appeared to be support for the contention that strong demand exists for consumerism.

Despite these favorable evaluations, public participation in organized consumer groups was weak, even though strong potential for involvement appeared to exist. Only six percent of the respondents indicated that they had ever taken an active part in a consumer group and only fourteen percent had ever personally contributed money to a consumer group. But two-thirds said they would certainly or probably support a consumer pressure group in their area under certain circumstances (Harris 1983).

The Harris survey also provided profiles of three groups that may be of interest to researchers and policymakers: black consumers, women, and the elderly. Overall, black consumers seemed particularly vulnerable to and concerned about consumer protection; they were an ally of those who press for more government regulation, but did not feel quite so well served by the movement as they might have been (Harris 1983). Similarly, women appeared to be more sensitive to consumer problems and less satisfied that these problems were being solved. They thought that government should be doing more to protect consumers (Harris 1983). Individuals over the age of sixty-five were more skeptical and less convinced that there had been progress in the marketplace, that the impact of the consumer movement was good, that government regulation was desirable, and that the benefits of consumerism were worth the costs (Harris 1983). In general, the lower-income and less-educated groups were proconsumerist with regard to worrying about consumer problems, perceiving deterioration in the marketplace, and preferring more government regulation and protection.

How effective do consumers perceive policymakers and consumer organizations to be? Respondents perceived Consumers Union and the Better Business Bureau as far superior at protecting the interests of consumers than the current Washington administration, state governments, and private industry. Congress received lower ratings than the White House. The Consumer Product Safety Commission was the only arm of government receiving a positive rating, while the Federal Trade Commission received only a twenty-six percent confidence vote. Overall, the ratings remained stable over a five-year period, except for Ralph Nader, who had dropped fifteen percentage points.

Clearly, consumers' perceptions of the consumer movement, its impact and accomplishments were more favorable than their opinion of its leadership. There was a widespread perception (sixty-six percent) throughout the public that the consumer movement was stronger than it had been five years previously (Harris 1983). There were, however, some complaints about consumer leaders. Forty-eight percent of the respondents thought the leaders were "out of touch" with consumer feelings and forty-nine percent did not think the leaders considered the cost of what they were asking for. Even though this criticism did not result in unfavorable evaluations, the shifting opinions were clear and should represent an early warning to consumer groups.

Another area that showed diminishing public support was government regulation of business. Only twenty-one percent thought there should be more regulation, thirty-three felt the same level is needed, and forty-one percent preferred less regulation of business. Consumers were overwhelmingly in favor, though, of protective intervention—ninety-four percent favored approving new drugs, eighty-eight percent were for approving new toys, and sixty-seven percent were for regulating misleading television advertisements. It is important to note that forty-two percent of the respondents felt that government regulation had not done enough to protect consumers, twenty-eight percent had mixed views, and twenty-seven percent thought it was about right. Only three percent felt government regulation had gone too far.

Middle Atlantic State Poll

Residents of a selected Middle Atlantic state hold similar views to their cohorts nationwide. Many seem to disagree with the current administration's policy of pulling back from consumer issues. These results were obtained from a small telephone poll (where questions on a diverse set of topics were asked) that surveyed a cross-section of state residents. A random sample was obtained by using the random-digit dial method of selecting telephone households and a probability selection of individuals within a household. One hundred forty-two individuals were interviewed during October 1982. The sample was representative of the state residents, when compared to the state's demographic profile.

When asked to respond whether the government should exercise more, less, or about the same level of responsibility as it now does for regulating the advertising, sales, and marketing activities of manufacturers, thirty-two percent of the sample preferred more, thirty-eight percent preferred about the same, and thirty percent indicated less government responsibility. These results are not identical to those found in the Harris study, but seem to indicate a stronger preference for more government regulation. This question, however, specifically probed concerns about marketing activities, in contrast to the Harris question, which dealt with the regulation of business in general.

The survey also identified differing attitudes across racial, educational and income groups. Black respondents overwhelmingly indicated the need for more government responsibility, in sharp contrast to the views of most of the state's white residents. Fifty-six percent of all black respondents preferred more regulatory responsibility, while only twenty-five percent of the white respondents felt this way. Likewise, only nine percent of the blacks indicated

Table 5–1
Middle Atlantic State Poll

Q: Do you feel the government should exercise more, less, or about the same level of responsibility as it now does for regulating the advertising, sales and marketing activities of manufacturers?

	Overall	Race		Income		Education	
		White	Black	≤$10,000	>$10,000	0–11 yrs.	12 yrs. or more
Base	142	104	32	59	67	19	123
More	32%	25%	56%	41%	24%	47%	30%
Same	38	40	35	34	40	21	40
Less	30	35	9	25	36	32	30

a desire for less regulatory responsibility, as compared to thirty-five percent for the white population. Similar results are obtained for lower-income and less-educated subsegments of the state's population. Table 5–1 presents the summary of percentages. Over one-half of those individual who earned less than $10,000 annually felt that the government should exercise more responsibility, as compared to one-third of those with incomes exceeding $10,000. Comparable feelings about government responsibility can be seen among those who are less educated. These data are in general agreement with the Harris study.

Survey of Washington Policymakers

A telephone survey was conducted of individuals in staff and administrative positions of Congress, the executive branch and independent regulatory agencies during June of 1982. Table 5–2 presents the questions and overall responses to each. (Responses are based on five point Likert-type scales.) The questions specifically examined perceptions of the continued viability of consumerism and the effectiveness of various consumer groups.

Generally speaking, most Washington policymakers (eighty-two percent) felt the consumer movement has been good for the public. There was, however, less enthusiasm about its impact on business. Only fifty-six percent of the respondents felt the movement has been good for business, and over one-quarter of the sample indicated that it has been bad for business. In addition, over one-half of the people surveyed agreed or strongly agreed that the consumer movment seemed to be running out of steam. This belief may, in part, be based on their perceptions that the current administration and Congress are not proconsumer. Only twenty percent of the respondents agreed or strongly agreed that the administration is proconsumer, while thirty-seven

Table 5–2
Survey of Washington Policymakers

Please state whether you STRONGLY AGREE, AGREE, ARE NEUTRAL, DISAGREE, or STRONGLY DISAGREE with each of the following statements:

Statement		Agree[a]	Disagree[b]
1.	On the whole, the consumer movement has been good for the public.	82.0%	8.0%
2.	On the whole, the consumer movement has been good for business.	56.2	25.4
3.	The consumer movement seems to be running out of steam.	51.3	35.3
4.	The current mood of the public is anticonsumer.	5.0	82.6
5.	The current Administration is proconsumer.	22.4	57.7
6.	The current Congress is proconsumer.	36.8	40.4

Statement		Good[c]	Poor[d]
7.	Are (the following organizations) VERY EFFECTIVE, GOOD, AVERAGE, POOR or VERY INEFFECTIVE?		
a.	National Consumer Organizations such as the Consumer Federation of America, the National Consumers League or Public Citizen.	40.0%	10.0%
b.	Federal Consumer Protection Agencies such as the FTC, FDA, and CPSC.	42.3	19.4
c.	The White House	12.9	53.6
d.	U.S. Congress	31.4	21.4
e.	State and Local Government Consumer Protection Offices	43.3	14.4
f.	State and Local Consumer Organizations such as citizen utility boards and campus public interest research groups	41.8	14.4
g.	Trade and Professional Associations	26.9	25.9

Statement		Increasing	Remaining the Same	Decreasing
8.	Looking ahead 5 years, do you see the overall level of consumer activism INCREASING, DECREASING, or REMAINING THE SAME?	44.3%	32.8%	21.4%

[a]Agree = Strongly Agree + Agree
[b]Disagree = Strongly Disagree + Disagree
[c]Good = Effective + Good
[d]Poor = Very Ineffective + Poor

percent assessed Congress as proconsumer. Thus, Washington policymakers had mixed views on the continued viability of the consumer movement, despite the current proconsumer mood of the public. One optimistic note is that almost eighty percent of them indicated that they expected to see the same or an increasing level of consumer activity in five years.

It is also interesting to consider how these policymakers viewed the effectiveness of their cohorts and various consumer organizations in responding to the consumer movement. From the percentages in table 5–2, the most effective groups in descending order are: state and local consumer protection agencies, state and local nongovernment agencies, national consumer organizations, U.S.Congress, trade and professional organizations, and the White House. While none of the groups received majority support, there is a clear distinction in the perceived effectiveness of consumer protection agencies versus policymaking bodies (i.e., both government and private business concerns). These results are very similar to the ratings obtained in the Harris survey.

Public Activists Survey

To gather more direct evidence on the effectiveness of certain consumer groups, fifteen organizations were examined to obtain information about the sizes of their staffs, memberships, and budgets. Data were obtained through both primary and secondary resources. Telephone interviews were conducted during October 1982 in order to collect current figures. Trend data was taken using *Public Interest Profiles,* compiled by the Foundation for Public Affairs (1977, 1980, 1982) in Washington, D.C.

The consumer organizations selected for review were judged to be the most visible and influential in recent years. They do not, by any means, represent an exhaustive list of consumer interest organizations, but they provide a reasonable estimate on which to examine growth patterns. The organizations are listed in table 5–3. It should be noted that the term "consumer organization" is used here to refer to an organization that has as a stated mission improving the satisfaction consumers obtain from individual market transactions. Such groups are concerned with the safety, quality, effectiveness, and price of consumer products and services.

Table 5–4 provides an aggregation of staff, membership, and budget data across various types of consumer organizations. Overall, between 1978 and 1982 staff sizes had decreased, while membership and budget levels had risen. A better understanding of changing patterns is seen, however, by examining data for each of the three types of consumer groups studied—national organizations, community/grassroots groups, and corporate/government accountability groups. These titles are somewhat broad in scope, but capture the nature of the programs emphasized by the groups classified in the categories.

Table 5–3
Data on Selected Consumer Activist Organizations, 1982

Group	Staff	Membership	Budget
National Consumer Groups (n = 8)			
Center for Auto Safety	15	3,000 +	$ 300,000
Center for Science in the Public Interest	16	35,000	900,000
Community Nutrition Institute	20	Nonmembership	1,300,000
Consumer Alert	4	5,000 +	102,000
Consumer Federation of America	10	220 organizations	320,000
Consumers Union of United States, Inc.	240	242,000	40,000,000
Health Research Group	8	Nonmembership	190,000
National Consumers League	10	1,500	n/a
Community Grassroots Consumer Groups (n = 5)			
Association of Community Organizations for Reform Now (ACORN)	130	50,000	1,700,000
California Campaign for Economic Democracy	21	11,000	500,000
Center for Community Change	40	Nonmembership	1,500,000
Citizen's Choice	15	78,000	1,500,000
National People's Action/National Training and Information Center	16	300 groups	510,000
Corporate/Government Accountability Consumer Groups (n = 2)			
Congress Watch	15	Nonmembership	280,000
Tax Reform Research Group	5	Nonmembership	n/a

Note: n/a = unable to ascertain.

National consumer groups appeared to have been most affected by changing patterns in the social movement. Staff positions had been cut by over forty-four percent since 1978. These reductions no doubt reflect the relatively small increase (three percent) in membership. Despite the limitations on growth in these two areas, budget levels continued to maintain strong growth—a forty-nine percent increase over 1978. These figures seem to suggest that national consumer organizations were effective in managing their resources and mobilizing monetary resources.

Community and grassroot organizations also appear to be extremely effective in developing support for their programs. Staff positions had increased by twenty-four percent over 1978, membership had increased by seventy percent, and budget levels by fifty-two percent. This supports Bloom and Greyser's (1981) contention that "locals" should have considerably more success

Table 5–4
Trend Data on Categories of Consumer Activist Organizations

	n	*1978–1982 (% change)*	*1982*	*1980*	*1978*
Staff Size					
National	8	− 31	323	498	466
Grassroots	5	24	222	226	179
Accountability	2	5	20	14	19
Membership					
National	8	3[a]	286,720	276,870	n/a[b]
Grassroots	5	70	139,300	83,300	42,300
Accountability	2	—	—	—	—[c]
Budget					
National	8	49	$43.1 million	$32.7 million	$22.0 million
Grassroots	5	52	$5.2 million	$4.5 million	$2.5 million
Accountability	2	33	$.3 million	$.2 million	$.2 million

[a]change calculated from 1980 base.
[b]n/a = unable to ascertain.
[c]Nonmembership organizations.

in selling their products in the consumerism industry. Local organizations offer direct and tangible benefits in the form of redress assistance, education, and information. Thus, it appears, community and grassroot organizations have a reasonably bright future.

Corporate/government accountability groups appear to be holding their own. Staff positions showed modest gains and budget levels were up by thirty-three percent between 1978 and 1982. Despite these seemingly encouraging gains, this category shows the smallest growth of the three categories presented. It is probably safe to say that a stable level of support exists for these organizations.

Discussion

The four studies provide some interesting answers to the five research questions introduced previously. They reflect assessments of the vitality of consumerism from varied perspectives. The remarks in this section interpret the common threads running through these studies. In general, the following conclusions can be drawn:

1. Public attitudes toward consumerism are extremely favorable and should remain strong for at least the next several years.

2. There is a willingness to engage in activism (e.g., join consumer groups), even though actual participation is limited.

3. Certain subsegments of the population are more favorable toward and have greater demand for the "products" of the consumerism industry. Their needs, unfortunately, have not yet been effectively met.

4. Policymakers in Washington do not appear to be accurately assessing the public's attitudes and do not seem to be doing a good job of reacting to the needs of the public in the area of consumer protection.

5. Some consumer groups are competing more effectively than others in the consumerism industry but, overall, the accomplishments of the industry are rated highly.

Attitudes toward Consumerism

The public opinion polls presented here consistently indicate consumers' considerable dissatisfaction with their situation in the marketplace and their sustained support for consumer protection initiatives. Survey respondents say that they want consumer protection and are willing to pay to get it. The evidence provided in these four studies suggests there is a great deal of strength and depth in the consumer movement. The movement has no traditional, social, demographic, or political lines. According to Harris, "If there were no movement up to now, let me assure you that the American people would go out and organize one" (Sinclair 1983:A21). A wide variety of individuals and groups want their interests better represented in the marketplace.

Attitudes versus Behavior

The potential for translating attitude into behavior is growing stronger, as consumers grow increasingly unhappy with the quality of goods and services, with the way government protects their interests, and with consumer leaders. This supports the proposition by Greyser, Bloom and Diamond (1982) that consumerism is shifting from a spectator activity to a participative activity. Smaller, local organizations serving the needs of select target groups, as opposed to larger organizations and national celebrities, will apparently epitomize the consumer movement in the latter half of the 1980s. So while current participation in the organized consumer movement is low, the potential for future involvement is extremely high.

Needs of Subsegments in the Population

Evidence illustrating the problems of the poor and disadvantaged was brought to light in both the Harris and the Middle-Atlantic state polls. In the face of current economic and financial conditions, the number of disadvantaged consumers may actually be increasing. Andreasen defines disadvantaged consumers as those "who are particularly handicapped in achieving adequate value for their consumer dollar in the . . . marketplace because of their severely restricted incomes, their minority racial status, their old age, and/or their difficulties with the language" (Andreasen 1975:6). It is clear that future programs and policy initiatives will have to more specifically target these consumers.

Assessment of Washington Policymakers

There is an obvious gap between the public's needs and expectations and policymaker's assessment and reactions to them. Data suggest that the public does not want a change in the proconsumer stance of government. Individuals, more than ever, want and are demanding consumer protection. The Harris survey illustrates people's criticism of government leaders for not doing a good job in this area. A clear majority does not rate any of the federal agencies positively.

Washington's less-than-accurate assessment of public attitudes is further demonstrated by the severe budget and employment cutbacks faced by the federal agencies responsible for consumer protection. According to *The Washington Post,* the Federal Trade Commission will be taking an 8.3 percent cut before inflation with the 1984 proposed budget. It has lost personnel steadily in the past two years and will lose another ten percent of its staff by 1984. The proposed budget of $32 million for the Consumer Product Safety Commission is "below its spending level of 1975, when the buying power of a dollar was almost twice as great." (Barringer 1983), and its work force will be lower than when it opened its doors in 1973.

Effectiveness of Consumer Groups

Approval of the consumer movement's accomplishments is high, and very widely and evenly spread across the population. Yet consumers feel the movement's leaders are out of touch with their needs. This may explain the marginal increase in the growth of national consumer organizations while community and grassroots groups are growing much more rapidly. Better responses to specific needs may be the reason why individuals are contributing to and joining such organizations. With the onslaught of increased competition, organizations now have to mobilize their limited resources to position themselves to take advantage of the widespread discontent. All organizations, not just local/community grassroots groups, can provide people with selective benefits in return for their support.

Research Implications

At this time, it seems reasonable to emphasize both evaluative and descriptive research. More empirical studies need to be devoted to the reasons why individuals join and support groups. With the current high level of unhappiness with the marketplace, it would be worthwhile to investigate the gap between people's attitudes and behaviors. Do fear of embarrassment, lack of confidence, insufficient information, or other variables explain why only a small percentage of individuals engage in behavior (i.e., joining consumer groups) consistent with their attitudes?

Another area for future research is the effectiveness of consumer organizations. More extensive studies are needed to assess the strength and vitality of the specific components of the consumerism industry (e.g., national groups, grassroots organizations). In-depth interviews and larger sample sizes would be useful in examining the changes over time in funding and membership, the level of support given to these organizations by other interest groups (e.g., political, labor and private business concerns), and their abilities to mobilize resources and support.

Not only can research describe and explain the problems faced by individuals and consumer groups, but it can serve as an evaluative tool as well. The effectiveness of existing programs and mechanisms initiated by government and consumer groups needs to be critically examined and alternative policy actions need to be provided. In particular, substantial research on the disadvantaged consumer is required. Studies must examine both the qualitative and quantitative problems faced by the subsegments in society who have a greater need for consumer protection, education, and redress. Such findings can help guide government and consumer group initiatives to help the disadvantaged consumer.

Conclusion

Consumerism is most definitely alive. In spite of (or perhaps because of) the recent actions of Washington policymakers, public attitudes toward consumerism are favorable and participation in consumer group activities, though limited overall, is growing—particularly on the local level. Continued research on consumer activism and consumer problems should therefore be welcomed by public policymakers, business firms, and consumer groups themselves.

References

Andreasen, Alan R. 1975. *The Disadvantaged Consumer.* New York: The Free Press.

Barringer, Felicity. 1983. Major regulatory agencies facing more cuts in fiscal '84. *The Washington Post* (Feb. 9):A17.

Bloom, Paul N., and Stephen A. Greyser. 1981. The maturing of consumerism. *Harvard Business Review* 59 (Nov.–Dec.):130–139.

Cohen, Stanley E. 1981. Peterson sees new coalition of consumers. *Advertising Age* 52 (Jan. 26):10, 72.

Greyser, Stephen A., Paul N. Bloom, and Steven L. Diamond. 1982. Assessing consumerism: The public's and the expert's view. *Consumerism and Beyond,* 4–10. (Proceedings of the workshop presented by the Marketing Science Institute and the Center for Business and Public Policy, University of Maryland, April.)

Herrmann, Robert O., and Rex H. Warland. 1981. Does consumerism have a future? In *Proceedings of the Twenty-Sixth Conference of the American Council of Consumer Interests,* edited by Norleen M. Ackerman. Columbia, Mo.: American Council on Consumer Interests, 12–17.

Harris, Louis, and Associates, Inc. 1983. *Consumerism in the Eighties.* Study no. 822047. Los Angeles: Atlantic Richfield Co.

Metzen, Edward J. 1982. Consumerism in the evolving future. *Consumerism and Beyond,* 16–20.

Molitor, Graham T.T. 1982. Worldwide search for consumer trends. *Consumerism and Beyond,* 95–103.

Public Interest Profiles. 1978, 1980, 1982. Washington, D.C.: Foundation for Public Affairs.

Sinclair, Molly. 1983. Consumer unhappiness growing. *The Washington Post* (Feb. 17):A21.

6

Evolution of Consumer Attitude toward Business, 1971–1984: A Replication

John F. Gaski
Michael J. Etzel

The assessment of general consumer attitudes toward business practice has been of interest to marketing researchers for a number of years. The literature contains some notable efforts to develop global measures of consumer satisfaction with business in general, including Barksdale and Darden (1972), Hustad and Pessemier (1973), and Lundstrom and Lamont (1976).

Hustad and Pessemier (1973) measured "consumers' opinions about marketing practices" based on the reactions of 912 husband/wife pairs from Lafayette, Indiana to twenty-one questionnaire items such as:

American businesses are honest.

Products and services are of high quality.

Business is responsive to the consumer.

Businesses are concerned about the public they serve.

There are too many brands and products available today.

Cluster analysis was used to develop demographic and psychographic profiles of the probusiness and antibusiness segments. The antibusiness segment was found to be considerably smaller (eighteen percent of the sample population) than the probusiness group (forty-two percent).

Lundstrom and Lamont (1976) provided a thorough exposition of the development and validation process for a comprehensive measure of con-

The authors extend their sincere appreciation to Market Facts, Inc., and especially to Verne Churchill and Norman Kane for their assistance in data collection in this research project. They also acknowledge the research support provided by the Gallo Fund and the Business Partners Fund.

sumer discontent with business, with this construct operationalized to include four components, or marketing-related factors:

The product strategies of business

Business communications and information

The impersonal nature of business and retail institutions

Socioeconomic and political forces such as an inflationary economy and concern over pricing practices

Lundstrom and Lamont used an eighty-two item, six-point Likert scale.

At two-year intervals during the period from 1971 to 1979, Barksdale, Darden, and Perreault (Barksdale, Darden, and Perreault 1976; Barksdale and Darden 1972; Barksdale and Perreault 1980) measured overall consumer attitudes toward manufacturers using a national mail sample survey and a five-item Likert scale. The survey consisted of these items:

Most manufacturers operate on the philosophy that the consumer is always right.

Despite what is frequently said, "let the buyer beware" is the guiding philosophy of most manufacturers.

Competition ensures that consumers pay fair prices.

Manufacturers seldom shirk their responsibility to the consumer.

Most manufacturers are more interested in making profits than in serving consumers.

They also measured attitudes toward particular marketing phenomena, including product quality and advertising. In general, it was found that

In the 1970s, there was substantial stability in consumer attitudes concerning . . . the business sector . . . . [C]onsumers were as skeptical about the operating philosophy of business in 1979 as they were nine years earlier. (Barksdale and Perreault 1980)

Since it has now been five years since such a general measure of consumer attitudes toward business practice has been reported, and the intervening period has been one of conspicuous shifts in national sentiment toward various institutions, we decided that a reprise of the Barksdale-Darden-Perreault work would be of interest. This study, conducted in February 1984, and its results are reported in the following sections.

Methodology

The Sample

The consumer sample used for this replication of the Barksdale-Darden-Perreault study was the Consumer Mail Panel of the research firm Market Facts, Inc. This mail panel contains a pool of over 200,000 households that is continually updated to reflect the most recent U.S. Census data in terms of geographic region, annual income, population density, age, sex, and family size. The sample size was 2,000, with a response rate of 71.4 percent (n = 1,428) achieved.

The Instrument

The mail questionnaire items used in this research constitute a near-identical replication of the Barksdale-Darden-Perreault (B-D-P) survey. These items are:

Most businesses operate on the philosophy that the consumer is always right.

Despite what is frequently said, "let the buyer beware" is the guiding philosophy of most businesses.

Competition between companies keeps prices reasonable.

Most businesses seldom shirk their responsibility to the consumer.

Most businesses are more interested in making profits than in serving consumers.

As can be seen, the only differences are substitution of the more general term "businesses" for "manufacturers," and a slight, but equivalent, restatement of the third item.[1]

The items were presented using a five-point Likert scale, as in the B-D-P research, with response options "agree strongly," "agree somewhat," "neither agree nor disagree," "disagree somewhat,' and "disagree strongly." Responses were scored from +2 to −2, with the most favorable answer (i.e., "agree strongly" with a positive statement, "disagree strongly" with a negative statement) receiving the highest score, indicating the most favorable attitude. Item scores were then summed for a scale ranging from −10 to +10.

Validation

The validity and reliability of the replication instrument as a measure of general attitude toward business were assessed by conventional techniques.

Cronbach's coefficient alpha for the scale was found to be .614, which is in the acceptable range. This demonstration of internal consistency or reliability can be regarded as indirect evidence of validity, as a necessary but not sufficient condition (Churchill 1976:251–252).

Convergent validity for the measure was established by correlating it with four alternative measures of the same construct. These measures can be described, briefly, as follows:

1. A four-item, five-point Likert scale assessing "overall satisfaction with each marketing area":

The quality of most available products.

The prices of most products.

Most of the advertising read, seen, and heard.

The selling conditions at most retail stores.

Response options here were "very satisfied" to "very dissatisfied," scored from $+2$ to -2.

2. A four-item, five-point Likert scale measuring the frequency of problems with products, prices, advertising, and stores, respectively. Responses were reverse scored, from 5 for "very seldom" to 1 for "very often," as an inverse measure of satisfaction with, or approval of, business. That is, frequent problems are equivalent to unfavorable attitude.

3. An index consisting of the sum of four five-item, five-point Likert scales, each used to measure general attitude toward "product quality," "price of products," "advertising for products," or "retailing or selling." This measure is thoroughly described elsewhere (Gaski and Etzel 1985).

4. The same index, with each category weighted for importance according to questionnaire responses to a five-point importance scale ("extremely important" to "not at all important").

Correlation coefficients between the B-D-P replication measure and each of these four alternative measures were found to be .527, .486, .608, and .606 respectively (all significant at $p < .001$), which seems to indicate an adequate degree of convergence, especially considering the limited number of items in B-D-P and the first two alternate measures, as well as the fact that most of the scales did not include importance-weighting of components.

Results

The mean score on the B-D-P replication measure was $-.8715$. By itself, this indicates very little except that aggregate consumer attitude toward business is slightly unfavorable (range $= -10$ to $+10$). However, this value can also be compared to the historical 1971–1979 results reported by B-D-P (Barksdale and Perreault 1980), and reproduced in tables 6–1 and 6–2. The comparison is shown graphically in the figure 6–1.[2]

Table 6–1
Attitudes toward Business, 1971–1979

Statements	Year of Survey	Percentage of Consumers				
		Strongly Agree	Agree	Uncertain	Disagree	Strongly Disagree
Most manufacturers operate on the philosophy that the consumer is always right.	1971	2	21	16	47	14
	1973	2	15	18	54	11
	1975	2	16	18	53	11
	1977	2	15	22	51	10
	1979	1	15	16	55	13
Despite what is frequently said, "let the buyer beware" is the guiding philosophy of most manufacturers.	1971	6	32	25	34	3
	1973	7	33	28	31	1
	1975	7	31	29	30	3
	1977	6	33	29	30	2
	1979	8	33	28	29	2
Competition ensures that consumers pay fair prices for products.*	1971	12	45	12	26	5
	1973	10	47	12	25	6
	1975	12	41	12	26	9
	1977	15	45	9	24	7
	1979	16	42	11	25	6
Manufacturers seldom shirk their responsibility to the consumer.	1971	1	20	20	47	12
	1973	1	24	22	43	10
	1975	1	25	20	45	9
	1977	1	24	23	43	9
	1979	2	20	23	47	8
Most manufacturers are more interested in making profits than in serving consumers.	1971	22	52	12	12	2
	1973	20	54	13	12	1
	1975	25	53	10	11	1
	1977	24	54	10	11	1
	1979	25	54	10	10	1

Source: Barksdale and Perreault, "Can Consumers be Satisfied?" *Business Topics*, vol. 28 (Spring 1980), table 1. "Attitudes toward Philosophy of Business, 1971–79." Reprinted by permission.

*Tau β significant ($p \leq .05$).

Table 6–2
Summary of the Barksdale, Darden, and
Perreault and the Replication Results

Year	Mean Attitude Score
1971	−1.50
1973	−1.58
1975	−1.69
1977	−1.50
1979	−1.74
1984	−0.87

There appears to have been some improvement in consumer sentiment toward business in recent years. (Raw data were not available from the B-D-P authors at the time of writing, so significance of the difference between the 1984 and earlier observations is not computed.) If this finding is valid, it could be an indication that (1) business practice has improved, (2) business's public relations efforts are paying off, (3) environmental circumstances have changed in a way that produces less consumer hostility toward business, or (4) some evolution of consumer sentiment has taken place so that consumers are less inclined to blame business for their problems.

Another finding of interest is that the attitudes of male and female respondents are not significantly different. The mean attitude score for men was $-.8306$, $-.9184$ for women, with the difference not significant ($t = .445$). Apparently, there is no gender gap between men and women in terms of their attitudes toward business.

Interpretation of the previous B-D-P results is also possible. A low point of measured consumer attitude toward marketing occurred in 1975, a time that marked the end of a decade of public disaffection with national institutions. Aside from experiencing the Vietnam War and Watergate, respondents had recently endured the first oil shortage, a period of rapid inflation, and a severe recession. This was also a period of intense consumerism. The 1977 measure, on the other hand, may have reflected the economic recovery and the sizeable reduction in the inflation rate achieved during the Ford administration. Then, the 1979 nadir signaled "Oil Crisis II," another period of rapid inflation, an impending recession, and the national "malaise" reported by President Carter.

Of course, there may be some concern that the B-D-P replication has produced a spurious result. Reasons for this could include: (1) Sampling differences—although B-D-P also conducted a national mail survey, their response rates were lower (between forty-two and forty-five percent). Also, it

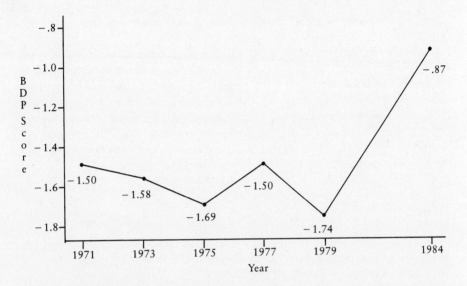

B-D-P = *Barksdale-Darden-Perreault* measure and replication.

Figure 6–1. Historical Pattern of Consumer Attitude toward Business

may be that their respondents, on average, were more involved in the issue because of more dissatisfaction, and this could be responsible for the lower sentiment ratings reported. However, it appears that both the B-D-P and Market Facts procedures produced representative national samples. (2) The slight differences between the original and replicated instruments—although the survey questions appear vitually identical, it is possible that "manufacturers" is a more negatively charged term for consumers.

The seasonal factor does not appear to be a problem. The B-D-P surveys were all conducted in around February-March, with the initial mailing during February, which is compatible with the present study.[3]

In spite of the possible limitations, we hope the longitudinal information provided here is of some value and interest. Thanks to the work of Barksdale, Darden, and Perreault, a historical perspective is available. The main finding of this study—that consumer sentiment has apparently improved toward business—is somewhat contrary to other evidence. As mentioned previously, Hustad and Pessemier (1973) found attitudes to be generally probusiness. Yet, in B-D-P and this replication, aggregate attitudes have consistently been in the negative range, and were more intensely so during the time of the Hustad and Pessemier research. Also, the improvement in consumer attitudes seen in the present study is in contrast to the Harris (1983) data reported by Smith and Bloom in chapter 5. That data showed, if anything, a negative trend in consumer satisfaction with marketplace conditions between 1976 and 1982.

Of course, differences in sampling and measurement could account for these discrepancies. The lack of construct validation in most of the work in this field could also be a factor. But perhaps as more research into such global consumer attitudes is conducted, this study and the other works cited will contribute as mosaic pieces to the understanding of general consumer sentiment toward business. Ultimately, it is hoped, our understanding of consumer attitudes will yield a clear enough picture to be of interest to researchers and consumers, and useful to business and public policymakers.

Notes

1. The replication instrument was not identical to the original because the items used in our survey were part of a larger project and, thus, performed dual functions. Had replication of B-D-P been the only purpose of our research, the original instrument would have been reproduced precisely. However, the differences are likely to be inconsequential and the items used in this research amount to an adequate replication of B-D-P.

2. Barksdale, Darden, and Perreault did not report these mean scores, presumably out of concern that data were not ratio-scaled and, therefore, not amenable to division. However, since the principle is well-established that ordinal data may be treated as interval (Kerlinger 1973:426–427), and since the neutral response ("neither agree nor disagree") may be considered a natural origin, the authors believe it is reasonable to treat responses to the Likert scales as quasi-ratio data. There is precedent for this approach in the literature (Harrell and Bennett 1974).

3. The authors extend their gratitude to Professor Hiram C. Barksdale of the University of Georgia for providing this and other helpful information.

References

Barksdale, Hiram C., and William R. Darden. 1972. Consumer attitudes toward marketing and consumerism. *Journal of Marketing* 36 (Oct.):28–35.

Barksdale, Hiram C., William R.Darden, and William D. Perreault, Jr. 1976. Changes in consumer attitudes toward marketing, consumerism and government regulation: 1971–1975. *The Journal of Consumer Affairs* 10 (winter):117–139.

Barksdale, Hiram C., and William D. Perreault, Jr. 1980. Can consumers be satisfied? *MSU Business Topics* 28 (spring):19–30.

Churchill, Gilbert A., Jr. 1976. *Marketing Research: Methodological Foundations.* Hinsdale, Ill.: The Dryden Press.

Gaski, John F., and Michael J. Etzel. 1985. A proposal for a global, longitudinal measure of national consumer sentiment toward marketing practice. In *Advances in Consumer Research,* vol. 12 edited by Elizabeth C. Hirschman and Morris B. Holbrook. Association for Consumer Research, in press.

Harrell, Gilbert D., and Peter D. Bennett. 1974. An evaluation of the expectancy/ value model of attitude measurement for physician prescribing behavior. *Journal of Marketing Research* 11 (Aug.):269–278.

Harris, Louis and Associates, Inc. 1983. *Consumerism in the Eighties.* Study no. 822047.

Hustad, Thomas P., and Edgar A. Pessemier. 1973. Will the real consumer activist please stand up: An examination of consumers' opinions about marketing practices. *Journal of Marketing Research* 10 (Aug.):319–324.

Kerlinger, Fred N. 1973. *Foundations of Behavioral Research,* 2nd ed New York: Holt, Rinehart and Winston.

Lundstrom, William J., and Lawrence M. Lamont. 1976. The development of a scale to measure consumer discontent. *Journal of Marketing Research* 13 (Nov.):373–381.

7

Consumer Activism, Community Activism, and the Consumer Movement

Rex H. Warland
Robert O. Herrmann
Dan E. Moore

T hose who have written recently about the consumer movement have suggested that there are several significant changes occurring. Both Bloom and Greyser (1981) and Herrmann and Warland (1980) indicate that the consumer movement is moving into a new phase, in which activity at the national and federal level is declining and likely to continue to decline.

Bloom and Greyser (1981) have suggested, however, that consumerism at the local level is alive and well. They have predicted continuing activity at the local level in the future. This view has also received support from Esther Peterson (Cohen 1981), who has stated that she expects to see new coalitions at the state and local level. She suggests that these coalitions of local socially concerned business groups, church groups, consumerists, environmentalists, and others are likely to support and participate in the consumer movement. It is our belief, however, that in order for such coalitions to occur and for the consumer movement to be viable at the local level, some of those who are currently most active in the community will have to become involved. Significant action on consumer rights is most likely to occur at the local level if those most experienced in community and political activities participate.

Over the last several years, our research in the consumer area has focused on the linkage of community and political actions with consumer-redress actions. Specifically, we have been interested in determining if those who are active in local community and political groups are also likely to seek redress for consumer problems. We have been primarily concerned with the breadth of the experiences these citizens have in community problem solving and consumer redress, rather than in the frequency of any one particular action.

Review of Past Research

In our national study of consumer unrest ten years ago (Warland, Herrmann, and Willits 1975), we found evidence that those who seek redress for consumer problems are also those most likely to be active in community organizations and political affairs. We found that those who complained shared several characteristics (Warland, Herrmann, and Willits 1975; Warland 1977).

They used several channels for consumer redress.

They shared an interest in consumer issues and consumerism.

They embraced the ideology of consumerism.

They were more aware and informed about consumer issues and consumer leaders than others.

They were upscale and relatively young.

They belonged to a number of voluntary organizations.

They were politically active.

This profile indicated that complaining behavior was related to broader consumer interests and concerns, and that those who complained were an identifiable segment of the population.

In this earlier study, only a few political actions were measured and no community actions were considered. As a result, our conclusion about the links between community and political actions and consumer-redress actions were tentative. Even though the empirical evidence was questionable, we believed that these two kinds of actions could be related on theoretical grounds (Warland, Herrmann, and Moore 1984). We based our ideas on Smith's (1980) theory, which proposes that there is a predictable pattern to how people use their discretionary time. Smith's thesis is that discretionary activities are positively correlated. Therefore, a person who is involved in community organizations is also likely to be involved in political, recreational, and cultural pursuits, and active in other areas of social life. Smith argues that higher-status persons are particularly likely to participate in a wide range of social, political, and economic activities because they live in social environments that enhance participation. They are encouraged to use their time in active rather than passive ways, and their association with others who are active helps them to obtain the skills, motivation, confidence, and knowledge necessary to be active in several areas.

In 1980 we had an opportunity to investigate more thoroughly the linkage between community actions and consumer-redress actions, using a more extensive set of actions. Analysis of the 1980 data indicated that an index of consumer complaining actions and an index of local community and political actions were related ($r = .36$). Even after age, education, income, and consumer grievances were controlled, the relationship between these two types of actions remained (Warland, Herrmann, and Moore, 1984).

There are several reasons why this relationship is relevant to the consumer movement. Recent social movement theories based on the resource mobilization perspective hold that the life and well-being of a social movement depend on organizational structure and social solidarity (McCarthy and Zald 1977). Oberschall (1973) has argued that those most likely to participate in social movements are those who have been active and relatively well integrated in the community. These individuals often have the resources and skills necessary to make the social movement successful (McCarthy and Zald, 1977). Furthermore, Jenkins (1983) has suggested that the consumer movement fits the resource-mobilization model quite well. It follows that the participation of citizens who have a wide range of experience in dealing with community issues and problems, a wide range of experience in complaining about consumer problems, and better-than-average educational and income levels, would certainly enhance the viability of a local consumer movement. The results of our early studies suggested that such a group does exist.

However, much is concealed by statistical summaries. It is also useful to determine if there are patterns to community activism and consumer-redress action. Is there a group of people who have a broad range of experience in both consumer-redress actions and community and political actions? Are there others who specialize in only a few particular actions? Are there people who do virtually nothing in terms of community or consumer redress actions?

Such questions were addressed by Verba and Nie (1972) in their study of political participation. They recognized that there are various ways in which citizens can participate. Rather than looking at participation as a unidimensional concept, they suggested that participation be viewed as a multivariate concept. We adopted this view and focused our analysis on types of actions that people take, rather than assuming a single continuum of action.

It is difficult to predict the exact nature of such a typology of actions. There are, however, several types of consumer-redress actions and community and political actions that have been previously identified and can aid in our interpretation of the results of the data analysis. With respect to consumer-redress actions, the classification offered by Day and his associates (1981) appears useful. He separated complaining behavior into personal actions and public actions. Private or personal actions included personally boycotting products, brands, and sellers, or complaining privately to family and friends. Public actions included complaining to business, taking legal action, seeking redress directly from firms, and so on.

The types of community and political actions delineated by Verba and

Nie (1972) also are useful. They suggested that some community actions are communal or group oriented; in these activities citizens work with others. Other actions are individually initiated. In these activities individuals, on their own, contact those whom they believe created the problem, or a third party whom they believe can help. Verba and Nie also argued that some activities, such as voting or signing a petition, require only low involvement, whereas other actions, such as participating in groups to bring about change, requires high involvement. In our interpretation of the types of activities, we will use these categories to help classify the differences between the groups identified.

Data and Procedures

Data for the analysis were taken from a large-scale mail survey of adults in the state of Pennsylvania. The survey was conducted in January, February, and March 1980. The sample was selected randomly from a statewide list of licensed automobile drivers and was apportioned by county, sex, and age. Over seventy-three percent of those who received the survey returned usable forms. The characteristics of the 9,367 respondents closely resembled the 1978 population estimates for age, but women were slightly overrepresented.

Involvement in community and political affairs was measured by a group of twelve items, based in part on Verba and Nie (1972). These items covered a variety of activities: voting in the last election, attending meetings on some community issue, discussing public issues with friends, giving time or money to a political party or candidate, writing to an elected official, and so on. The time referent for all measures was the previous two years.

Consumer-redress actions were measured by another group of nine items. These items covered a range of behavior from talking to family and friends about a problem and ceasing use of a service or product to refusing to pay for goods and beginning legal action. Thus, both private and public actions were considered.

Twelve different consumer grievances were also investigated. The respondents were asked to indicate if they had experienced problems such as difficulties with auto repairs, defective products, utility rates, mail order sales, or health insurance claims in the previous two years.

A cluster analysis was conducted on the community and political affairs measures and the consumer-redress action measures. Because of the large number of observations, it was necessary to use the optimization technique referred to as K-MEANS in the CLUSTAN program. Even this program is limited to 1,000 cases, so it was necessary to take repeated samples of the 9,367 respondents to assure that the same cluster structure was obtained. A similar structure was found in twelve of the fourteen samples selected.

Results

The groups produced by the cluster analysis are presented in table 7–1. Only eight of the twelve community actions and seven of the nine consumer-redress actions were included in the cluster analysis. The six actions omitted from the analysis (contacting media about local issue, participating in public demonstration, serving on local government board, running for public office, contacting media about a consumer problem, and initiating legal action because of a consumer problem) were excluded because less than five percent of the respondents indicated they had done any of these things.

Four groups emerged from the cluster analysis. The first group, labeled the complete activists after Verba and Nie (1972), contains respondents who had engaged in both community and consumer action. The breadth of their experience in community and consumer-redress actions is most impressive. Not only did a majority report private actions (table 7–1, numbers 1, 2, 6, 9, and 11) but also public actions (numbers 3, 4, 5, 10, and 12). Furthermore, they were the most likely to engage in both group actions (number 4, 5, 7, and 8) as well as those which require initiation on their part (numbers 6, 10, 12, 13, 14, and 15). The complete activists had the highest level of participation on fourteen of the fifteen actions. They represented seventeen percent of the sample.

The counterparts to this group were termed the inactives. This group was the largest of the four groups (thirty-six percent). The only action in which a majority of these respondents had engaged was voting in the last election. This group had the lowest level of participation on fourteen of the fifteen actions. Their consumer-redress activity was particularly low.

Those categorized as mainstream activists were citizens who tended to participate in the most popular and conventional community and consumer actions. They were more likely to participate in private actions (numbers 1, 2, 9, and 11), those public actions that did not require a high level of involvement (numbers 1 and 3), and the most conventional of the public consumer complaint actions—complaining to a store manager. What is striking about this group when compared to the complete activists is their very low levels of participation in any group actions. The mainstream activists represented twenty-two percent of the sample.

The fourth group, labeled the community specialist (twenty-six percent of the sample), primarily participated in community and political actions. Few reported consumer-redress actions. A majority had discussed public issues with friends, voted in the last election, signed a petition, and attended meetings about some community issue. This group was second only to the complete activists in their rates of participation in the other community and political actions. On the other hand, they were very similar to the inactives in their low level of consumer-redress actions. It is likely that the correlation

Table 7–1
Community Involvement and Consumer-Redress Action Profiles

Actions	Groups Produced by Cluster Analysis			
	Complete Activists	Mainstream Activists	Community Specialists	Inactives
Community and Political Actions				
1. Voted in last election	89%	54%	88%	58%
2. Discussed public issues with friends	88	78	79	40
3. Signed a petition	84	50	81	15
4. Attended meetings about some community issue	81	9	56	6
5. Worked with others to solve a community problem	64	9	35	5
6. Wrote to or personally contacted a government agency or elected official	58	14	34	7
7. Gave time and money to political party or candidate	45	9	34	7
8. Joined an organization that takes stand on public issues	28	8	22	3
Consumer Redress Actions				
9. Stopped using service, product, or store	84	80	19	15
10. Complained to a store manager	77	55	11	9
11. Talked about consumer problem with family or friends	72	79	14	9
12. Contacted a manufacturer	50	22	10	8
13. Contacted the Better Business Bureau or the Chamber of Commerce	32	15	7	5
14. Refused to pay for goods or service	27	16	5	2
15. Complained to local or state government agency or official	24	7	4	3
Percent of sample in type	17	22	26	35

Table 7–2
Consumer Grievances Reported, by Activist Group

Grievances	Complete Activists	Mainstream Activists	Community Specialists	Inactives
Defective products	64%	59%	20%	18%
Misleading advertising	62	50	28	21
Poor quality of auto repairs	56	55	29	26
No attention paid to consumer complaints	51	40	18	12
Misleading packaging and labeling	48	36	18	12
Misleading mail order sales	37	30	15	10
Utility rate charges	31	26	17	14
Poor workmanship in home improvements	30	20	16	8
Problems in dealing with or getting service from local government	34	18	11	6
Poor medical service	19	12	8	6
Problems with health insurance claims	16	12	8	7
Discriminated against in getting credit or loans	11	8	6	6
Total number of grievances				
0 to 1	10	14	45	58
2 to 3	28	38	34	27
4 or more	62	48	21	15

reported earlier (Warland, Herrmann, and Moore 1984) between the number of community actions and consumer-redress actions was attenuated by this split-level type of activist. The cluster analysis results strongly suggest that the relationship between these two types of actions is far more complex than a simple linear association.

Table 7–2 summarizes the consumer grievances expressed by each of the four groups. As would be expected, a higher percentage of the complete activists and the mainstream activists reported grievances than did the other two groups. In addition, nearly two-thirds of the complete activists reported four or more grievances, suggesting that these respondents had perceived a wide range of consumer problems.

A demographic profile of the four types of activist is presented in table 7–3. Statistical tests are not presented, since such tests are not very meaningful given the large sample size. Although many of the differences among the groups resemble those reported in past studies of political participation and complaining behavior, a comparison of the four groups revealed several new insights. The complete activists had the highest incomes and the highest levels

Table 7–3
Demographic Profile of the Four Activist Groups

Demographic Profile	Complete Activists	Mainstream Activists	Community Specialists	Inactives
Education				
Less than high school graduate	8%	13%	18%	28%
High school graduate	29	31	27	40
Vocational school or some college	23	32	29	21
College graduate and more	40	24	26	11
Income				
Less than $9,000	7	13	18	29
$9,000 to $17,999	30	31	29	29
$18,000 to $24,999	26	27	22	24
$25,000 or more	37	29	31	18
Age				
Under 30	20	50	15	27
31 to 61	67	43	58	47
Over 61	13	7	27	26
Marital Status				
Never married	18	30	12	17
Married	72	60	76	65
Divorced or separated	5	5	3	6
Widowed	5	5	9	12
Sex				
Male	50	46	47	34
Female	50	52	53	66
Employment Status[a]				
Employed	67	72	57	49
Homemaker	26	22	30	28
Student, unemployed, disabled	12	20	6	8
Retired	9	5	24	20
Years Lived in Community				
Less than 10	16	18	13	15
11 to 20	14	22	10	15
21 or more	70	60	77	70

[a]Since respondents could hold more than one status, totals exceed 100.

of education, but they were not greatly different from the mainstream activists or the community specialists in these two demographic characteristics. The complete activists were primarily middle-aged and divided equally between males and females. They had lived in their communities for a long time. With respect to education, income, age, and sex, the complete activists of this study are similar to the complete activist type reported by Verba and Nie (1972).

The mainstream activists were the youngest of the four types. One-half of the group were under thirty, nearly one-third of them were single, and nearly three-fourths of them were employed at the time of the study. They had above-average levels of income and education. The negative relationship between age and consumer complaining reported in earlier studies apparently may have been based on consumers who had consumer-redress action patterns and demographic profiles similar to those of the mainstream activists.

The community specialists differed primarily in age. They typically were the oldest group, had lived in their communities the longest, and proportionally had the most retired members.

The inactives were clearly a downscale group. Their education and income levels were well below the other three groups, and were disproportionately older and younger. Nearly two-thirds of the inactives were female, and less than half were employed. Relatively large proportions of the inactives were widowed or retired. The profile of this group is similar to Verba and Nie's (1972) inactive group.

Discussion

The results of the data analysis reveal that a significant number of individuals have a wide range of experience both in community and political action and in consumer-redress action. The members of this group appear to be middle to upper-middle class (better than average incomes and education), middle aged, and long-time residents of their communities. It also is noteworthy that this group reported a large number of consumer grievances.

We believe that the discovery of the complete activist type has important implications for the future of complaining activity as well as for the consumer movement. In light of our findings, it is little wonder that many studies during the last decade have reported extensive complaining activity. The profiles of both the complete activists and the mainstream activists suggest that momentum for complaining has come from very active middle-class consumers or from relatively young consumers with substantial consumer grievances. With high levels of economic strain and continuing pressures on real incomes, the number of grievances may remain relatively high. And these two groups are likely to continue to be very active, at least on the individual level, in consumer-redress activities. These groups already have extensive experience in complaining actions and the knowledge and skills needed to voice their grievances.

The implications of these results to the future of the consumer movement are more difficult to state because of limitations of the data analyzed. On the one hand, the results of the study suggest that there is a pool of people in local communities whose previous community and consumer activism, resources (education and income), and social integration make them an ideal group for mobilization in the consumer movement. This conclusion is supported by recent studies by Useem (1980) and Walsh and Warland (1984), who suggest that those who have been previously active in the local community are the most likely to become involved in a social movement once a crisis has occurred. Walsh and Warland (1984) also found that those most involved in the Three Mile Island social movement were primarily middle and upper-middle class people who had been politically active and highly involved in both local and extralocal community organizations. The profile of consumer complainers obtained from our 1972 national survey indicated that complainers were socially integrated and politically active, were interested in the consumer movement, embraced a consumerism ideology, and were knowledgeable about the issues and leaders of the consumer movement. On the basis of these studies, it would appear that the complete activists—if not already involved in the broader consumer movement—are likely to become so if and when circumstances precipitate their involvement.

Based on the data presented here, we cannot support such conclusions. We do not know if the complete activists have any interest in broader consumerism issues or embrace consumerism ideology. More importantly, we do not know what experience, if any, they have had in consumer groups or organizations. Nor do we know if they know people who are involved in such groups, or if they would be willing to join such groups. Furthermore, we are not sure whether they would devote already-limited time and resources to support group consumer actions.

Even so, it is important to know that the complete activist type exists in local communities. Their existance suggests some hope for the future of the consumer movment at the local level. Smith and Bloom's review of recent consumerism studies (chapter 5) suggests that public attitudes are very favorable toward consumerism, but there is still a gap between people's attitudes and behavior. Perhaps a crisis will be necessary to mobilize these consumers, as has been the case in other social movements that have been studied recently (Jenkins 1983). Nonetheless, we suspect that some of these complete activists are already involved in some local consumerism issues like resistance to condo conversions, landlord–tenant conflicts, and control of cable television franchising. Further data are needed to assess more precisely to what extent these activists are currently involved or are likely to be involved in future local consumerism.

References

Bloom, Paul N., and Stephen A. Greyser. 1981. The maturing of consumerism. *Harvard Business Review* 59 (Nov.–Dec.):130–139.

Cohen, Stanley E. 1981. Peterson sees new coalition of consumers. *Advertising Age* 52 (Jan. 26):10, 72.

Day, Ralph L., Thomas Schaetzle, Klaus Grabicke, and Fritz Staubach. 1981. The hidden agenda of consumer complaining. *Journal of Retailing* 57 (fall):86–106.

Herrmann, Robert O., and Rex H. Warland. 1980. Does consumerism have a future? In *Proceedings of the Twenty-Sixth Conference of the American Council of Consumer Interests,* edited by Norleen M. Ackerman. Columbia, Mo.: American Council on Consumer Interests, 12–17.

Jenkins, Craig J. 1983. Resource mobilization theory and the study of social movements. *Annual Review of Sociology* 9:527–553.

McCarthy, John O., and Meyer N. Zald. 1977. Resource mobilization and social movements: A partial theory. *American Journal of Sociology* 82 (May):1212–41.

Oberschall, Anthony. 1973. *Social Conflict and Social Movements.* Englewood Cliffs, N.J.: Prentice-Hall.

Smith, David Horton, Jackqueline Macaulay, and Associates. 1980. *Participation in Social and Political Activities.* San Francisco, Calif.: Jossey-Bass.

Useem, Bert. 1980. The Boston anti-busing movement. *American Sociological Review* 45 (June):357–369.

Verba, Sidney, and Norman H. Nie. 1972. *Participation in America: Political Democracy and Social Equality.* New York: Harper and Row.

Walsh, Edward J., and Rex H. Warland. 1984. Social movement involvement in the wake of a nuclear accident: Activists and free rides in the TMI area. *American Sociological Review* 48 (Dec.):764–780.

Warland, Rex H. 1977. A typology of consumer complainers. In *Consumer Satisfaction, Dissatisfaction and Complaining Behavior,* edited by R.L. Day. Bloomington, Ind.: Indiana University, 144–146.

Warland, Rex H., Robert O. Herrmann, and Jane Willits. 1975. Dissatisfied consumers: Who gets upset and who takes action. *Journal of Consumer Affairs* 9 (winter):148–163.

Warland, Rex H., Robert O. Herrmann, and Dan E. Moore. 1984. Consumer complaining and community involvement: An exploration of their theoretical and empirical linkages. *Journal of Consumer Affairs* 18 (summer):64–78.

Part III
Emerging Issues

8
The Elderly Consumer: A Perspective on Present and Potential Sources of Consumerism Activity

Ruth Belk Smith
George T. Baker

I n spite of the increasing concern of policymakers (Howard 1967; Waddell 1976), marketers (Phillips and Sternthal 1977; Schiffman 1971,
1972a, b), and consumer affairs specialists (Burton and Hennon 1980)
about the elderly population, little is known about this group other than the
impressive demographic statistics shown by the U.S. Bureau of Census
(1980). The older population has been increasing at twice the rate of the rest
of the population for the last two decades. This trend is expected to increase
well into the next century. According to U.S. Census projections, the total
U.S. population is expected to increase 33 percent between 1982 and 2050,
while the group aged fifty-five and over will grow at the rate of 113 percent.
In 2010, one-fourth of the total U.S. population (74.1 million) is expected to
be at least fifty-five years old and one person in seven will be over sixty-five
(U.S. Bureau of the Census 1980).

The percent of "old-old" individuals is also expected to continue to grow
(see figure 8–1 and table 8–1). As the figure and table show, persons over
seventy-five will comprise almost 28 percent of the total U.S. population. The
most rapid increase, however, is expected between the years 2010 and 2030
when the baby boom generation reaches sixty-five. Currently, there are more
individuals over age sixty-five than teenagers, whose numbers are projected
to decrease by 17 percent by the turn of the century. Thus it is vital to advance
our understanding of elderly consumers.

Although the elderly consumer is of much concern, there has been little
empirical or theoretical research in the area. The research that is available
tends to be fragmented and primarily descriptive. Much of the research interest has been among policymakers. In addition to obvious needs to protect
the elderly from deceptive and/or misleading advertising, high pressure sales
tactics, and outright fraud ("Consumer interests of the elderly" 1967; Smith
and Moschis 1985), policymakers realize that the elderly are an increasingly
powerful political force (Waddell 1976). They are becoming more vocal, de-

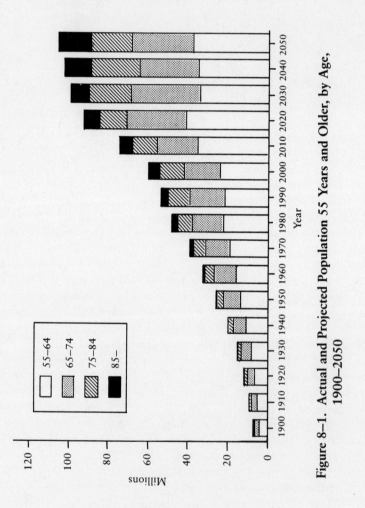

Figure 8–1. Actual and Projected Population 55 Years and Older, by Age, 1900–2050

Table 8–1
Actual and Projected Growth of the Older Population, 1900–2050
(numbers in thousands)

Year	Total Population, All Ages	55 to 64 Years		65 to 74 Years		75 to 84 Years		85 Years Plus		65 Years Plus	
		Number	*Percent*	*Number*	*Percent*	*Number*	*Percent*	*Number*	*Percent*	*Number*	*Percent*
1900	76,303	4,009	5.3	2,189	2.9	772	1.0	123	0.2	3,084	4.0
1910	91,972	5,054	5.5	2,793	3.0	989	1.1	167	0.2	3,950	4.3
1920	105,711	6,532	6.2	3,464	3.3	1,259	1.2	210	0.2	4,933	4.7
1930	122,775	8,397	6.8	4,721	3.8	1,641	1.3	272	0.2	6,634	5.4
1940	131,669	10,572	8.0	6,375	4.8	2,278	1.7	365	0.3	9,019	6.8
1950	150,697	13,295	8.8	8,415	5.6	3,278	2.2	577	0.4	12,270	8.1
1960	179,323	15,572	8.7	10,997	6.1	4,633	2.6	929	0.5	16,560	9.2
1970	203,302	18,608	9.2	12,447	6.1	6,124	3.0	1,409	0.7	19,980	9.8
1980	226,505	21,700	9.6	15,578	6.9	7,727	3.4	2,240	1.0	25,544	11.3
1990	249,731	21,090	8.4	18,054	7.2	10,284	4.1	3,461	1.4	31,799	12.7
2000	267,990	23,779	8.9	17,693	6.6	12,207	4.6	5,136	1.9	35,036	13.1
2010	283,141	34,828	12.3	20,279	7.2	12,172	4.3	6,818	2.4	39,269	13.9
2020	296,339	40,243	13.6	29,769	10.0	14,280	4.8	7,337	2.5	51,386	17.3
2030	304,339	33,965	11.2	34,416	11.3	21,128	6.9	8,801	2.9	64,345	21.1
2040	307,952	34,664	11.3	29,168	9.5	24,529	8.0	12,946	4.2	66,643	21.6
2050	308,856	37,276	12.1	30,022	9.7	20,976	6.8	16,063	5.2	67,061	21.7

Source: U.S. Bureau of the Census, *Decennial Censuses of Population, 1900–1980 and Projections of the Population of the United States; 1982 to 2050* (advance report); *Current Population Reports,* series P–25, no. 922, October 1982. Projections are middle series.

manding their rights, and getting results (e.g., the Grey Panthers). Similarly, consumer educators are interested in developing programs to aid the acquisition and use of consumer skills by the elderly. Evidence of this interest is found in the growing number of special programs for elderly consumers (Diamond 1974: Fox 1980; Waddell 1976).

The public and private sectors have only begun to attempt to understand the elderly consumer (Burton and Hennon 1980). The elderly have been forced to be conscientious shoppers (Mason and Bearden 1978), and they would appreciate special treatment, as befits their age, from salespersons, but they do not perceive that they obtain such treatment (Lambert 1979). Most promotion-related research has focused on the negative stereotyping of the elderly in advertisements (e.g., Aronoff 1974; Gerbner et al. 1980; Smith, Moschis, and Moore 1984). Although the elderly represent over eleven percent of the population, programming and advertising (particularly television advertising) underrepresents them (about five percent of actors are old) (Schreiber and Boyd 1980). Elderly consumers have also been found to be less sensitive to unfairness and less likely to complain (Krosk and Srivastava 1977, Mason and Bearden 1978, Bernhardt 1981).

The elderly consumer is generally healthy and financially independent; less than five percent of elderly persons are institutionalized (Maddox and Douglas 1973). However, they have definable consumer needs that differentiate them from younger people. Normal aging processes such as a decline in sensory acuity, lessened mobility, and redistribution of proportions of body fat and lean muscle mass cause the elderly to have physically different needs. For instance, about thirty three percent of older Americans are limited in their major activities by chronic physical conditions, and need special information on necessary products such as wheelchairs, eyeglasses, and hearing aids. Elderly consumers have different requirements for food, housing, and insurance, and a need exists for readable, timely, and understandable information that will aid them in selecting products and services. Other areas of concern include specific buying situations. For instance, the National Retired Teachers Association/American Association of Retired Persons (NRTA/AARP) receives more complaints from older persons about mail order transactions than about any other single business category (Waddell 1975).

Older people no more fit a stereotype than members of other arbitrary groupings of people. Indeed, as persons age they become much more heterogeneous in terms of both physiological and psychological traits. The only blanket assertion that applies to all older people is that they have lived longer. They have come from every strata of society, are active in their communities, have friends and families. They encompass all economic levels; affluent, middle class, and poor. Most older people (over seventy-six percent have adequate incomes (NRTA/AARP 1981). Income stretching (e.g., Medicare, senior citizen discounts) and the fact that most older persons (about eighty percent) own their homes outright also deny the stereotype of the poverty-stricken old person (Gelb 1978).

In spite of this, poverty is prevalent among elderly people, particularly women and minorities, who account for most of the aged poor.

Some Areas of Particular Interest and Debate

As table 8–2 shows, some categories of expenditure are relatively more important to consumers over age sixty-five. Health care and food eaten at home, for example, represent major expenditures for elderly consumers. The areas addressed in this report are food, health care, insurance, credit, services, and technology, and the reader must keep in mind that most so-called problems of the elderly (failing eyesight, hearing, etc.) are part of normal aging. These areas, therefore, represent some issues that could potentially spark debate among consumer and elderly-rights groups, industry, and policymakers.

Food

A 1979 U.S. Department of Agriculture study on the food expenditures of the elderly shows that persons over sixty-five spend about twenty-two percent of their pretax income on food, compared to seventeen percent for persons under sixty-five (in NRTS/AARP 1981). This percentage grows to as much as forty percent among the poor elderly. Many elderly persons face a fixed and/or shrinking income, which can create problems when they try to acquire and store nutritious foods. Older people want to buy smaller portions of food, both because they eat less and because of a fixed food budget. Thus, a demand exists for smaller offerings from manufacturers and food retailers.

Close to $2 billion is spent on food advertising; much of it on heavily processed foods. Because elderly consumers watch television more than any other population group and are thus exposed to more advertising (Real, et al. 1980), some concern exists that such advertising may significantly influence their food purchasing decisions. This influence may not be positive. One study found that increased exposure to mass media advertising may decrease the ability to differentiate evaluative advertising from more factual advertising (Smith and Moschis 1985). A consumer who is frequently exposed to advertising for heavily processed foods, may be encouraged to shift purchasing patterns toward these types of food. Since processed foods tend to be higher in fat, sodium, and sugar than others, their consumption in large amounts may make it more difficult for the elderly to follow controlled diets (e.g., low sodium). Advertisements for these foods may also overstate nutritional value and inadequately disclose information about ingredients that may present unforeseen risks. The elderly consumer may not wish to eat pro-

Table 8–2
Consumption Expenditures by Age of Family Head

Expenditure categories	Family Head 35 to 44		Family Head 65 and Over	
	Amount	Percentage of Total	Amount	Percentage of Total
Current consumption expenses, total[a]	$10,478.25	100.0	$4,866.50	100.0
Food, total	2,157.93	20.6	1,038.76	21.3
Food at home, total	1,570.04	15.0	828.45	17.0
Pork	137.53	1.3	77.99	1.6
Poultry	72.73	.7	41.87	.9
Dairy products other than milk and cream	87.23	.8	48.00	1.0
Fresh fruits	51.60	.5	42.68	.9
Fresh vegetables	62.58	.6	42.00	.9
Processed fruits	42.61	.4	32.33	.7
Housing, total	3,120.83	29.8	1,660.91	34.1
Shelter, total	1,549.28	14.8	795.61	16.3
Rented dwellings	468.27	4.5	353.36	7.3
Fuel and utilities, total	513.13	4.9	342.25	7.0
Gas, total	113.40	1.1	83.57	1.7
Gas, delivered in mains	94.87	.9	66.71	1.4
Gas, bottled or tank	18.53	.2	16.86	.3
Electricity	198.14	1.9	114.45	2.4
Fuel oil and kerosene	57.83	.6	55.91	1.1
Other fuels, coal & wood	4.87	.0	7.95	.2
Water, garbage, sewerage, trash & other	84.36	.8	49.60	1.0
Household operations, total	527.57	5.0	348.22	7.2
Telephone	201.11	1.9	124.00	2.5
Housekeeping and laundry supplies, total	173.76	1.7	94.50	1.9
Postage and stationery	46.33	.4	30.04	.6
Domestic and other household services	152.70	1.5	129.72	2.7
Dry cleaning and laundry	90.46	.9	47.59	1.0
Health care, total	566.61	5.4	507.10	10.4
Health insurance	195.60	1.9	196.54	4.0
Expenses not covered by insurance	311.92	3.0	251.83	5.2
Nonprescription drugs and medical supplies	59.10	.6	58.73	1.2
Personal care	210.74	2.0	114.86	2.4
Owned vacation home	10.47	.1	7.60	.2

Table 8–2 Continued

	Family Head 35 to 44		Family Head 65 and Over	
Expenditure categories	Amount	Percentage of Total	Amount	Percentage of Total
Vacation and pleasure trips, total	286.59	2.7	193.99	4.0
Lodging	45.96	.4	39.54	.8
Transportation other than gasoline	55.16	.5	48.74	1.0
All-expense tours	29.97	.3	40.96	.8
Television	51.67	.5	27.73	.6

Source: Bulletin 1992, "Consumer Expenditure Survey, Integrated Diary and Interview Survey Data, 1972–73," table 3, Bureau of Labor Statistics, 1978.

Note: These data represent categories of consumption expenditures for which the percentage of consumption expenses in larger for households with family heads over 65 than for households with family heads 35–44. The data cover all urban and rural families in the 1972–73 Consumer Expenditure Survey.

[a]Details will not add to totals becuase of items omitted.

cessed food if aware of the controversies and possible health risks posed by the ingredients (NTRA/AARP 1981).

Deshpande and Zaltman (1978) found that the elderly utilize fewer information sources than younger consumers. This may be because the elderly tend to have fewer social contacts (Schiffman 1972b) and are less physically mobile (Finch and Hayflick 1977), or because less information is available for the elderly. Mason and Bearden (1979) found that the elderly make less-than-average use of unit pricing and open-code dating. A 1976 Michigan State University study concluded that shoppers in stores without conventional item pricing were at a significant disadvantage, and several states have passed regulations and laws to require price marking (NTRA/AARP 1981).

Labeling on food products is another area of concern with elderly consumers. Although much has been accomplished in providing more comprehensive information on labels, Silvenis (1979) has found that elderly consumers have problems using this information. Size of print, unfamiliarity with chemical ingredients' benefits and possible hazards, and certain color combinations of letters and background prevent the elderly from making optimal use of information on labels.

Proper usage of nutritional information can help prevent disease and promote good health. Food labeling is usually the only source of diet-related information at the point of purchase, and the elderly would prefer more such information on packaging (Baker et al. 1982). It is extremely important to enhance the availability of packaging information through the use of larger print, easily understandable terms and contrasting colors, such as yellow and red, in the spectra best perceived by the older eye (Silvenis 1979). Then information that would be useful to an elderly consumer with hypertension, on a fat- and salt-restricted diet, or on taking certain drugs that may react with food ingredients, would be more readily accessible.

Health Care

As table 8–2 shows, elderly individuals spend a larger proportion of their total income on health care than younger people. Among people over sixty-five, ninety-four percent experience vision problems, forty percent suffer from hearing problems, and about fifty-one percent need denture-related services.

Access to and quality of vision care is an area of concern for elderly consumers. Preventive vision care is extremely important, yet studies by the Federal Trade Commission (FTC) reveal substantial differences in the thoroughness of eye examinations among practitioners. Glaucoma is a common opthomological problem with elderly people, yet only about twenty-five percent of those over forty-five years receive a test for glaucoma in any given year, less than sixty percent had ever had such a test, and only slightly more than half the practitioners may be administering the exam routinely. Thus standards should be set for the quality of eye examinations (NRTA/AARP 1981).

Poverty is a major characteristic of the elderly population with hearing impairments. The elderly who have become hearing-impaired late in life are "at a distinct disadvantage in dealing with the numerous unfair high pressure sales tactics that have often characterized hearing aid sales" (NRTA/AARP 1981:41). Much of the abusiveness of such practices is in claims to restore hearing ability to normal, when amplified hearing is neither normal nor natural.

Other documented misrepresentations include unsupported claims of superiority and uniqueness, false claims that hearing aids can be prescribed as are eyeglasses, claims that aids can slow or halt progressive physiological degeneration of aural capacity, and various claims that the user needs special features or more than just aid (NRTA/AARP 1981). Since over sixty percent of hearing aids are sold in the home, the possibility of high-pressure sales tactics, misinformation, and fraud is high. Although the FTC has issued a rule allowing a thirty-day trial period, disclosures in sales transactions or complete representations about what the aid can do are not required.

Currently, the elderly pay about ninety-seven percent of their dental costs themselves (no medical assistance or insurance). People over sixty-five are five times more likely to need denture-related services than younger people (NRTA/AARP 1981). Little information exists on the health problems caused or potentially caused by inadequate dental care; however, sixty-two percent of people over sixty-five have not seen a dentist in over two years. The high price of dental care, difficult access to care, lack of adequate information, physical or mental infirmities, and dissatisfaction with previous care contribute to this problem. It has been found that elderly consumers tend to complain less than younger consumers (Deshpande and Zaltman 1978), exacerbating the lack of information available on the possible harm suffered by the elderly.

Health Care Providers

The current health care system may not be able to meet the increasing demand of aging Americans. Nursing home patients are underserved by physicians, while many uninstitutionalized elderly may have inadequate health care due to inaccessibility and expense. As health care costs spiral upward, certain health care givers, such as nurse practitioners, need to be given extended functions. Research is needed to determine the impact on the current health care system of expanding the use of physician extenders. Extending the responsibility of nurse practitioners and other health care providers may help the elderly cope with medical costs.

Health care providers who also sell medical appliances or devices should be obliged to disclose such information and be qualified by a licensing board. Such suppliers should be monitored for accuracy in promotion of their services, quality of equipment, and safety of installation and maintenance.

Insurance

A 1974 survey of 2,000 members of the National Retired Teachers Association/American Association of Retired Persons who used prescription drugs showed that at least ten percent of their income was spent on medication. Much of this amount is out-of-pocket expense for the elderly because little is covered by third-party health insurance and state assistance. Attention should be devoted to the promotion of drugs, so that elderly consumers, some of whom must go without costly medication to pay for other necessities, may receive accurate price and comparison information. There should be a study of whether or not television advertising encourages the use of unnecessary nonprescription drugs, both to protect elderly from the expense and from potential harm. Research should also be conducted on possible false claims about medical results and cost savings.

The FTC has identified specific problems with health insurance for the elderly that fills gaps created by Medicare, yet has a limited right to investigate. Although federal legislation on supplemental health insurance does exist, it is voluntary. Thus the legislation's success depends on elderly consumers' understanding of it, and clear information about such policies should be required in promotion. Problems like overlapping policies should be made more evident to consumers. This is true for life insurance as well as health insurance. Not only should the promotion of such insurance be more clearly informative, but the policies themselves should be written in easily understandable language (Baker et al. 1982).

Credit

Many older Americans experienced the Depression and have tended to pay debts in cash rather than use credit (Elder 1974). Criteria used by creditors to determine whether a person is creditworthy include prior credit history, income, assets, employment, insurance, and life expectancy. Having no credit history is a major problem for those elderly who wish the convenience of credit purchases. The personal safety resulting from not carrying cash is also important to elderly people because they tend to fear robbery and assault more than younger people (Dowd et al. 1980). Although older borrowers are more likely to repay loans than younger people, and the Equal Credit Opportunity Act (ECOA) prohibits discrimination, "elderly borrowers can expect to pay higher interest rates and to receive smaller loans because less credit is available to them than to nonelderly borrowers" (Meyers 1983:32–33). A 1976 report to Congress noted that borrowers sixty-five and older have a repayment record approximately five times better than those twenty-one to twenty-four years old and twice that of those thirty-five to forty-four years old (NRTA/AARP 1981). However, as one study found, even when control is made for default risk, there appears to be credit discrimination against elderly borrowers. In fact, this study found that credit discrimination faced by older borrowers has possibly increased as a result of ECOA. "When control is made for default risk, the astonishing result is that the difference [the residual gap in interest rates or amounts financed between elderly and nonelderly borrowers] *increases* between the amount lent to elderly borrowers and the amount elderly borrowers would have been lent had they faced the same market conditions that nonelderly borrowers face" (Meyers 1983:32).

Because many elderly people are retired, their income is not easy to verify; thus they face the dual problem of not being employed and not being able to easily prove regular income. Also, since life expectancy is considered by creditors to help determine likelihood of loan repayment, the elderly borrower faces yet another barrier to receiving credit. Finally the fact that many elderly live on fixed incomes, receiving monthly checks, means that a lack of coordination in billing cycles may result in consistent late payments and a lack of good credit history (NRTA/AARP 1981).

One mortgage instrument that is becoming increasingly common is the reverse annuity mortgage, which enables the elderly homeowner to sell this asset while retaining the right to remain in the home for some period of time. If structured properly, this type of mortgage can greatly benefit the elderly consumer. If the term of the reverse annuity mortgage is limited, however, the old person could lose his or her home. Information should be very clear to elderly homeowners who may wish to sell their homes this way, both regarding the terms of the sale and the impact on their taxes, eligibility for public assistance, and estates.

Services

As table 8–2 shows, the consumer aged sixty-five and over spends a large proportion of income on home-related expenses. About eighty percent of elderly own their homes (Allan 1981) and often require home repair services. In most states, contractors, subcontractors, and material men hold an automatic lien or security interest in any real property that they build or repair, and in some states this lien may go to providers of more minor home services. Some of these providers take advantage of elderly consumers by coercing them into purchasing unneeded repairs or performing unsatisfactory work (NRTA/AARP 1981).

In other service areas, such as television and small appliance rental, the poor elderly may be taken advantage of by nondisclosure. If the rental contract can be cancelled by the consumer at any time, then it is not subject to Truth in Lending or Consumer Leasing acts (NRTA/AARP 1981). Therefore, the poor elderly customer may pay more for the appliance than if it had been bought in a retail store, and never be aware of it. There should be a mechanism for ensuring that these consumers, who are often not well educated, make more informed consumer choices.

Technology

In a recent survey on the aged consumer and the use of technology by the National Retired Teachers Association/American Association of Retired Persons, respondents indicated a surprising receptivity to technology. This is contrary to the stereotype of the elderly as unteachable or set in their ways. Corporations, however, seem to be ignoring an age-related shift in product service needs. A recent study (Baker et al. 1982) found six areas in which elderly consumers face inadequacies or potential for harm in existing products or services: communications and electronics, food, health and safety, home building and design, appliances, clothing, and transportation (Baker et al. 1982).

These consumers expressed a need for information about electronic shopping and bill paying, personal emergency response systems, obtaining devices to help around the house (e.g., grippers, reachers), cooking only top-of-stove for one or two, and special diets. They also wanted existing products, such as smoke alarms and security systems, to be adapted for the requirements of the elderly; for example, alarms for the hearing-impaired. They expressed a need for smaller, more energy-efficient appliances with knobs and buttons that are easier to manipulate. In the area of transportation, the elderly respondents preferred cars with greater visibility and mechanically assisted steering, windows, and so on (Baker et al. 1982). Products that meet the special physiological requirements of aging individuals are scarce, and an elderly consumer has no means of receiving information about these few products and services. Even retail stores in some respects inhibit optimal shopping by the elderly. The older shopper has expressed need for warmer stores, benches, and more readily available shopping information (Lambert 1979).

Conclusion and Implications for Future Practice and Research

These are a few of the areas of concern in marketing to the elderly consumer. Little research exists on this topic, and much more work needs to be done in identifying potential concerns and problems of elderly consumers since by the year 2030, around 10 percent of the Gross National Product will consist of services to the elderly (Waddell 1975). The small body of extant work shows substantial differences between older and younger consumers and among elderly consumers themselves and indicates several areas in which public policy and corporate responses are needed. It has been suggested, for example, that social factors such as education, income, and exposure to mass media advertising can produce measurable differences in consumers' ability to differentiate between factual and evaluative claims and in their motivations for consumption (Smith et al. 1984). The problems faced by elderly consumers today, of course, will become more pressing as the American population steadily ages, unless steps are taken now to ensure a safe environment for the increasing population of normally aging persons.

References

Allan, Carole B. 1981. Measuring mature markets. *American Demographics* 3 (March):13–17.

Aronoff, C. 1974. Old age in prime time. *Journal of Communication* 24 (1):84–87.

Baker, G.T., B.C. Griffith, F. Carmone, and C.K. Krauser. 1982. *Report on Products and Services to Enhance the Independence of the Elderly.* Commonwealth of Pennsylvania, Department of Aging.

Bernhardt, K. 1981. Consumer problems and complaint actions of older americans: A national view. *Journal of Retailing* 57 (3):107–125.

Burton, J.R., and C.B. Hennon. 1980. Consumer concerns of senior citizen center participants. *Journal of Consumer Affairs* 14 (2):366–382.

"Consumer Interests of the Elderly." 1967. (Hearing before the Subcommittee on Consumer Interests of the Elderly, Special Committee on Aging, U.S. Senate, 90th Congress, Washington, D.C.)

Deshpande, R., and G. Zaltman. 1978. "The Impact of Elderly Consumer Dissatisfaction and Buying Experience on Information Search." (Presented to third annual conference on Consumer Satisfaction/Dissatisfaction and Complaining Behavior, (October).

Diamond, S.L. 1974. "Consumer Education: Perspectives on the State of the Art." (Unpublished paper, Harvard University, Graduate School of Business Administration.)

Dowd, J., R. Sisson, and D. Kern. 1980. Socialization to violence among the aged. *Journal of Gerontology* 36 (3):350–361.

Elder, G.H., Jr. 1974. *Children of the Great Depression.* Chicago: University of Chicago Press.

Finch, C., and L. Hayflick, eds. 1977. *Handbook of the Biology of Aging.* New York: Van Nostrand.

Fox, J.A. 1980. Consumer protection and the elderly. In *The Elderly Consumer.* Rosslyn, Va.: Consumer Education Resource Network.

Gelb, B. 1978. Exploring the grey market segment. *MSU Business Topics* 26:41–46.

Gerbner, G., L. Gross, N. Signorelli, and M. Morgan. 1980. Aging with television: Images on television drama and conceptions of social reality. *Journal of Communication* 30:37–47.

Krosk, N., and R. Srivastrava. 1977. "Preliminary Examination of the Sources and Handling of Consumer Problems by the Elderly." (Unpublished manuscript, University of Pittsburgh.)

Lambert, Zarrel V. 1979. An investigation of older consumers' unmet needs and wants at the retail level. *Journal of Retailing* 55 (winter):35–37.

Maddox, G.L., and E. Douglas. 1973. Self-assessment of health: A longitudinal study of elderly subjects. *Journal of Health and Social Behavior* 14:87–93.

Mason, Barry J., and William O. Bearden. 1978. Satisfaction/Dissatisfaction with food shopping among elderly consumers. *The Journal of Consumer Affairs* 13 (winter):359–369.

Meyers, S.L. 1983. *Age Discrimination in Credit Markets,* Working Paper no. 99. Washington, D.C.: Federal Trade Commission, Bureau of Economics.

National Retired Teachers Association/American Association of Retired Persons. 1981. *Consumer Problems of Older Americans: New Directions for Government and Business.* Washington, D.C.: Consumer Affairs Section.

Phillips, L., and B. Sternthal. 1977. Age differences in information processing: A perspection on the aged consumer. *Journal of Marketing Research* 14:444–457.

Real, M.R., N. Anderson, and M. Harrington. 1980. Television access for older adults. *Journal of Communication* 30:74–76.

Schiffman, L. 1971. Sources of information for the elderly. *Journal of Advertising Research* 11:33–37.

―――. 1972a. Perceived risk in new product trial by elderly consumers. *Journal of Marketing Research* 9:106–108.

―――. 1972b. Social interaction patterns of the elderly consumer. In *AMA Combined Conference Proceedings*, edited by B.W. Becker and H. Becker. Chicago: American Marketing Association.

Schreiber, E., and D. Boyd. 1980. How do elderly perceive television commercials. *Journal of Communication* 61–69.

Silvenis, Scott. 1979. Packaging for the elderly. *Modern Packaging* 52 (Oct.):38–39.

Smith, R.B., and G.P. Moschis. 1985. A socialization perspective on selected consumer characteristics of the elderly. *Journal of Consumer Affairs* 19 (1):74–95.

Smith, R.B., G.P. Moschis, and R.L. Moore. 1984. Effects of advertising on the elderly consumer: An investigation of social breakdown theory. In *Proceedings*, American Marketing Association, edited by R. Belk et al.

Waddell, F. 1975. Consumer research and programs for the elderly—the forgotten dimension. *Journal of Consumer Affairs* 9:164–175.

―――. 1976. *The Elderly Consumer.* Columbia, Md.: The Human Ecology Center, Antioch College.

9
Disadvantaged Consumers in the 1980s

Alan R. Andreasen

Three critical features of the current environment of consumer policy provide a discouraging backdrop for this paper. First, despite the fact that the marketplace problems of disadvantaged consumers have occupied a central place in the rhetoric of consumerism since the early 1960s, it is debatable whether there has been significant improvement. The problems I outlined in my 1975 book, *The Disadvantaged Consumer,* still exist, and in many ways have worsened. Second, complicating the persistent and worsening position of disadvantaged consumers, the nature of the problems they face has changed in important and often little-appreciated ways. Finally, it is particularly disheartening to see these changing and worsening problems subject to sustained neglect on the part of academic researchers. As I pointed out in a 1978 *Journal of Marketing Research* essay, interest in the area was in decline as early as 1973. I see no evidence that this has changed today. Further, the forces determining the direction of future academic research leave me pessimistic about the likelihood of a resurgence of interest very soon.

Permanence and Decay

In the following sections, disadvantaged consumers are defined as those "who are particularly handicapped in achieving adequate value for their consumer dollar in the . . . marketplace because of their severely restricted incomes, their minority racial status, their old age, and/or their difficulties with the language" (Andreasen 1975:6). It is, of course, well understood that these factors often go together; that, for example, whether one is poor depends on one's racial or ethnic status and/or one's age. Being black means that one is three times as likely as a white to be poor and to be twenty percent poorer in average household income. Further, as can be seen in the more detailed date in table 9–1, being black and living in an urban poverty area increases the likelihood of being poor by thirty-five percent!

It is distressing that there has been surprisingly little reduction in the

Table 9–1
Selected Detailed Characteristics of Persons in Poverty, 1980

Characteristics	Number (thousands)	Poverty Rate	Percentage of Poor
All persons	29,272	13.0	100.0
White	19,699	10.2	67.3
Black	8,579	32.5	29.3
Spanish origin	3,491	25.7	11.9
65 years and over	3,871	15.7	13.2
White	3,042	13.6	10.4
Black	783	38.1	2.7
Spanish origin	179	30.8	.6
In metropolitan areas	18,021	11.9	61.6
In central cities	10,644	17.2	36.4
In poverty areas	4,284	38.1	14.6
White	1,384	30.9	4.7
Black	2,843	43.8	9.7
Spanish origin	815	43.6	2.8
Worked in 1979	7,792	6.7	26.6
White	5,714	5.6	19.5
Black	1,826	16.3	6.2
Spanish origin	780	13.1	2.7
Worked 49 weeks or less	5,441	12.7	18.6
White	3,940	10.6	13.5
Black	1,323	28.9	4.5
Spanish origin	564	22.9	1.9
Southern states	12,353	16.5	42.2

Source: U.S. Bureau of the Census, *Current Population Reports,* Series P–50 (1981) and P–60 (1982).

incidence of poverty in the last ten years, despite the massive programs of the 1970s. As shown in table 9–2, the absolute number of poor families rose in the decade between 1969 and 1979 (and it rose an additional twelve percent in 1980!). The patterns of change, however, vary across major disadvantaged groups. The number of elderly poor declined significantly in the last decade, suggesting that they may have been the main beneficiaries of the poverty programs of the 1960s and 1970s. Whites as a group also held steady in absolute numbers of poor. On the other hand, the number of black families in poverty rose twenty-two percent from 1969 to 1979 (and a further 6.6 percent in 1980). The situation for Hispanic families in poverty was even

Table 9–2
Selected Characteristics of Poverty Families, 1969 (or 1974) and 1979

	All Families		Whites		Blacks		Spanish Origin	
	1969	1979	1969	1979	1969	1979	1969	1979
Number in poverty (thousands)	5005	5320	3574	3515	1365	1666	(526)[a]	610
Percentage in poverty	9.7	9.1	7.7	6.8	27.9	27.6	(21.3)	19.7
Mean size of family	3.83	3.65	3.53	3.47	4.58	3.96	(4.52)	4.19
Mean number of children[b]	2.95	2.45	2.71	2.33	3.36	2.65	(3.06)	2.73
Percentage of poor families								
Householder[c] 65 + years	25.5	15.9	29.0	16.7	16.4	12.3	(8.4)	6.6
Householder less than high school education	(37.3)	32.4	(38.2)	33.0	(35.4)	30.7	(59.3)	48.2
No workers	35.8	41.2	38.1	39.0	29.6	45.9	(39.9)	41.6
Two or more workers	21.3	20.2	18.0	22.0	30.1	16.1	(17.5)	19.0
Percentage of working householders working full time	39.4	33.6	40.8	36.3	35.7	26.8	(31.2)	35.4

Source: U.S. Bureau of the Census, *Current Population Reports*, Series P–50 (1981) and P–60 (1982).
[a]Figures in parentheses are for 1974.
[b]Families with children.
[c]"Householder" is head of household.

worse. Poverty in this group increased fourteen percent in only five years from 1974 to 1979 (earlier data are unavailable), and a further twenty percent in 1980. Supporters of past poverty programs, however, hasten to point out that since all three of these racial/ethnic groups are growing in aggregate numbers, rates of poverty have declined for whites and Hispanics, although not for blacks.

There has been relatively little change in the other characteristics associated with poverty since the late 1960s. The poor continue to have larger families, and are more likely to be in households headed by a female, to have relatively less education, and to live in poverty areas of major urban centers. As outlined in *The Disadvantaged Consumer,* each of these factors, as well as minority status and lack of income, has serious direct negative effects on the consumption abilities of the disadvantaged. A particularly important factor that continues to contribute to their problems as consumers is the fact that the disadvantaged have steady jobs much less often. In 1979 only one in six poor households had a head who worked full time fifty or more weeks a year. One in three heads of poor households worked part time, and one in two did not work at all. The significance of this is that not only do the disadvantaged lack adequate absolute incomes, but they also lack predictability of income, which would allow them to effectively manage their limited expenditures, or continuity of income, which would allow them to carry out obligations under credit contracts (Bowers and Tabor 1977). This income instability often brings the disadvantaged into bankruptcy or subjects them to the often-traumatic legal measures meted out to defaulting debtors by our court system (Caplovitz 1974).

Given these consequences, it is further distressing to note that since 1969 the incomes of the disadvantaged poor have become more unstable. In 1969, 21 percent were working full time. In 1979, as just noted, this figure had dropped to 16.4 percent, the difference being taken up by those who had not been employed at all during the year. The burden of increased income instability had fallen almost totally on black families. Only 11 percent of poor blacks were employed full time in 1979, compared to 21 percent in 1969. The 1979 figure is also much lower than the 19 and 17 percent for whites and Hispanics, respectively. This once again seems to justify my conclusion in 1975 that "being black and poor is both different from and worse than just being poor" (Andreasen 1975:73).

In summary, then, although there was some modest progress in the "war on poverty" in the 1970s, when population growth is taken into account, there remains the stark fact that there are still more poor households today than in 1969. Further, the facts that whites and the elderly have apparently benefited most from poverty programs and that blacks and Hispanics are worse off now than in 1969, underline a second distressing point: race and language also continue to compound one's disadvantage as a consumer.

Other Changes

While poverty is undoubtedly the single most important source of disadvantage, old age, race, and language are also significant contributors, even when one is not poor. Thus, an increase in the incidence of consumer disadvantage is also signaled by the fact that in the last decade aged, ethnic, and racial minorities grew faster than the general population and will continue to do so in the 1980s. For example, from 1975 to 1979, the three groups grew as follows:

	Percent change 1975–1979
Total population	+ 3.3
Over 65 years	+10.1
Blacks	+ 5.8
Spanish origin	+ 7.9

And, as is generally well recognized, the rate of growth for Spanish-origin individuals is seriously understated, since it does not take into account the substantial influx of "undocumented aliens" in the past decade, principally from Mexico and South America. (This also means that the poverty statistics for Hispanics cited in the previous section also seriously overestimate their relative economic position.) Indeed, it is predicted that by the year 2000, Hispanics will be America's dominant minority.

Poverty, race, language, and age are, of course, only objective determinants of consumer disadvantage. It has by now been established that the attitudes and values associated with these objective conditions are also major sources of disadvantage. For example, many researchers and sociologists have shown that the poor—and to some extent the elderly, racial, and ethnic minorities—see themselves as powerless, alienated, relatively deprived, and externally manipulated. As a consequence, in the marketplace they may feel insecure, helpless, and fatalistic, and they are likely to have a present rather than a future orientation. These factors tend to make the disadvantaged cautious and narrow in their shopping habits; more easily victimized by merchants; and unwilling to redress market wrongs when they are encountered. Rose describes these responses as "normal adaptations to the frustration which comes from adherence to the cultural goals and values of a broader society in which the social structure imposes barriers to goal attainment" (Rose 1972:57).

This conclusion is not, however, universally accepted. The opposite view emphasizes the distinctiveness of the various subcultures. Oscar Lewis (1965) was one of the first to argue that the poor live in a separate "culture of poverty" that derives its norms, values, and behaviors internally rather than from the broader society—as the aforementioned theory maintains. More recently Wilson (1971) has extended this view to racial minorities. In the present context, these theorists would argue, for example, that the frequently noted narrower shopping scopes of the poor, blacks, and Hispanics is due not so much to a conscious or unconscious fear of venturing out into the broader marketplace but to a desire to remain among their own, to support local business, and to engage in the social contacts that local markets provide. However, in one sense this debate is abstract: whatever the cause, it is agreed that the observably more-restricted shopping scopes of the disadvantaged, their less-frequent complaining about their consumer problems, less use of formal protection mechanisms by the disadvantaged, and so forth collectively contribute to the higher prices, shoddier products, and more frequent encounters with deception to which these consumers are subjected. Thus, whatever the reason, these groups clearly get less value for their consumer dollars. On the other hand, whether they are satisfied with the condition—or in some sense whether they ought to be—depends on which of the above theories is applicable.

Whatever the underlying social cause may be, the narrower shopping scope that leaves many of the disadvantaged to shop in atomistic and inefficient ghetto markets results in the second major source of consumer disadvantage. Because of lower-quality management, limited patronage, and diminished physical facilities, such markets are characterized by high prices, limited selection, and an absence of mass merchandisers.

Market Determinants

The third and final source of consumer disadvantage arises not from the consumers' own characteristics, nor from the structural properties of the markets they patronize, but from the exploitative behavior of the merchants who inhabit these markets or who are willing to prey upon the fallibilities and fears of the disadvantaged elderly, poor, and minorities wherever they find them. Incidences of fraud, misrepresentation, deceit, and high-pressure selling, along with willingness to exploit language difficulties, the failing health of old people, fears of racial and ethnic slights, and the hopes of the disadvantaged to someday achieve a better life (either for themselves or for their children) are well documented, if mainly by anecdotal evidence (Caplovitz 1967; Magnuson and Carper 1968).

Policy Alternatives

It is clear from this brief outline of the three-pronged structural sources of the consumer problems of the disadvantaged that future policy could focus on three broad areas to improve conditions. First, attempts could be made to change the characteristics of the disadvantaged themselves, both their socioeconomic circumstances and their attitudes and values. Programs with this focus would necessarily concentrate on income and employment opportunities, family planning, educational enrichment (including consumer education), housing, language skills, and consumer mobility.

Second, policymakers could assume that programs focusing on characteristics will take a long time to bear fruit, and reluctantly decide to concentrate on improving inner-city market structures and performance—granting that for some time to come, the disadvantaged will be served disproportionately by ghetto enterprises. Or, finally, policymakers could focus on exploitative marketer behavior, recognizing that not all disadvantaged consumers live in areas with depressed markets, and that although such areas seem to be major hotbeds of deception, the nonghetto disadvantaged are also seriously at risk.

Before discussing these alternatives, a first question must be asked: What will be the policy environment of the 1980s? This environment necessarily determines what will be *possible*. Although other papers in this book focus on the nature of the future consumer policy environment in more detail, several assumptions about future solutions seem reasonable here:

1. In general, free market alternatives will be preferred to government intervention.
2. New government interventions (if any) will be preferred if they do not require additional spending.
3. The closer a policy initiative is to the local level, the more it will be preferred.
4. Policy alternatives that reduce government intervention will be preferred to those that continue or enhance intervention.

Since I contend that these assumptions reflect the present public mood, I believe that they will hold no matter what administration is in office nationally or locally. On the other hand, it is likely that the relative attention given to the problems of the disadvantaged will be much less under Republican than under Democratic administrations.

The Characteristics Problems

A major concern of recent administrations is inflation. Conservative leaders would argue that nothing is more damaging to the spending power of disadvantaged consumers than runaway, double-digit inflation. By cutting government spending and personal and corporate taxes, and by cooling off the economy, consumers will be given more spending power. At the same time, as corporate taxes are reduced, business will be encouraged to invest, the economy will rebound, and the federal budget will become more nearly balanced.

A question is whether the disadvantaged are more or less often injured by inflation. John Davenport supports the conservative position, arguing that the cruelest tax on the poor is inflation, from which the rich have loopholes of escape—from real estate to money market funds" (Davenport 1981:91–92). A contrary conclusion, however, was reached in a recent study by the Economics Unit of the *U.S. News and World Report* (1981b:72). "Indexing and cost-of-living clauses lift benefits and wages automatically with the rising consumer price level. For that reason . . . the elderly, the poor and union workers have not paid the tax of inflation to the same degree other Americans have."

A second question is whether the disadvantaged will be made relatively worse off by the budget cuts proposed by conservatives. Again, Davenport points out the positive aspects of budget cuts, noting that the disadvantaged in the United States are not really all that badly off. Welfare payments increased 273 percent from 1965 to 1975, during a period when prices rose 69 percent. Further, "such spending will keep rising under Reagan, though a bit less rapidly than prices. . . . The Reagan initiatives are decelerating the programs: they are not throwing the poor through the windshield." Besides "poverty by Americans standards [equals] unimaginable comfort by the standards of Bangladesh" (Davenport 1981:92).

It is nevertheless true that many programs that directly benefit the disadvantaged have been cut back, including food stamps and school lunch subsidies, and that additional cuts in welfare and Medicaid are proposed. One repeated conservative proposal is to shift responsibility for many government program to the states. Two key variables determining the impact of such a shift on the disadvantaged are its effects on the level of absolute spending and on the allocation of available funds across programs. Federal grants to cities are already being cut back; it is highly unlikely that states or individual cities will make up the difference. Certainly not all will, either from philosophical antipathy to many of the programs, political fears of a middle-class backlash, or concern that raising state taxes will put them at a competitive disadvantage in the bidding for new industries or the retention of old. The latter seems particularly likely, as states and cities are increasingly forced by federal cutbacks to develop their own revenue sources. It is clear, therefore, that consumers in some states may be worse off, especially those not in energy-rich or sunbelt areas. *U.S. News and World Report* (1982) concludes that "The gap between prosperous and ailing regions will widen" and quotes Congressman Henry Reuss, Chairman of the Joint Economic Committee, that "[federal] cuts are most pronounced in cities with high unemployment and slow growth."

However, the impact might be mitigated if cutbacks can be concentrated on those who might be classified as marginally disadvantaged (those not covered by a safety net). If a loss of aid forces these disadvantaged into self-supporting employment that could increase their earnings, they may well be much better off in the long run. (The latter outcome, of course, will be more likely if the hoped-for rebounding of the economy and the job market also occurs.) On the other hand, greater reliance on wages as opposed to government support may make the incomes of the disadvantaged more *unpredictable*, especially if they enter marginal occupations. As already noted, this presents a major problem for the disadvantaged in planning purchases and maintaining credit. We may see the paradoxical outcome of a significant increase in delinquencies and bankruptcies among the disadvantaged in the short run, even while the economy improves.

Finally, if—as is also likely—states vary not only in absolute allocations but also in basic approaches and allocations to the economic and social problems of the disadvantaged, then a variety of experiments should ensue. This may well yield a much greater chance of learning how to bring people permanently out of poverty than we have now under monotholic federal programs. Certainly the need for marketing scholars (and other researchers) to monitor these experiments for their impacts on the disadvantaged as consumers is quite clear.

Market Structure

One type of program widely discussed as a means of bringing about inner city economic development is popularly known as the "enterprise zone" plan for urban revitalization (Raines 1982; Beman 1981). Enterprise zones could be in rural areas and on Indian reservations as well as in urban areas.

A zone would be eligible for such assistance as:

1. Tax reduction on the construction or rehabilitation of commercial, industrial, or rental properties, on wages paid to disadvantaged individuals, and on capital gains on zone property;
2. tariff and import duty relief for goods subsequently exported out of the zones;
3. guaranteed continuation of industrial development bonds, even if such programs are discontinued elsewhere;
4. possible relief from other federal regulations (except those involving discrimination or public safety).

State and local governments would be expected to provide additional tax and regulatory relief, as well as improved local services—possibly including job training and minority business assistance. Finally, the enterprise zone concept typically entails a vaguely defined involvement in the program by neighborhood organizations.

Principal criticisms of these programs focus on the relative weight the program gives to capital investment incentives. Critics argue that the programs will do little to directly improve retail and service institutions, which tend to be smaller and more labor-intensive. Nor will the programs provide much help to minority business people, who are much more likely to run or manage small businesses. Further, it has been suggested that, since the programs would not abolish minimum wages in enterprise zones or set a lower minimum for certain target populations, such as teenagers, there will little impact on the most disadvantaged groups. One such group is black teenagers who, according to Glenn Lowry of the University of Michigan, "are simply not worth $3.35 an hour to an employer" (*U.S. News and World Report*, 1982:54).

On the other hand, if employment and wages of residents in such zones are increased, growth in demand may lead to improved business structures, unless residents use their augmented incomes to shop outside the area more often. Further, if new commercial and industrial construction brings a sense of renewal to an area, and workers and managers with money to spend are imported each day from outside the zone, this may provide sufficient incentive for retail investment without government aid.

From the administration's standpoint, the program has the advantage of not requiring new federal outlays (although it does result in a loss of tax revenues, at least in the short run), while fitting in with its broad preference for private-sector, competitive-market solutions to social problems. On the other hand, if at the same time the administration cuts back other forms of aid to cities and states, it will stimulate more competition for industry between cities in different regions and between cities and suburbs in specific metropolitan areas. It may be that in the latter battles, cities with major urban problems and slow growth will still not attract new businesses, even if they offer enterprise zone incentives. Certainly, if present inner-city businesses are lured away from areas not securing an "enterprise zone" designation, these areas may well be worse off under enterprise zone programs.

Consumer Exploitation

Recent administrations appear committed to extending the trend toward regulatory reform begun during the Carter administration. Antitrust activity at the Federal Trade Commission (FTC) and the Justice Department has been deemphasized, and new consumer protection regulations from any agency now will require much more extensive cost justification than in the past. Several major projects at the FTC, such as the children's advertising rule, have already been dropped, and the commission has largely abandoned its "unfairness" test for market practices, a test that covers many ghetto exploitation problems.

In my judgment, whether or not current regulatory reforms benefit or harm disadvantaged consumers depends upon the extent to which reforms recognize the special problems of these groups. FTC Chairman Miller claims to be sensitive to the differences. Although basing many of his proposals for narrowing FTC jurisdiction on the concept of an average "reasonable consumer," Miller recognizes that, for example, an advertisement that does not deceive a reasonable consumer could deceive "vulnerable" consumers. However, Miller feels that the FTC should only intervene in cases where there is demonstrable injury or where there is a compensating social benefit. Miller would further require that, in order to justify regulatory action, the seller should "know or should have known" that a practice would deceive vulnerable consumers (*Advertising Age* 1982).

There are three potential difficulties with the new regulatory thrust at the FTC. First, there appears to be a strong presumption that consumers are, in general, already looking after themselves very effectively (the reasonable consumer concept) and that the FTC need only intervene when there is compelling evidence this is not the case. This stance presumes that consumers can detect exploitation and will act on the information. However, the fact that the disadvantaged often have limited education, older age, language problems, or limited mobility makes it less likely they will detect mistreatment

(Magnuson and Carper 1968). Further, it is by now relatively well documented that even when they detect mistreatment, the disadvantaged are much less likely to complain to the seller or to third-party complaint handlers (Best and Andreasen 1977). Given this lower likelihood that the vulnerable can and will look after themselves, it is significant that, in the face of recent budget cuts, the FTC has eliminated a program initiated under the Moss-Magnuson Act whereby funding was available for testimony from groups not normally appearing in FTC proceedings. In recent years these funds have been used extensively for the disadvantaged or their representatives.

A second problem with the new FTC approach is the need to prove that the seller had prior knowledge of impact on the vulnerable and that there was actual injury. These tests can only lengthen any intervention procedures by the commission, if not prevent them entirely. Delay may not be particularly hard to bear for a middle-class consumer; it is decidedly so for the disadvantaged. There is the further question of whether a cost–benefit orientation can fully recognize the real economic and psychological impact of seemingly small-dollar losses on the disadvantaged. To insist that a ghetto fraud involving a $200 set of furniture is half as important as a $400 mail-order land fraud aimed at the middle class is to ignore the impact of official neglect on the feelings of helplessness of the disadvantaged. Such treatment will only reinforce their reluctance to look out for themselves.

Finally, given that the FTC budget will fall, it is reasonable to expect the agency to focus more on nationwide problems rather than on those at the local level where, as we have seen, the major problems of the disadvantaged are to be found. Certainly, we have already noted recent administration's preference for leaving local problems to local authorities.

However, it seems unlikely that local governments will pick up the slack, given their other budgetary needs and given the risk that extending local or state regulatory action may repel prospective industrial and commercial investors. It is further possible that the Washington administration may not be entirely dismayed by this reduced activity at the local level if it accepts the protestations of Better Business Bureaus and various firms and industries that the latter are already effectively policing their own economic houses.

Thus, whether the disadvantaged will receive better or worse protection from exploitation in the coming decade may depend on how well local organizations, business and nonbusiness, take up the slack and how sensitive such organizations are to the particular problems of the disadvantaged. Bloom and Greyser are optimistic on this score. In the 1980s they expect continued public support by individuals for consumerist organizations, particularly at the local level. They believe that local groups will grow because they have demonstrable benefits to sell in terms of "redress assistance, education, information, and services from which people receive direct, personal benefits" (Bloom and Greyser 1981: 137). However, since these organizations tend to be dominated by middle-class interest, I continue to be skeptical about whether they will be any more effective in meeting the needs of the disadvantaged than they have been in the past (Andreasen 1976).

Research Implications

Since research interest in the subject of disadvantaged consumers has declined dramatically in recent years, we now face what might be called a "remarketing task." In the past, researchers have believed that the area attracted quick-and-dirty studies with which they didn't want to be associated, that the few good studies had cleared up the major issues, and that the remaining problems were either uninteresting intellectually or intractable because of the difficulties of carrying out field research in disadvantaged communities. If we see ourselves faced with a marketing strategy problem, a useful place to begin is to briefly assess the needs and wants of the relevant target groups: academic and other research groups that can supply needed research on disadvantaged consumers, and corporate, governmental, and nonprofit agencies that can demand and financially support such research. Presumably more research will be forthcoming if both these groups perceive that the costs of carrying out research on disadvantaged consumers have been reduced and the benefits enhanced.

Costs

Several of the major costs that were encountered in researching disadvantaged consumer problems have been mitigated with time:

1. Ignorance about broad consumption, attitudinal, and market structure differences between disadvantaged and nondisadvantaged consumers has declined since the early 1970s (Hodges 1982). Similarly, technical understanding of how to do sampling, construct questionnaires, and conduct interviews in disadvantaged areas has improved significantly. Thus, researchers in the 1980s no longer lack testable hypotheses or tested methodologies with which to field the needed research.

2. As noted, several burning research issues of the 1970s, such as whether ghetto supermarkets charge more for worse food (they don't—at least now they don't) or whether putting minorities in advertisements hurts sales to nonminorities (it doesn't), have been resolved. Thus, researchers today need not fear they will proceed down blind alleys (i.e., toward insignificant differences) or "reinvent the wheel" and thus waste their own limited resources.

3. The hostilities encountered by many of us doing research in these markets in the 1960s and 1970s appears to have considerably dissipated, making the psychological costs less severe.

4. The recent broad acceptance in marketing of research dealing with social issues ought to have banished the feeling many of us had in the 1970s of being odd and clearly out of the mainstream of marketing academic research. Researching the disadvantaged in the early 1970s meant risking being labeled as a "with-it" scholar who tagged onto any currently fashionable topic. This should no longer be the case.

Despite these improvements, a major cost to the researcher that has increased in the 1980s is the effort now necessary to find and secure needed research funding. As is well known, funding for behavioral science research by federal agencies had declined markedly. And it is unlikely that private or local foundations will make up the difference, given the pressures on them to increase their action rather than research programs. These environmental parameters may be irreducible, at least in the short run. Thus, in the near term prospective researchers may well be required to reduce the scope of their enterprises (e.g., to that supportable by in-house funding or modest pilot grants and/or by the researcher's volunteered time and talents) and compete much more vigorously for shrinking outside funding. Success at the latter means making a stronger case for the benefits of research on the disadvantaged. In my opinion, such a case can be made.

Benefits

It is clear from the analysis in the earlier sections of this paper that the challenge of improving the status of America's disadvantaged is still with us. Indeed, as I have outlined, the challenge is even more pronounced in the early 1980s because of worsening economic conditions and cutbacks in traditional sources of support. Thus, the magnitude of the benefits to society from alleviating these problems has, in my judgment, substantially increased.

It can also be argued that the potential personal benefits have also been increased by recent social and political trends. This is, it is increasingly clear that the country and its leaders are turning to private—often voluntary—efforts to help the unfortunate. Thus, for those taking up the gauntlet, the challenge of finding ways to help the disadvantaged make their real income go much farther can offer important personal satisfaction.

A third beneficiary of future research in this area is "the academy." As I have pointed out in many forums, the remaining critical research issues in this domain are intellectually very important not only to solutions to the social problems we have been discussing but also to our understanding of basic consumer behavior. A sampling of these research issues was outlined in a 1980 *Marketing News* article (Andreasen 1980).

1. How do disadvantaged families respond to economic downturns through their consumption behavior? Do they shop more diligently, buy less on credit or more on credit, bargain more over prices, engage in more home production, or consider more potential sources? Or does a downturn cause them to restrict their shopping to high-priced outlets where they know they can get credit if things really get tough? Are there economizing techniques they don't use often but could?

2. Why do the disadvantaged use credit to the extent they do (or at all), given the uncertainty of their future incomes? Why do some have consumer debt payments amounting to 20 percent or more their monthly incomes? How far from FTC Commissioner's standard of reasonable consumers do the disadvantaged fall and in what directions?

3. What happens as the disadvantaged become economically advantaged? Do they retain old "bad habits?" Do they become overprivileged (relative to their lower-class aspirations) and spend on frivolous products, or do they change their aspirations and become underprivileged relative to the acquisitive middle class?

4. Where do the disadvantaged get their consumer goals? For example, a recurring question with respect to ethnic minorities is: Do they aspire to emulate other minority members or the often more-affluent nonminorities with whom they are in contact in the neighborhood or at work? (Mitchell 1980; Stein 1980)

5. What is the current status of ghetto market structures? Are they more underdeveloped economically, more dominated by small, overpriced, understocked, unprofitable outlets than when they were studied in the early 1970s? (This seems quite likely, given economic conditions and benign neglect over the last decade.) Have any more retailers set up successful ventures in the ghetto over this period and, if so, what secrets do they have to share with others?

6. How have exploitative merchants changed their tactics in economic hard times and under the harsh spotlight shone on their practices earlier in the decade? Are new regulations, or simply new approaches, needed by regulators in the 1980s?

7. How successful were the reforms that public and private regulators adopted in the 1970s? Have changes at some Better Business Bureaus (for example, introducing required arbitration in some areas) led to more help for the disadvantaged? What reforms have worked and need to be diffused elsewhere? Which have failed and need to be put aside to free energies for newer, more imaginative efforts?

8. How do the problems of the elderly or Hispanics differ from those of

blacks and poor whites? What differences exist across the three major Hispanic groups?

It may be argued that the disadvantaged do not really merit special attention, that the general advances in consumerism that Bloom and Greyser believe will be forthcoming and the research on the marketplace problems of all consumers will have a trickle-down effect on the disadvantaged. However, as noted previously, my fifteen years of research and activism in this area have convinced me that the problems of disadvantaged consumers are both quantitatively and qualitatively different from those of the middle class. We simply cannot leave their problems to be resolved by so-called mainstream programs.

As this paper demonstrates, the 1980s present a considerable challenge to the research community—both to its intellect in confronting important but often difficult research questions and to its resourcefulness and energy in overcoming past inertia and the impediments of recent funding cutbacks. It is a challenge I wish others would join me in taking up. However, I confess that past experience also leaves me rather pessimistic. Perhaps the publication of this volume will, indeed, mark a new beginning.

References

Advertising Age. 1982. Miller's FTC plan draws fire. *Advertising Age* (March 22):1, 84.

Aldrich, Howard, and Albert Reiss. 1976. Continuities in the study of the ecological succession. *American Journal of Sociology* 81 (Jan.).

Andreasen, Alan R. 1975. *The Disadvantaged Consumer*. New York: The Free Press.

———. 1976. "The differing nature of consumerism in the ghetto. *Journal of Consumer Affairs* 10 (winter):179–189.

———. 1978. The ghetto marketing life cycle: A case of underachievement. *Journal of Marketing Research* (Feb.):20–28.

———. 1980. Marketing educators still face disadvantaged consumer challenge. *Marketing News* (July 25):1, 16–17.

Beman, Lewis. 1981. Reorganizing the inner cities. *Fortune* (Dec. 14):98–103.

Best, Arthur, and Alan R. Andreasen. 1977, Consumer response to unsatisfactory purchases: A survey of perceiving defects, voicing complaints, and obtaining redress. *Law and Society Review* 11:701–742.

Bloom, Paul N., and Stephen A. Greyser. 1981. "The maturing of consumerism. *Harvard Business Review* 59 (Nov.–Dec.):130–139.

Bowers, Jean, and Joan Tabor. 1977. Factors determining credit worthiness of low income consumers. *Journal of Consumer Affairs* 11 (winter):43–51.

Caplovitz, David. 1967. *The Poor Pay More*. New York: The Free Press.

———. 1974. *Consumer in Trouble*. New York: The Free Press.

Davenport, John A. 1981. Measuring the pain in Reagan's cuts. *Fortune* (Nov. 2):91–100.

Hodges, Lloyd. 1982. "Race and Clothing: An Examination of the Effects of Race on Consumption." (Unpublished doctoral dissertation, College of Business Administration, University of Illinois, Urbana, Ill.)

Lewis, Oscar. 1965. *La Vida: A Puerto-Rican Family in the Culture of Poverty—San Juan and New York*. New York: Random House.

Magnuson, Warren G., and Jean Carper. 1968. *The Dark Side of the Marketplace*. Englewood Cliffs, N.J.: Prentice-Hall.

Mitchell, Ivor S. 1980. Cultural dimensions of marketing strategies. *The Review of Black Political Economy* 10, 3 (spring):247–261.

Raines, Howell. 1982. Reagan offers enterprise zone plan for urban revitalization. *The New York Times* (March 3):1, 16.

Rose, Stephen. 1972. *The Betrayal of the Poor*. Cambridge, Mass.: Schenkman Publishing Co.

Stein, Karen F. 1980. Explaining ghetto consumer behavior: Hypotheses from urban sociology. *Journal of Consumer Affairs* 14, 1 (summer):232–242.

U.S. Bureau of the Census. 1976. *Statistical Abstract of the United States: 1976*. Washington, D.C.: U.S. Government Printing Office.

———. 1981. *Current Population Reports, Series P-50, No. 130, Characteristics of the Population Below the Poverty Level: 1979*. Washington, D.C.: U.S. Government Printing Office.

———. 1982. *Current Population Reports, Series P-60, Money Income and Poverty Status of Families and Persons in the United States: 1980*. Washington, D.C.: U.S. Government Printing Office.

U.S. News and World Report. 1982. Black teenagers without jobs: Time bomb for U.S. *U.S. News and World Report* (Jan. 18):52–54.

———. 1981b. Hispanics make their move. *U.S. News and World Report* (Aug. 24):60–64.

———. 1981c. Signs of hope—the battle on inflation. *U.S. News and World Report* (Nov. 2):70–72.

Wilson, Robert. 1971. "Anomie in the ghetto: A study of neighborhood type, race and anomie. *American Journal of Sociology* 77 (July):66–87.

10
The New Technologies: Some Implications for Consumer Policy

Philip A. Harding

My purpose in this paper is to describe two of the new video-based technologies with which CBS and other communications companies have been experimenting for the past several years: teletext and videotex. The development of these technologies has generated some enormously complex questions and issues, and it is helpful to have at least some sense of that complexity. I want also to set forth some thoughts I have about the implications of these technologies for future consumer policy concerns.

First, a disclaimer. The observations presented here are entirely my own and certainly are not to be construed as representing official statements or positions of CBS. The perspective I bring to this area is that of the social sciences—which is, I think, useful for looking at these kinds of innovations, and one that has not been conspicuously present to date.

Let me start by briefly describing teletext, which is the generic name for systems that transmit letters, numbers, and characters to the home television receiver. The information is transmitted simultaneously with the normal television picture, either by over-the-air broadcast or by cable. Equipped with a special decoder, a television receiver can extract and translate that information to appear as letters, numbers, and graphics on the television screen. With the use of a hand-held control unit, much like a small calculator, the user can select from a variety of subject matter: news, weather, stock prices, traffic conditions, listings of community events, retailer catalog information, tips on gardening and home repairs—just about anything.

Turning now to videotex: From a physical standpoint, a videotex system does not look much different from teletext. Videotex also uses the home television receiver (or sometimes a separate display terminal) and a keyboard or keypad with which the user summons up various kinds of information to the screen. Both rely primarily on textual material; graphics are still fairly primitive. But, in actual use, there are major differences between the two systems:

1. Videotex offers a vastly greater amount of information to the user—literally hundreds of thousands of individual screen pages, compared with a maximum of perhaps 2,000 for cable-delivered teletext systems and perhaps 250 for broadcast teletext.

2. Whereas teletext is a one-way system that transmits information only to the user, videotex is two-way, which means that the user not only receives information but can also send it. This interactive capability of videotex is what enables such from-the-home transactions as shopping, bill-paying, and banking.

3. Cost: once the teletext-equipped television receiver has been purchased, there are no further costs to the user. Videotex's pricing, in contrast, will probably be something like that of the telephone, with a basic monthly charge plus usage fees that vary with particular categories of service.

There, in a rather small nutshell, are the two electronic technologies I will be discussing. On first impression, they seem to hold great promise for revolutionizing the ways Americans meet their information needs, engage in banking transactions, shop, pay their bills, and so forth.

Former president Lyndon Johnson once observed, in a quite different context, that, "Today our problem is not making miracles, but managing them." And the prospect of managing these technologies, if and when they become widely available, has raised some incredibly complex issues. To name only a very few:

1. Regulatory policy. Attempts to define AT&T's role in this field have been getting headlines in recent years; but there are other regulatory issues, just as tough, that have not been much publicized. Questions of access, which come down to whether these systems must operate on common-carrier principles, available to all comers, or whether the system operator should be allowed to exercise control and selectivity. Questions of protecting the security and privacy of the individual user. Questions of regulatory jurisdiction: Congress, the Federal Communications Commission (FCC), the Justice Department, the Federal Trade Commission (FTC), state public utility commissions—all conceivably have a role in formulating and implementing regulatory policy in this area.

2. Advertiser response. Will the advertising community perceive these technologies as important vehicles for reaching their target markets?

3. Evolution of competing media. I'm thinking here particularly of cable television and video cassette recorders, which obviously are not going to remain in their present stages of development. They will continue to evolve, broadening the range of services they offer. A crucial question then becomes whether that evolution will reach a point in the future

where the benefits most important to the public are provided adequately, and at less cost, by these established in-home technologies, thereby undercutting prospects for teletext and videotex.

4. Social impact. Some very significant questions have arisen about the impacts these technologies will have upon the well-being of society at large, including the ability of consumers to function in the marketplace.

There are, of course, other issues: pricing for various services, who is going to manufacture the hardware and to what specifications, copyright protection, and on and on. So one begins to get a sense of the turmoil accompanying the gestation and birth of these technologies. It is certainly not the old test-market and roll-out game we normally associate with new product launches.

What I find interesting, and a little peculiar, about the issues that have so far dominated discussion in this area is that so many of them are essentially supply side in character. "Supply side" in the sense that they implicitly assume a level of market demand for these products, and then move quickly on to matters having to do with regulatory policy, or advertiser support, or societal impact, or whatever. So you have a kind of skew in the way the issues have been framed, plus something close to obsession with the sheer technological "whiz-bang" of these things—what the trade refers to as bells and whistles.

As a consequence, demand side questions have been accorded a distinctly second-class status.

> Questions of which—if any—of the informational and transactional services offered are likely to meet real public needs.

> Questions of the market segments initially most receptive to these technologies and to specific services on them.

> Questions of whether the public is willing to change entrenched habits of information-seeking, shopping, banking.

> And, basic to everything else, questions of whether these technologies will be perceived as offering benefits justifying their dollar costs to the consumer.

In short, questions aimed at establishing the existence of a residential market for teletext and videotex. For, if such a market does not exist and is not likely to materialize in the near-term future, then most of the other issues become moot.

Because these questions have thus far received so little serious attention, forecasts of marketplace acceptance and year-by-year penetration inspire a level of predictive confidence roughly comparable to that accorded tea leaves and the entrails of owls. But in trying to anticipate the future social environment—and, more particularly, consumer issues in that environment—I think we have to assume some in-home presence in some form for teletext or videotex or both.

Once these technologies begin to appear in homes, it seems to me that the public will have at its disposal something with the potential to facilitate dramatically the tasks involved in being an informed and effective consumer. A means to simplify and make more efficient the performance of these tasks—tasks that, in an era of increasingly severe constraints on time, might otherwise not be performed at all. So I think that, to the extent that these electronic technologies become widely available, one major result will be a significant increase in consumers' knowledgeability and sophistication about the marketplace and about individual products and services within it. Indeed, when we get to the stage of actually marketing these technologies, I suspect that this is going to be a key selling point—both to the public and prospective advertisers.

Let me amplify on that last point, because it has some important implications for future consumer policy. Both teletext and videotex are systems by which the home television receiver can be used to obtain on-demand information of almost any conceivable kind. But videotex also uses the television set (or perhaps a separate terminal) to enable transactions of one sort or another. It is this transactional, or two-way, capability that seems to have captured everyone's imagination: the idea that while sitting at home pressing buttons, someone can pay bills, move funds between checking and savings acounts, participate in what are loosely referred to as public opinion surveys. And, particularly relevant to future forms of consumer behavior, he or she will also be able to place direct orders of merchandise from stores and catalogs, and have the price automatically charged to a credit account.

At this point, I am not personally persuaded that the transactional capabilities in general, and merchandise-ordering in particular, are going to justify their advance notices. From the consumer's standpoint, I do not yet see that the ordering feature represents a quantum leap in benefit beyond the ways presently available for making nonstore purchases. And there will always be products that simply do not lend themselves to this mode of buying—either because the shopping experience offers gratifications of its own or because, for certain products, people want to see what they're getting before they put their money down. In any case, whatever utility the American consumer will ultimately find in this kind of pushbutton purchasing, the transactional feature comes down essentially to a means for streamlining the mechanics of the buying process.

But the consumer movement, as I understand it, has traditionally been more concerned with what precedes and follows the act of purchasing than with the purchase mechanism itself: more concerned with the flow of honest and useful information about products and services before the decision to buy is made, and with procedures for redress should something go wrong after purchase.

So when I suggest that teletext and videotex may turn out to be profoundly positive forces in advancing certain of the consumer movement's objectives, I see that resulting more from these technologies' information capabilities than from the transactional ones. For what these devices will have the capacity to do is something that all of us—advertisers, the advertising media, consumer groups, policymakers—have long sought. Namely, to facilitate the flow to the consumer of complete, practical, and truthful information about all manner of products and services. And, just as important, to deliver that information on demand—when the consumer most needs it and is thus in a state of mind most able to benefit from it.

The kinds of consumer-relevant information these systems will be able to provide range from the very simple and straightforward to the detailed and complex. For example, by keying in to such a system, the user could quickly find out where particular goods and services are available—whether what is needed is lawn and garden equipment, a twenty-four hour plumber, or a three-star French restaurant with free parking and Master Card. The system could also be used for making price comparisons of what local retailers or supermarkets are charging for the same item.

Where and how much are fairly basic forms of consumer information. But far more extensive product data could be obtained as well. For major purchases, such as a washing machine or home stereo equipment, the consumer could easily learn the features and characteristics of different manufacturers' models, objective evaluations of product quality, frequency-of-repair—and, of course, relative prices.

At a more general level, and this probably applies more to videotex than to teletext, these systems will be able to offer lessons or even whole courses of instruction on how to function as a rational consumer in an increasingly complex marketplace: advice on budgeting and money management, how to seek redress, things to watch out for—in short, consumer education in the home. And not only for adults but conceivably for young people as well, providing an important supplement to their limited exposure to this type of material in the schools.

Of course, much of this information is already available to the consumer. But it comes in such disparate, fragmented, and perishable forms—and at times when he or she has no immediate use for it—that in a very real sense the consumer usually is not available to the information. And when such information is needed, it takes time—an increasingly rare commodity—to track down.

It is not my intent to beat the drum for teletext and videotex. None of us can say, at this early juncture, whether either one will establish a significant presence in the marketplace. Moreover, even in the consumer-information applications I have been talking about—which, on their face, seem to have substantial utility—all of us can foresee problems. Clearly, measures will have to be devised to gain and maintain public trust in these services; to the extent that abuses occur and go uncorrected, the integrity of the entire system is threatened. A policy of reporting, on the system itself, instances of proven deception could do a great deal to deter such practices—but that, of course, might open a rather large legal can of worms for the system operator.

There is another, even more basic question to think about. Much has been made of the possibility that the anticipated revolution in information technologies is going to superimpose yet another class distinction upon American society: the information-rich and the information-poor. The information-rich will be those with the means to acquire and benefit from these technologies. The information-poor will not—and to their impoverishments will now be added residence in a kind of information netherworld, whose resources will be limited.

As a generalization, the case for the information-rich versus the information-poor seems overdrawn. And yet, as regards the kind of consumer-relevant information we have been considering, there may be something to it. Because people are going to have to pay to have information delivered in this way, and it may be that those with the least financial resources—the very ones who might benefit most from these services—will find the cost too high. And if, under a worst-case scenario, the success of such pay services results in less consumer-relevant information being offered by traditional media, then the people who cannot afford the services will indeed have been disadvantaged. But that issue, like so many others raised by the emergence of the home-information technologies, has not yet been seriously confronted. Meanwhile the technologies continue to develop and evolve, promising between them to deliver into the homes of those who can pay a truly enormous variety of informational and transactional services.

When I think about all the goodies we are told we will be able to have at the touch of a button, I do wonder how many of them the public will perceive as affording significant advantages over the ways they now perform these same information-gathering and transactional tasks. It seems to me, however, that for the kinds of consumer education applications I have been describing, there is a very nice fit between the needs of an increasingly well-educated, consumer-savvy, time-constrained public and certain attributes unique to teletext and videotex. Three of these impress me as particularly useful and important:

First, their convenience, by which I mean the advantage of having marketplace information available from one central in-home source, accessible instantaneously and for as long as it is needed.

Second, timeliness: information about prices, specials, new services being offered, and so forth can be updated as frequently as necessary.

Finally, and in some ways the most important, informational efficiency. The information available from these systems reaches the consumer only in response to his or her initiative. The audience for such information is thus limited to those who seek it out—which is a reversal of the present situation wherein consumer-targeted messages must seek out a receptive audience.

Users of teletext and videotex will by definition be receptive to the content of the services. Given that state of mind, they should be optimally able to learn and to benefit from that content. And so I would suggest that what these technologies could ultimately accomplish is something that too often eludes us today: namely, the objective not only of increasing the amount of consumer-relevant information available to the public, but also of delivering it when the consumer is actively in the market for various products and services. It is that capacity of teletext and videotex—to make information available at a point in the purchase-decision process when it is particularly likely to be used—that will, I suspect, be a very significant contribution these technologies will make to consumer welfare in the future.

11

Wanted: Consumer Perspectives on the New Technologies

Mary Gardiner Jones

One way to consider the future research needs of the consumer movement is to examine the important developments now emerging in our society that will engage consumer concerns over the next decades. We are at the beginning of the information society and the service economy. The immensity of the changes that this society will bring in its wake—changes in our ways of learning, thinking, working, and living, and changes in the infrastructures of law, employment, and perhaps even of government are akin to the revolutions wrought by Gutenberg and Marconi.

Toffler, in *The Third Wave* (1980), and Jean-Jacques Servan-Schreiber, in *World Challenge* (1980), have laid out some of the more global and historical dimensions of the information society that the new telecommunications and electronic technologies have facilitated. My purpose in this paper is somewhat narrower in scope. I want to sketch out some of the characteristics of the new technologies and their applications to our daily lives, evaluate the opportunities and the problems that these technologies will pose for consumers and consumer organizations, and identify some of the areas to which consumers will likely be directing their concerns. We will then be able to determine just what questions a consumer-oriented research agenda must address in order to be assured that the research results will focus first on those information issues that are of significance to consumers, and, second, on those solutions that can best address consumer interests and concerns.

The Dimensions of the New Information Technologies

At the outset, it is important to understand the integral connection between the information society and the new technologies that have made it inevitable. The information society is essentially the product of computer miniaturization, made possible by the microchip, the laser beam, fiber optic technologies, and developments in satellite and digital transmission. These technologies have radically transformed the quantity of information that can be stored, the speed with which it can be transmitted, the ease with which it can be captured as byproducts of other transactions, and the number of uses for which the same item of information can be made available. There is no difficulty today in storing an entire encyclopedia on a small thin disk the size of a normal greeting card, which can be accessed on a home terminal the size of an ordinary office typewriter. Two video disks, the size of ordinary records, can record an entire opera or movie. Or one disk can provide dance or cooking instructions, which can be easily controlled to repeat any sequence or to freeze any frame that requires closer attention—all at the command of the user. Satellite and digital transmission enable data to be transmitted in nanoseconds. It is possible to compose graphics on the computer and transmit them to points anywhere in the world. Very soon computer voice recognition will be a standard feature of our electronic equipment.

For the home user, which is our concern in this paper, these new technologies can provide consumers with an extraordinary range of information services and transaction opportunities, such as messaging, banking and shopping transactions, computing games and entertainment, and telemonitoring of home energy use or security systems. By using simple keyboard commands, consumers can have the information and knowledge of the world at their fingertips—as well as the marketplace of goods and services.

Without undue elaboration of the technological developments involved in this revolution, the hardware configuration required for the home user to utilize these new systems for information retrieval or service applications is relatively simple. Users can participate in one-way information systems—generally referred to a teletext systems—through their television console, which can be equipped with a special adapter and a key pad that enables them to cue in numbers corresponding to information menus contained in the limited teletext database. Some of these services will be provided by cable systems, which—with their greatly enlarged channel capacities—could offer the television viewer an infinite menu of essentially one-way information and other specialized services to choose from. Two-way systems—known as videotex systems—require only a home terminal and a telephone modem and line to enable home users to reach almost any compatible database in the country. In the future, direct-broadcast satellite systems will present another method for transmitting information from the source to the home, without the need for cable or telephone links. With peripheral equipment like disks, cassettes, and printers, the home terminal can act as a word processor; a center for sending, receiving, and storing messages; an electronic record or filing system, indexed to the user's special needs; a library accessing and disseminating system; a home-based educational training source, or as an order processing and bill paying center.

Among the institutions and organizations likely to be affected by the emergence of videotex and teletext systems are all retailers; banks; insurance companies; educational institutions and libraries; the travel, film, and paper industries; newspaper, book, and periodical publishers; legal services; the U.S. Post Office; and the telephone, telecommunication, computer, cable, and broadcast industries—not to speak of the business and household users. It is probably not an exaggeration to predict that some part of almost every service we use in our everyday life will be available to us, alternatively or exclusively, through some type of home-based electronic information system.

The Impact of the Information Technologies on Consumers

One of the principal motivating forces behind the consumer movement in the 1960s was consumer's need and demand for information. Whether their needs were to find out how to apply for social security, employment, or medicare benefits; how to utilize the range of social welfare services available; how to take advantage of the emerging financial assistance programs for education or housing; or how to be an effective purchaser of goods and services in the marketplace, consumers in the 1960s, of all incomes or educational levels, recognized that their key to effective action or to simple survival was access to information and knowledge. These information needs continue to be of critical importance to consumers today.

The incredible ability of the new technologies to create and generate information, both independently and as a byproduct of other transactions. These impacts affect the nature of information as a public or private good and, hence, who ultimately will have access to it. Those who provide information are making strenuous efforts to centralize the management and control of these information systems, although the technologies could equally facilitate a wide fragmentation of information providers. In either case, what information will ultimately be provided and by whom will be directly affected by who owns and manages these systems.

Finally, the quantity and quality of information and the technical skills required to participate in these systems, as users and as information providers, will determine how realistically and effectively consumers will be able to utilize these information systems.

The impacts of the new technologies must be understood before consumers can identify what steps need to be taken in order to ensure their effective participation in and their enjoyment of the information society.

The Commercialization of Information

Information has traditionally been regarded as both a public and a private good. Our public education system and our long tradition of public libraries reflect our belief as a nation in the importance of knowledge and information.

Indeed, when demands for information were not met by the private sector, government and nonprofit organizations moved to meet the needs. Many government agencies and nonprofit organizations regarded the dissemination of information as one of the primary tools to accomplish their aims. Information as a public good has been widely accepted.

Today, information, because of the ease with which it can be created and disseminated, has become a commercially valuable property. This development has serious consequences for the continued status of information as a free good. In addition, information—because of its special properties—presents complex problems to the society that handles it as a normal item of commerce. Unlike ordinary products, information can be possessed by many persons simultaneously and is not destroyed when it is consumed. Once public, it is available to all who hear it or learn it.

Inability to restrict information tends to reduce its value. Hence, sellers are wary of disclosing too much about their product; as a result, consumers have difficulty knowing what is being offered. Since the value of information cannot be displayed without disclosing the information itself, sellers confront difficulties in marketing information effectively without giving it to the buyer. Because information is in many respects a public good, putting it up for sale raises serious problems of public policy toward the free flow of information.

The special properties of information create enormous dislocation in our traditional institutional mechanisms for dealing with information in terms of its ownership and monopolization and in terms of its status as a public or private good.

Unlike raw materials such as bauxite, steel, and products made from steel, the various states in which information can be available are difficult to define and identify. Information can be an individual fact or statistic, an intermediate stage of data reflecting someone's aggregation, or a finished product such as an article or book. A database of information about nursing homes could consist of raw facts and a system of organizing and describing these facts in ways that are meaningful and easy to use. Nursing home information could also encompass evaluative analyses about nursing homes, such as might be found in a consumer report or in a how-to book. The same basic facts about nursing homes are of interest to prospective patients, their families, doctors, nurses, and to the community as a whole. Thus, how the facts about nursing homes are organized and presented can be of the critical element that distinguishes nursing home databases from each other and from books. Yet how these different states of information are defined can directly affect consumer access. Thus the ambiguities attached to distinguishing between raw data, facts, information, and knowledge (to try out one possible classification) throw into question our traditional legal and commercial concepts of property; we may not wish to attach traditional concepts of property to each of these states of information. In this light, freedom of access to government-generated raw data now becomes an important concept to consider. Does, can, or should ownership attach to raw data, and who is the owner—the nursing home or the researcher observing the nursing home?

Once information becomes commercially valuable, its status as a free service could suddenly cause charges of unfair competiton between the public and private sectors. Arguments may wax furiously over the proper role of government and the nonprofit sector, which may be seen as "competing," at taxpayers expense, with the private sector in the dissemination of information. In addition, the private sector is finding the battle over information control emerging within its own ranks. A serious consequence of this battle is the threat that it presents to treating information as a public good and the impact of this threat on the type of information that is made available and the persons who can have access to it.

The current fight between the producers of movies and the manufacturers of video tape recorders illustrates one of the dilemmas created by the new information technologies. The movie producers argue that the video tape recorder manufacturers are taking their property, since the manufacturers are depriving movie producers of the television market and also destroying the mechanism for compensating the authors and artists who helped make the movie, because their compensation depends on the number of viewings that the networks or movie houses give to the product. Whatever the merits of the arguments, the battle points up the dislocations that the new technologies are creating in traditional market mechanisms for the selling of what in the past has been categorized as intellectual property and today is part of the broader information society.

We see the *Yellow Pages* of the telephone companies, which used to be a free service provided to telephone subscribers and paid for by advertisers, now becoming the target of a bitter struggle for control between AT&T and the newspaper publishers. Why? Because, rather than continuing to be simply a source of revenue from local advertisers who wish to advertise to telephone subscribers or as an easily providable service to AT&T subscribers, the names and addresses of the local advertisers in the *Yellow Pages* have become a valuable article of commerce in themselves. Imaginatively indexed and packaged in a variety of categories, these names, addresses, and telephone numbers of local businesses become a valuable database that can be marketed to a whole host of information providers or users. For users with home terminals capable of order taking and money transfer, the *Yellow Pages* can be a central database for messaging, teleshopping, or restaurant listings with menu previews or reservation capabilities. One consequence of the newly found commercial value of this electronic database that it would be self-defeating to provide the names free to local telephone since to do so would depreciate part of the value of the list by eliminating one potential user market.

One of the most cogent arguments for the market system points to the incentive of profit and the discipline of cost as the most effective tools to ensure that the economy produces the goods and services for which a real demand exists. Society, in this sense, consists solely of those individuals whose needs constitute a viable market and who can afford to pay for the goods produced. When information is the product, this rationale may be neither applicable nor appropriate.

Education developed outside the market system as a public good and a public service, because society determined that an educated and informed citizenry was essential and that, therefore, education should not be available, only to those who could afford to pay for it.

I believe that an additional dynamic contributed to the development of education as a public good—a realistic recognition of the structure of people's needs and individuals' realization of their own priority of needs.

Maslow characterized basic human requirements as physiological and safety needs, and needs for love, esteem, and self-actualization. He stressed that all are important to indivduals for their human fulfillment. Yet the amounts of effort and money that human beings expend for the satisfaction of those needs are very different, depending on their incomes and education levels, and on their levels of awareness of the relationship between their needs and the communal resouces available to fill these needs. People do not need to be pressured to attend to material needs such as housing, food, and clothing. These are basic needs required to survive. Attending to such needs will always take precedence over demands for goods and services that are not regarded as so essential, or whose benefits are seen as less immediate, less certain, or even as less safe.

Thus, because the benefits that individuals perceive in education, information, and other nonmaterial goods are intangible, it is not clear to what extent that market system of supply and demand reliably indicates all consumer needs. The market may only reflect how citizens allocate what monies they have. If they need housing more than information, or if they refrain from buying information out of an insufficient understanding of what it could mean to their lives or out of fear that they will waste their money, their failure to buy only says something about their state of mind, not about their needs or desires.

Given the realities of consumer needs and choice parameters, the rapidly developing commercialization of information confronts consumers—and the country—with the renewed dilemma of reconciling our notions of the public good and the proper role of government with our equally firmly held notions about the role of the marketplace. Further, we need to determine the applicability of our marketplace concepts to the production and dissemination of information to the citizenry. It is clear that treating information as an article of commerce will limit information made available to that which can be paid for. Moreover, since commercially offered goods and services and "free" goods and services can not realistically compete, as soon as a commercial use is developed for information, its free status is jeopardized. Despite the advantages of market-oriented distribution systems, the consequences of restrictions on the free availability of information must be carefully and prayerfully examined before they are accepted or rejected.

Ownership and Control of Information Systems

At present the leading contenders for bringing the new information systems to the public are the media: cable television, the networks, and public television, as well as newspaper chains, AT&T, and a few service retailers who are experimenting with the technology and measuring consumer demand for their various services. In addition, a few commercial database systems are offering consumer information to home terminal owners for a fee. Some of these information systems are available to consumers on their television screens and others plan for access via home terminals.

Those who manage the systems will directly affect the standards that will determine which information providers have access to the system. If the information database system is created by the media, the system probably will be operated on the basis of media's constitutionally protected rights to be the sole decisionmakers on what information providers and what information will be provided on the system. If, on the other hand, the system is managed by private entrepreneurs, whose business is the purchase and sale of information products, then what information will be available will be essentially determined by market forces. A common carrier information system, with its obligation to confidentiality and neutrality of information, would focus on a third parameter, volume of use, and would probably provide the most value-free choice of information content. In a similar way, the method of financing the information system may also affect the information content of the system and the breadth of access afforded to different types of information providers. Advertiser-supported media can be expected to make different decisions about information content than entrepreneurs who charge for their information products on a subscription or usage basis. Common carrier systems, at least as they have developed in Great Britain, permit the information provider to set the user fee, and simply charge the information provider a fee for using the system.

Thus consumers have a vital interest in the way information systems develop, since each alternative will affect which consumer information providers have access to the system and hence will affect the diversity of the information that will be available to consumers.

Information Overload and Information Quality

One of the important characteristics of the new information technologies is their ability to deliver data instantly to the consumer on command, at any level of interest and in whatever detail the consumer selects. A consumer concerned about nursing home care could, with the proper database and software, dial up the nursing homes in a specific geographic area, or with particular characteristics (coed, hospital associated, for ambulatory, or nonambulatory patients), or within designated cost ranges. Or more generalized information could be accessed, such as questions that persons interested in nursing home care should ask, indicators of quality that should be considered or alternatives to nursing home care that may exist.

A second and related characteristic of this new electronic world is its interactiveness—its ability to respond on command to consumer needs and desires. One of the most deeply felt needs of individuals is a desire to feel recognized, to feel effective, to see instant results for one's efforts. This new medium has a special propensity for reinforcing these needs. We have but to look at the popularity of the electronic game today to get some appreciation of the excitement generated by the instant responsiveness and interactiveness of the new medium. I believe that some part of this excitement is due to the immediate visible response that this interactiveness gives to individuals' actions and skills. Educators who are successfully experimenting with microcomputer terminals in their classrooms, with students as young as three or four years of age, are seeing this same phenomenon of excitement and responsiveness as the terminal reacts to the students' manipulations. It is not too far afield to assume that this characteristic can generate the same responsiveness and excitement among consumer users.

However, as the consumer marketplace of the 1960s taught us so graphically with its explosion of new types of goods and services, too much abundance can bring to consumers severe problems of overloading and confusion. Without adequate indicators to separate the wanted from the unwanted, the good from the bad, the accurate from the inaccurate, the useful from the useless, the new media can as easily generate feelings of helplessness and inadequacy as they can of effectiveness and self-mastery.

All of these potentials are magnified by the new electronic information technologies. Thus, one problem faced by users of the new technologies is the need to develop new indicators of quality, so that consumers can learn how to evaluate the various database offerings available to them on their television or home terminal screens. As electronic graphics on the screen replace the printed word, the shiny pages of our favorite magazines will be gone, along with the familiar variations of print, paper, format, and graphics of newspapers and magazines, which we have come to associate with certain levels of reliability, quality, and interest. Distinctions between content and advertisement also may largely disappear in the new media. Indeed, advertisers have already responded to the new media's informational role by adding "information" to their promotional messages and calling them "infomercials"!

A look at some of the information menus offered on databases currently available to a household user illustrates some of these problems. At the present time, there are two general-purpose databases being offered commercially to a home terminal owner, The Source and Compuserve.[1] Prestel in Great Britain also currently offers to consumers a broadly based information/transaction service, which is being used by some 1,500 British households.

A look at these three systems provides us with some idea of the magnitude of the information potential of the new electronic information technologies and also with some caveats for consumers on their current usefulness in practice. The information offered on each of these three systems encompasses a minimum of 400 items, ranging from news, sports, weather, airline schedules, restaurants, theaters, and movie and television reviews in specific cities to so-called general-purpose consumer information about such subjects as gardening, home budgeting, energy conservation, or babysitters.

On Prestel, the catalog somewhat resembles a medium-sized telephone book, with offerings separately cataloged by subject matter and information provider. The indexing of The Source and Compuserve databases is far less comprehensive and gives no indication of the information provider. The thrust of the consumer-oriented offerings of all three systems is essentially textual, covering several pages, or screen frames, that require the user to scroll the text in order to read through the complete item.

At the present time, the information retrieval systems relevant to consumer needs that are on-line in the United States contain a small amount of what one might term Washington Checkbook or Consumers Union type information. Both organizations are involved in several of the pilot programs, but their data is not yet available on current commercial systems.

We do not have any experience of the types of consumer information that may be generated by information providers who see consumer information needs as a potentially profitable market to be served directly and not to be served as a byproduct of selling products or services or selling viewership to advertisers.

Computer Literacy and User-Friendliness

Another problem that consumers must confront in mining the maximum potential of the new technologies is the ease or difficulty of accessing and searching the informational and transactional databases available to them.

Using the home computer to access informational databases is not easy. Each database provider has its own procedures and command names, which must be learned before using the database. Once the commands are learned, the computer technology is so exact that simple errors such as omitting a hyphen or a space in a command renders the command useless. The commands that enable users to ask for help, return to a previous page, or go back to the original information category can differ in minor or major respects among the various systems. For example, on Compuserve, the user signs off by typing "bye" or "off." On The Source, you type "Q" for quit and then "off." On The Source each category has its own command that you type to leave one category and go to another. On Compuserve, you can reach another category by typing "T." All of this diversity is further complicated if you change terminals.

Once entered into an information category, you have an index of choices that enable you to browse through the data. You can also pinpoint the particular category of information you want by its specific number, which saves user time—and, more important, saves telephone and computer charges. However, more often than not the information provided in the chosen category is not what the user expected or wanted. Sometimes, it is preceded by information that the system provider thinks you need or wants to tell you about. Frequently, what appears are pages of text about the subject. This is because so much of the consumer information is simply an electronic reproduction of the information as it appeared in the newspaper. However, the point is that at the present time the searcher has little opportunity to know in advance the number of pages in the information category or, frequently, its source—whether newspaper or other. Moreover, it takes considerable skill and practice to move easily in and out of information categories, and these skills must be relearned for each database system, since each system has its own protocols and commands.

Difficulties in entering and exiting, scanning, and rejecting are important because they can cause deep frustration to the user—to the point of despair and helplessness—and because they are costly in terms of time spent.

Information providers have their own set of difficulties in trying to include their data in publicly available databases. Frame size, number of lines, graphics, and color capability all differ from system to system, so that information providers cannot generically program the data in advance to fit all data bases.

This birdseye catalog of difficulties is not meant to damn either the information system managers or the information providers, nor to discourage potential users. Rather, these difficulties point up the areas in which consumers will have to take an active, assertive interest in order to be sure that terminal producers and information system managers and providers will develop products that meet consumer needs and skill levels.

The Policy Alternatives—the Need for Consumer Research

The new electronic information technologies will have important consequences for consumers' participation in the society of the 1990s and beyond. Consumers could become newly empowered, with information geared to their interests and desires easily accessible to them. They could participate in all of the resources available to help them find and enjoy the services and products they need, as well as the full range of educational, entertainment, and cultural riches in the community. Or they could become a new disadvantaged segment of society, unable to access and enjoy the informational potential of the technology and resigned to a passive, nonparticipatory role in our society. Whichever scenario achieves reality will depend largely on the actions that consumers and their leaders take now to identify their needs and the policy decisions taken in order to those needs.

Consumers have opportunities to be heard. Their constraints lie in the difficulties they encounter in identifying and documenting their needs in objective and analytical fashions, and in presenting data or the consequences of policy actions or of the failure to take action. The key to taking effective action and obtaining a serious response is research carefully directed to consumer needs, interests, and concerns.

At present very little research and analysis is solely devoted to identifying consumer needs and framing public policy alternatives that can respond to these needs. Research in this area is concerned primarily with identifying the range of issues that the new technologies pose to particular sectors of our society or to society as a whole. These studies review the technical and economic aspects of developments and predict their likely shape over the next twenty years. Such research deals with questions like: who are likely information providers; what is access likely to cost; who will have access, and at what cost; what issues of security (for information providers) and privacy (for users) are likely to arise; and what constitutional, legal, and regulatory alternatives and government functions can be used to control or shape the consequences of the new technologies. Some researchers are particularly concerned with likely consumer demand and the applications likely to have the largest consumer acceptance and use. None focus on how to familiarize consumers with the new technologies so that they can signal their interests and concerns on a basis of knowledge and experience. Similarly, the accessibility of these systems by consumer information providers needs to be dealt with specifically. Analyses of what incentives and other aids may be necessary to ensure that consumers receive the full range of information they need and want is typically lacking in these studies. None of these research studies deals with what these technologies must look like in order to ensure that consumers enjoy them.

Consumers must see to it that their requirements for these systems are carefully researched and presented, so that they can participate in an informed way in the public debate on the actions best suited to meet the full range of consumer needs. Consumers must have opportunities to see for themselves what these systems can do for them. Consumers cannot signal their desires for information about financial aid for education or for nursing care services, for example, unless these services are available to them, and they are realistically equipped by information and experience to utilize the services. Certainly, consumers cannot signal, much less rank in order of importance, their preferences for transactional services, information retrieval, or other capabilities unless all offerings, actual and potential, can somehow be demonstrated. Consumers need databases developed for their specific interests, in order to determine for themselves the benefits—and problems—of these new technologies.

A research agenda would have to look at the hardware and software in these electronic information systems and examine public policy issues, with a view to identifying what aspects are of consequence to consumer's ease of use and enjoyment of the new technologies. An outline of this agenda can only be briefly suggested here.

The impact of market-driven information systems on the types of information provided and the segments of the consumer population most likely to be served must be carefully researched. This research must also analyse the impact on consumers of coexisting public and private systems of information generation and the forms they might take. Existing community resources must be examined for their potential role in providing information, managing information systems, and helping consumers who lack the skills, interest, or sophistication would impair their access to these systems without outside help. Research must also study the impact on consumer interests of the different ownership and management configurations and the opportunities and limitations each configuration might present to consumers for their information needs.

Another area of concern for researchers relate to the so-called electronic "environmental" problems that the database technologies will create for consumers. The applicability to the new technologies of existing constitutional and regulatory philosophies designed to ensure a free marketplace for ideas, promote competition, and avoid censorship, is an important issue for consumers, whom these philosophies were designed to benefit.

The role of libraries, community centers, municipal governments, and other local groups must be explored to determine what role they could play—either as managers of information databases and terminal centers or as sources of help and counsel, or both—in supporting consumers who do not or cannot own their own home systems, or who need assistance in utilizing their home systems.

At the other end of the spectrum of issues, consumers have an immediate need for opportunities to familiarize themselves with the operation of these systems and with the systems' potential for meeting their information needs. Consumers need data to evaluate existing terminals and to make certain that purchasing a terminal will not lock them into access to only certain database systems. Similarly, consumers should be able to pick their information system on the basis of full information about the information providers on the system and the standards of selection utilized by the system.

The software needed to access available databases must be simple to use and should ideally employ standard commands. Consumers will also need some indicators by which to evaluate the user-friendliness of a system.

Consumers will have a basic need for on-line information directories that fully disclose the sources of the information, the names of the providers, and probably the date of preparation. The directories should list whether the data is presented textually, and the number of pages. It is critical to the user whether a movie review is three lines or three pages. A listing of names, addresses, and telephone numbers of babysitters or day-care centers, or sources of listings of these services, is very different information from a three-page article about day-care centers or babysitting, or about the different age groups for which day-care and babysitting services are available, or about indicators of quality to look for when selecting one. At the present time, descriptions of the information item provide very few clues about its content.

Cues will need to be worked out for differentiating "infomercials," the information supplied by commercial providers of the product or service described, from information supplied by nonproducers or by nonprofit groups. Newspaper-generated information differs from advertiser-generated information, and both may be different from information generated by a consumer union or local consumer, or by environmental, senior citizen, or public health groups. Browsing through a series of electronic information offerings is a very different process from reading, and contains none of safeguards or quality indicators that consumers are familiar with in the print world. For such familiar information providers as Consumers Union or Washington Checkbook, the mere disclosure of their names will be enough to clue the viewer to the nature of their offerings. But new information providers will have no such ready recognition, and consumers will have to learn new ways of familiarizing themselves with the quality, reliability, and relevance to their needs of these new information providers. Some shorthand ways of disclosing the providers' backgrounds and relationship to the information provided will be essential.

Consumer-oriented information such as comparative prices, the characteristics of services and products, data about the quality of medical and legal services is not easy to generate. It requires special interests, skills, and resources. Moreover, it is information that other sectors of society frequently oppose. There must be special incentives for the creation and dissemination of information that some interest groups may not wish to see offered.

If consumers are afraid that computer records of their information retrieval or shopping orders may be used by others, research should focus on the feasibility of creating buffering structures that could retransmit individual consumer commands through some blind or aggregate ordering system. Consumer organizations should explore the possibility of providing computer security for their constituents, perhaps on a subscription basis. This could provide the organizations with a source of income and their constituents with a protective shield for their individual actions.

Consumers are realistic enough to recognize that the world can never be made perfect. Some solutions that might meet their interests will not be possible, economically or politically. But it is essential that consumers participate in the debate over new technologies, and that they understand and appreciate not only the potential of these systems but the steps that must be taken to realize this potential. Consumers' views must be heard by their state legislatures, their county and city authorities, and by their elected representatives in the House and Senate. Industry is searching for consumer input. It is essential for industry leaders to hear from knowledgeable and informed consumers, so that they can realistically assess what part of consumer needs can and will be effectively met by the private sector.

Consumer research, based on intelligently expressed consumer needs, is the key for consumers to assure themselves that the new technologies will serve their interests to the fullest extent possible.

Note

1. There are several information/transactions systems being offered in local or regional areas on an experimental basis to small groups of users. Bank One mounted one such experiment in conjunction with OCLC, Inc., a nonprofit computer network of libraries; WETA and New York University's Center for Media Alternatives have a two-year teletext pilot project underway in the District of Columbia. The pilot programs utilize teletext systems that essentially offer information on set frames or pages that can be called up by the homeowner for display on his or her television screen. These systems are relatively user-friendly and easy to manage, but have a limited volume of data available. Viewdata systems, which are more interactive, have also been the subject of pilot testing by the Knight Ridder chain in Coral Gables teamed with AT&T, and by the Times Mirror in Los Angeles teamed with Canada's Infomart. AT&T and CBS are testing a two-way home and business information system in Ridgeway, New York, that could ultimately bring in advertising and shopping services. American Express, owner of Warner Communications, is actively expanding Warner's Qube program in Columbus, Ohio. This program involves not only information retrieval but also opinion polling systems, and has been running since 1980.

The databases of all of these programs have included a limited amount of consumer information. Unfortunately, the details of the consumer information offerings and the results achieved are not publicly available.

References

Servan-Schreiber, Jean-Jacques. 1980. World Challenge. New York: Simon and Schuster.
Toffler, Alvin. 1980. The Third Wave. New York: Bantam Books.

12
Consumer Protection in Public Sector Marketing: A Neglected Area in Consumerism

Ben M. Enis
Dean L. Yarwood

A used automobile dealer in Miami, William Lehman, noticed that all of a sudden, in about 1960, there seemed to be an economic miracle among the Cuban used car dealers. Many dealerships sprang up; used autos became expensive and hard to find. As a member of the U.S. House Select Committee on Intelligence in 1975, Congressman Lehman heard allegations of fifty or more Central Intelligence Agency (CIA) proprietary organizations operating in Dade County. (U.S. House Select Committee on Intelligence 1975:143). The congressman was concerned about unfair CIA competition with small businesses. But what consumer protections does the CIA offer its customers?

Governments as Marketers

We believe that almost all governments function, at least to some degree, as marketers. In the broad sense that marketing is interpreted as exchange to expected mutual advantage (Kotler and Levy 1969; Bagozzi 1975), then governmental agencies at local, state, national, and international levels offer goods and services to consumers in exchange for payment. While there are many substantial differences between private sector marketers and government agencies that perform marketing activities, there are sufficient commonalities to characterize government fairly as marketers (Mokwa and Permut 1981). Here are a few examples.

At the local level, a number of municipalities provide utilities (electricity, gas, water); there are numerous community colleges; and from time to time municipalities sell surplus equipment (automobiles, office furniture and machines, even land and buildings). All state governments operate universities and hold auctions of surplus equipment; twenty-one operate or have approved lotteries, thirty have commissioned-controlled horse racing, and eighteen operate state-controlled liquor stores (Council of State Government 1984; Lindsey 1984). The U.S. federal government is by far the nation's largest publisher of books, and it operates the U.S. Postal Service and Amtrak as quasipublic corporations. The federal government also auctions surplus equipment and supplies, and from time to time operates businesses as a cover for espionage activities (U.S. House Select Committee 1975; Landauer 1979). In the international arena, the U.S. Department of Commerce promotes tourism and the National Aeronautics and Space Administration provides technical assistance to businesses. The British government markets coal and crude oil, and many governments have state-controlled flag airlines.

The dollar amounts involved in such transactions are difficult to determine, but a few examples demonstrate the magnitude of government marketing efforts:

Sales of federal surplus personal property by the Federal Property Resources Service came to $54 million in financial year 1983; proceeds from the sale of surplus real estate and buildings came to $191.3 million (General Services Administration 1983, table, inside cover).

During 1978, almost 1.68 billion visits were made to recreation areas managed by various federal agencies (Comptroller General 1981a).

In fiscal year 1980, the Department of Agriculture (DOA) provided over $3.5 billion in cash and donated commodities to support school lunch programs (Comptroller General 1981c).

In recent years the Department of Defense has spent well over $100 million annually to recruit an all-volunteer force. The services promise a career, interesting work, a chance to serve one's country, and educational opportunities. One service promises an adventure, not just a career (Yarwood and Enis 1982:38).

Compiling a complete listing of government marketing activities would be, to say the least, a challenging task. Perhaps these examples are sufficient to document the point: governments market much to many consumers.

This paper focuses on marketplace transactions in the form of government agencies selling to final consumers. It does not examine (1) issues involved in consumer complaints about transfers of goods and services (food stamps, veterans' hospitals, police protection); (2) activities of government agencies in factor markets (employers of labor; borrowers of capital; purchasers of land, buildings, durable goods, raw materials, component parts, etc.); nor (3) activities of government agencies as purchasers of goods and services. These are interesting and important areas, but the focus of this paper is consumer protection in marketplace transactions in which governments compete for consumer dollars with other private and nonprofit organizations.

Consumerism Issues in Government Marketing

Consumerism by definition seeks to protect the rights of buyers in exchange transactions, and to augment their satisfaction from such transactions (Kangun and Richardson 1978; Kotler 1972). Given the many and varied transactions that consumers have with government agencies, it is appropriate to examine such transactions for consumerism issues. In 1962, President Kennedy offered what has become the classic taxonomy of consumers' rights: (1) the right to safety, (2) the right to be informed, (3) the right to choose, and (4) the right to be heard (Kennedy 1962). This taxonomy is used to examine consumerism issues in government marketing transactions.

The Right to Safety

The consumer, noted President Kennedy, has the right to expect that products will be safe. He was primarily thinking in terms of physical safety. Consumers utilizing public utilities, for example, have the right to expect that electricity, natural gas, and water will be delivered to their premises in such manner that their use will not engender bodily harm. But Wilson and Rachal (1977) comment, "electric utility companies have been ordered by the government to take a number of expensive steps to clean up the gases they emit into the air. The Tennessee Valley Authority (TVA), a public agency, is not as vulnerable to the authority of the Environmental Protection Agency as, for example, Pacific Gas and Electric (PG&E). . . . PG&E has 'clear stacks,' and TVA does not."

Similarly, students attending community colleges expect campus security officers to insure the physical safety of their persons and property. But rapes and robberies occur regularly on college campuses. Each year a number of injuries and one or two deaths result from fraternity hazing. In one case, a student was seriously wounded by a gun fired at an instructor by another student. The student has recovered physically, but the university involved has to date refused to accept liability for the incident.

A more celebrated case results from government disposal of surplus property. The U.S. Postal Service uses vehicles known as jeeps, manufactured by American Motors Corporation. In an NBC broadcast (National Broadcasting Company 1981), it was noted that such jeeps would not meet U.S. Department of Transportation vehicular safety standards for sale to consumers. Yet they meet U.S. Postal Service standards for operation as delivery vehicles. The U.S. Postal Service annually auctions some 5,000 such vehicles, and many are purchased by household consumers. Several serious injuries have been recorded. The only response to date by the Postal Service has been to place a small plaque—very much reminiscent of the Surgeon-General's warning on cigarette packages—on the dashboards of the vehicles it sells.

Persons who use public park facilities have a right to assume that they meet federal and state health and safety standards. Yet, when the Government Accounting Office (GAO) evaluated twenty-two federal facilities that were operated by state and local governments, it found that thirteen did not meet these standards. Twelve of them had substandard sanitation systems, five had deficient water systems, and six each had several unsafe restrooms and/or picnic shelters (Comptroller-General 1981a:6–10).

The National School Lunch Act requires that lunches of schools participating in DOA's hot lunch program meet standards of nutrition set by the Secretary of Agriculture. The goal of this public policy is to safeguard the health of the nation's school children by assuring that they receive nourishing meals. However, a study of a sample of seven participating school systems employing different lunch formats, showed that none of them met the secretary's goal of providing one-third of the recommended dietary allowances as that standard was applied to fifteen- to eighteen-year olds. Most of the programs were deficient in at least half of the recommended nutrients (Comptroller General 1981c:1–6).

Consumers of government products also have the right to expect financial safety. In general, purchases of government bonds and real estate are assumed to be among the safest of investments. However, most financial counselors know that government bonds have historically paid unusually low interest rates, and an increasing number of government foreclosures on Veterans' Administration and Federal Housing Authority mortgages raises possible questions about the financial safety for consumers of these government products (Turk and Cook 1984; Comptroller General, 1982). And is the student who borrows federal funds to attend a state university obligated to repay the loan if the expected job opportunities resulting from that education do not materialize?

The Right to be Informed

As any citizen in modern society can attest, government documents tend to be overly complex and verbose. Government catalogs and merchandise descriptions are no exceptions to this generalization. Academicians know that university catalogs have among the highest fog indexes in the English language, and government descriptions of surplus property for sale are in many cases impenetrable. The potential buyer is forced to rely upon interpretations of such documents by government employees. For example, in his 1978 courtmartial defense, army Captain L.T. Davis claimed that contractual promises made by recruiters, advertising, and bulletins were false and deceptive (Turk & Cook 1984:329). Among the more common forms of malpractice, according to a study of the perceptions of 4,400 officials involved in military recruitment, are "misleading applicants about conditions of service of benefits" and "misleading applicants about which assignments or schools are available or for which they are qualified" (Comptroller General 1981d:5–17). Many a student has failed to graduate when planned, and many a buyer of surplus automobiles and office equipment has rued the consummation of that transaction.

For most families, the purchase of their home is by far the largest one they will ever make. Obviously, they need to be especially well informed about this transaction. In the 1970s, new legislation allowed the Department of Housing and Urban Development (HUD) to insure loans with graduated-payment mortgages. As of September 1980, HUD had insured 190,878 mortgages with graduated payments worth a total of $8.9 billion. In looking into these loans, GAO found that (1) HUD underwriters lacked the criteria necessary to establish the loan applicant's ability to meet the increasingly high loan repayments, and (2), though five graduated-payment mortgage plans were available, most prospective homeowners were only being informed of the most popular plan.

Under Section 245(b) of the National Housing Act as amended, potential home purchasers can get loans with lower down payments than they can under Section 245(a), though both sections provide for graduated-payment mortgages. This section causes concern at HUD because it seems to assume a rate of housing appreciation of six percent or higher to be actuarially sound. The Director of Financial Management at HUD worried in a 1980 memo "that many foreclosures might occur when buyers sell their property and learn they owe more than when they purchased their home." This is a case in which government underinforms citizens in transactions that are extremely important to the citizens (Comptroller General 1981b:1–6, 53–82).

Like all marketing communication, government promotional activities are susceptible to misunderstanding (Yarwood and Enis 1982). Consumerism efforts have been directed during the past decade toward reducing ambiguity and regulating deceptive promotion. Such regulations do not generally apply to government promotions. As noted above, government savings bonds are often promoted as safe and sound investments. Many consumers buy them, and accept the low interest rate in the name of patriotism. Other consumers, however, may not be well-informed about interest rates, and may feel that their government has duped them (Comptroller General, 1982). Then there is the classic case of the Illinois State lottery, which advertised a top prize of $1,000,000. That sum was not paid in a lump at time of winning, however, but rather in twenty annual installments of $50,000 each. In view of the present value of money, to say nothing of inflation rates, this at least borders on deception. *Newsweek* magazine (1975) commented, "government lottery operators do things that would land profit-seekers in jail." As a final example, it was noted above that some governments market games of chance and others sell alcoholic beverages through state-owned stores. Both products are addictive for some people. Do the governments marketing such products bear some responsibility to consumers who become addicted to them?

The Right to Choose

Many government marketers operate as monopolists: municipal utilities, state-owned liquor stores, the U.S. Postal Service. While there are substitute products, in a generic sense, for these government-marketed goods and services, the governmental restrictions on the particular product form offered by governmental agencies may limit consumer sovereignty. The U.S. Postal Service, for example, has many competitors (e.g., United Parcel Service, Federal Express, Western Union, AT&T, Xerox Information Net). But consumers who patronize those competitors also subsidize via their taxes the operation of the Postal Service. This is true of the consumer who patronizes a private security service, who imports liquor rather than buying it from the state-owned store, who supplements the public utility with bottled water or a propane generator. Perhaps the most vivid contemporary example of this point is education. Patrons of private schools from kindergarten through higher education not only pay for that product, but also subsidize their government-operated competitor schools. Perhaps this is why there is so much discussion about voucher systems and about educator accountability.

The right to choose, according to one conception, is predicated upon preserving competition and rules of fair play in the marketplace. This would suggest that government marketers should be held to the same rules as private sector marketers. However, such is not always the case. The Missouri Public Interest Group (MoPIRG) admonished Union Electric to cease displaying the American flag in its commercials on behalf of nuclear power. In support of its request, MoPIRG cited the U.S. Code, 36§176, which stipulates: "The flag should never be used for advertising in any manner whatsoever." (Missouri Public Interest Group 1982). Be that as it may, it is not especially unusual to see the flag prominantly displayed in military recruitment ads.

The Right to be Heard

Perhaps the most important consumer right is to be heard when problems arise. Most consumers in contemporary society recognize that products sometimes malfunction, that misunderstandings can arise between buyer and seller, that computers snarl bills. Trust, an essential ingredient of any exchange transaction, implies the right to have such grievances aired.

All professors are aware of the difficulties faced by the student who feels that he or she has been unfairly graded, or that the university library has levied an incorrect fine. Procedures for redress are time consuming and laborious, and too often are weighted against the student/consumer. Most municipal utility companies work diligently to restore service after a storm or flood, but the consumer not satisfied with that service can do little but hope that relief will soon come. The consumer whose reliance upon the U.S. Postal Service's promise to deliver overnight is disappointed can look forward to nothing more than a refund of postage. According to NBC, the injured consumer of a U.S. Postal Service jeep has no recourse against either the Postal Service, or the manufacturer, American Motors Corporation.

Governmental Responses to Such Issues

Ideally, a government's agencies are responsive to its citizens. With respect to consumerism issues, however, government responses are difficult to document, and to interpret. Attempts have been made to ascertain the possible government responses that could be expected by the ordinary consumer of government products. These studies involved library searches of pertinent documents and telephone interviews with officials in various government agencies. Such efforts were probably in excess of those typically expended by the ordinary citizen, but were by no means exhaustive. In general, the responses indicated that dissatisfied consumers of government products had no recourse from unsatisfactory purchases.

Executive branch offices at federal and state levels were consistent when it came to surplus equipment sales. Government liability extended only to explicit description of the products to be purchased. Military surplus is sold subject to a limited warranty based on catalog description for national sales (General Services Administration 1981). There is no guarantee as to condition; the property is sold "as is where is." Said an official of Marketing Support Branch of the Defense Logistics Services Center, "What you see is what you get." The contract provides that government makes no warranty expressed or implied as to condition or usage. The agency does try to give notification of defects when they are known. For example, a frozen engine or malfunctioning transmission is sometimes noted on the vehicle tag. But the agency cannot be certain that defects are known, nor does it perform safety checks on vehicles. Customers are told that army vehicles do not have to comply with Environmental Protection Agency (EPA) standards, but that customers will have to bear the expense of bringing items into EPA compliance prior to operation. A significant exception is that there is consumer recourse if the item received differs from its catalog description.

This pattern was reflected at the state level. A property control assistant for the state of Missouri reported that buyers of the state's surplus property had no recourse of any kind if something went wrong. The contract bears the statement "no guarantee of any kind is expressed or implied by any agency or the state of Missouri"; he noted, "You buy and take your chances." And a local Internal Revenue Service (IRS) official confirmed that property seized for nonpayment of taxes is sold to the public "as is, what is."

Thus, the consumer's rights to safety and to be heard appear to be less solid in dealing with government marketers than with private sector marketers. Moreover, notice of sale is published in catalogs whose circulation is restricted to those on the government agency's mailing list (although it is not difficult to be added to such a list), and/or to one newspaper in the local area. This means that the consumer's right to be informed may be abridged, or at least limited, when dealing with government marketers.

Statutes pertaining to consumerism issues are numerous at all levels of government. However, most exempt government marketers from their provisions. As noted above, U.S. Army and U.S. Postal Service vehicles do not have to comply with Department of Transportation and Environmental Protection Agency standards. When such vehicles are sold to the public, it is the buyer's responsibility to bring those vehicles into compliance. In Boston (Wilson and Rachal 1977), the Housing Inspection Department (HID) is responsible for responding to tenant complaints about unsafe housing conditions. HID is more successful in handling complaints against private landlords than against the Boston Housing Authority (BHA), which manages low-income, public housing projects in the city. "Though public housing complaints were more frequently well-founded, they were much less frequently corrected— only about 14 percent of the year's public housing cases, compared to at least ¾ of the private housing cases, were reported as corrected at the time of the survey. The difference did not arise because public-housing managers are callous, but because the BHA as a public agency is required (by legislation) to serve goals that, as it turns out, are inconsistent with good maintenance. It must keep rents low and it may not pass onto tenants increases in operating costs."

Although former Federal Trade Commission (FTC) Chairman Michael Pertschuk announced that his agency would monitor government advertising using the same standards as it applied to private sector advertising, the FTC has no authority to enforce such regulations. Maryland is the only state that operates a government-sponsored program to combat gambling addiction, and even it explicitly eschews legal reponsibility for such addiction.

In Missouri, the state Public Service Commission has no jurisdiction over publicly owned municipal utilities. According to a public relations officer for the commission, consumer complaints must be referred directly to the utility. Unsatisfied consumers can then appeal to the city council or other appropriate municipal governing body. There is no independent regulatory body to whom the consumer can turn. Again, the clear pattern is that legislated consumer rights are considerably less secure for buyers of government products.

In private sector transactions, many consumerism issues are adjudicated in municipal, state, or federal courts. Our admittedly limited, but specifically focused, research in the pertinent documents and our contacts with government officials and professors of law failed to identify even one instance of a successful consumerist suit against a government marketer. Such efforts confront the doctrine of sovereign immunity. According to one academic expert, the consumer must first convince the court that the agency was acting in a commercial rather than a sovereign manner. If successful, the consumer could then sue under existing consumer protection laws.

Wilson and Rachal (1977) conclude "the private sector is not without resources to resist government controls . . . but in the final analysis, the private sector cannot deny the authority of the state—if it were able to, the state would cease to exist. . . . A private organization can be sued or enjoined in court by a government agency; it is rare in the extreme for one agency to sue another."

Conclusions and Implications

Despite the enormous progress that has been made in consumer issues during the last decade, our overall assessment is that, in transactions with government marketers, *caveat emptor* must remain the consumers' guide. Since most consumerist groups and most government regulators have not focused upon this area of consumerism, buyers' rights are generally less well defined and less fully protected.

This paper has only tentatively explored this area of consumerism. It is an important, and insufficiently researched, aspect of the consumerism movement. Truly, further research is warranted. Further investigation in three areas appears appropriate. These are implications for: (1) consumers of government goods and services, (2) government marketers of such goods and services, and (3) public policy toward such transactions.

For Consumers of Government Products

It would be interesting to learn more about consumers' attitudes toward government marketers and their products. It may be that consumers feel that governments are so vast and so impersonal that any movement resembling the consumerist movement in the private sector would be doomed to failure. On the other hand, such research could uncover considerable discontent, and therefore document a pressing need for consumerist activity in this area. Of course, it is also possible that consumers of government products are completely satisfied with such transactions.

Government Marketers

Recognition by government agencies that they do indeed function as marketers is a relatively recent phenomenon (Enis 1981). Accordingly, one should not expect sophisticated organizational structures and procedures in government agencies for dealing with any aspect of marketing management, much less with consumerism issues in government transactions. But such issues will, in our opinion, increasingly be raised in this context.

It would be interesting, therefore, to determine empirically the extent of such structures and procedures in government agencies and of plans for them in the future. We hope that any government agency would be seriously considering instituting marketing structures and procedures, particularly consumer affairs. Our expectation, in contrast, is that there is relatively little such activity at the present. If this is the case, it would indicate a significant opportunity for academic research and professional practice in an important area of marketing activity.

For Public Policy

Public policy presents perhaps the most complex and therefore the most interesting set of implications. It is now all but universally recognized that marketing activities must be regulated in the public interest. Few believe totally in Adam Smith's "invisible hand." It is logical, therefore, that marketing by government agencies also should be regulated.

But this logical deduction is easier to state than to implement. Does society want, for example, one agency of the Executive Branch—say the Federal Trade Commission—regulating the advertising activities of another branch— for example, U.S. Treasury Department bond sales? What are the applicable legal precedents for consumer litigation, and what judicial procedures and constraints should apply? Should the current complex and far-reaching interpretations of product liability laws be applied to jeeps sold by the U.S. Postal Service? Marketing scholars with legal and regulatory expertise should find such questions interesting. Those questions are particularly pertinent in light of the focus of this paper upon products marketed by government agencies that have private sector substitutes. In short, government marketers compete at least indirectly with private sector marketers for all of the products mentioned in this paper. This raises rather fundamental questions about the nature of a mixed economy.

In their insightful recent article, Bloom and Greyser (1981) contend that the consumerism movement has entered the "mature phase of its life cycle and is experiencing market fragmentation." They comment, " in the same way that companies seek to extend the life cycles of their products and brands, the consumer movement can find creative strategies for remarketing its product."

An examination of consumerist issues in government marketing would seem to provide one such opportunity. Government agencies are an increasingly significant factor in the marketplace. Perhaps it is time for consumerists to focus attention on the rights of consumers engaged in such transactions. An official of the Marketing Support Branch of the Defense Logistics Services Center, Battle Creek, Michigan, commented, "consumerism in governmental sales is a fascinating topic. You should continue studying it." This appeared to be a new thought.

References

Bagozzi, R.P. 1975. Marketing as exchange. *Journal of Marketing* (Oct.):32–39.

Bloom, Paul N. and Stephen A.Greyser. 1981. The maturing of consumerism. *Harvard Business Review* 59 (Nov.–Dec.):130–39.

Comptroller General. 1981a. Health and safety deficiencies found at water recreation areas. In *Report to the Chairman, Committee on Appropriations, United States Senate* CED-81-88 (June 15). Washington, D.C.: U.S. Government Printing Office.

———. 1981b. New mortgages for financing homes need uniform and comprehensive consumer safeguards. *Report to the Congress of the United States* CED-81-53 (July 2).

———. 1981c. Efforts to improve school lunch programs—are they paying off? *Report to the Congress of the United States* CED-81-121 (Sept. 9).

———. 1981d. Recruiting malpractice: Extent, causes, and potentials for improvement. *Report to the Honorable Sam Nunn Member, Committee on Armed Services of the United States* FPCD-81-34 (July 20).

———. 1982. *Alleged Abuses in the U.S. Savings Bond Division of the Department of the Treasury* B208248 (July 26). Washington, D.C.: U.S. Government Printing Office.

Council of State Governments. 1984. *The Book of the States 1984–85*. Lexington, Ky.: Council of State Governments.

Enis, B.M. 1981. Government as marketers: Issues of management and public policy. In Mokwa and Permut:343–345.

General Services Administration. 1981. *Doing Business with the Federal Government*. Washington, D.C.: U.S. Government Printing Office.

———. 1983. *Operating Summary: 1983* (Nov. 8), A-28. Washington, D.C.: General Services Administration.

Kangun, Norman, Lee Richardson, eds. 1978. *Consumerism: New Challenges for Marketing*. Chicago: American Marketing Association.

Kennedy, J.F. 1962. *Message from the President, Relative to Consumers' Protection,* (Document no. 364, House of Representatives 87th Congress, 2nd session.) Washington, D.C.: U.S. Government Printing Office.

Kotler, Philip. 1972. What consumerism means for marketers. *Harvard Business Review* (May–June):48–57.

———, and S.J. Levy. 1969. Broadening the concept of marketing. *Journal of Marketing* (Jan.):10–15.

Landauer, Jerry. 1979. CIA has flown parts from auto makers to assembly plants. *The Wall Street Journal* (Feb. 16):1, 13.

Lindsey, Robert. 1984. Tax-cutting proposals defeated in three states. *New York Times* (Nov. 8):A-28.

Mokwa, M.P., and S.A. Permut. 1981. *Government Marketing: Theory and Practice.* New York: Praeger.

Missouri Public Interest Group. 1982. (News release, March).

National Broadcasting Company. 1981. *NBC Magazine* (Nov. 6).

Newsweek, Inc. 1975. Lotteries: States take the gamble. *Newsweek* (Dec. 12):90.

Turk, Michael A. and Ernest F. Cook. 1984. How the U.S. government uses deceptive advertising to manipulate the consumer to gain an unfair advantage over the consumer. *Proceedings, 1984 Educator's Conference.* Chicago: American Marketing Association, 319–323.

U.S. House Select Committee on Intelligence. 1975. *U.S. Intelligence Agencies and Activities: Intelligence Costs and Fiscal Procedures, Part 1.* Washington, D.C.: U.S. Government Printing Office.

Wilson, J.Q., and Patricia Rachal. 1977. Can Government Regulate Itself? *The Public Interest* (winter):3–14.

Yarwood, D.L., and B.M. Enis. 1982. Advertising and publicity programs in the Executive Branch of the national government: Hustling or helping the people? *Public Administration Review* (Jan.–Feb.):37–46.

13

International Consumerism in the Aftermath of the Infant Formula Controversy

James E. Post

International consumerism is a new frontier for business, the activist community, and governments. The reasons are not difficult to understand. U.S. businesses are increasingly caught up in global competiton. Competitive pressures in domestic markets have accelerated the search for international expansion. European, Japanese, and Third World competitors from nations such as Brazil, South Korea, and Taiwan are engaged in sharp and determined competition in numerous industrial and consumer product markets. To say that competition has become aggressive is to vastly understate the case. Competition has led to an extraordinary array of products and services, pricing pressures, and promotional innovations; and it is doing so in every developed and developing country.

This competitive "manifest destiny" worries consumer activists in industrialized and developing nations, because it threatens to distort consumer and industrial purchasing behavior on the one hand, and to imperil public health, safety, and economic stability on the other. At the International Consumer Congress held in Bangkok, Thailand, in December 1984, for example, the tragic consequence of the chemical leak at Union Carbide's plant in Bhopal, India, were extrapolated directly or by analogy to dozens of other consumer protection issues. While the parallels may be weak or nonexistent, international catastrophes such as that at Bhopal energize the consumer movement, encouraging activists to define problems, conduct research studies, and publicize concerns before tragedy strikes again. National governments are also recognizing the need for thinking out, and enacting new relationships between themselves and businesses of local or extranational origin. Economic development remains a governmental imperative as it has been for decades in the developing world, but it is decreasingly sought at any cost. Government officials are much more aware of and sensitive to the concerns of environmental protection, public health and safety, and consumer efficacy than ever before. Thus, the three sets of institutions that will shape the social and economic future for so much of the world's population are drawn inexorably toward confrontation and conflict in the international consumerism arena.

One issue that illustrates the potential of this convergence of institutional interests for serious confrontation and conflict, and the limited prospects for negotiated harmony, is the infant formula controversy. For nearly fifteen years, this issue engaged the international activist community, some of the world's largest consumer product companies, and most of the international health community. For a decade, the confrontations between industry and its organized critics were strident and without mercy. For more than six of those years, a consumer boycott engaged hundreds of thousands of citizens in ten nations in a drive to alter the marketing behavior of Nestlé, the industry's largest seller of the formula, and one of the world's largest multinational food companies. The results of this consumer campaign have been hailed by many consumerists. Esther Peterson, in Bangkok in December 1984, called it "the most significant victory in the history of the international consumer movement."[1] Rhetoric aside, the campaign for international consumer health and safety has been greatly influenced by the infant formula controversy. It has been a surrogate for a host of health and consumer protection issues in the Third World, and has helped define and redefine the essential concerns of business, activists, governments, and international agencies.

The consumerism movement, which appears relatively dormant in the United States, today is burgeoning in the developing world. Through the efforts of the International Organization of Consumer's Union (IOCU) and church organizations, grassroots consumer groups have been formed in Latin America, Africa, and Southeast Asia. Monitoring of corporate social performance is increasing, and networks of publication groups reach across national boundaries in unprecedented ways. Public action groups are now receiving official Non-Governmental Organization (NGO) status in international forums such as the World Health Organization. These institutional changes signal an increasingly vigorous international consumer movement and presage an ever-closer scrutiny of the impact of developed world products and practices in Third World markets. Most importantly, these institutional changes all derive from the international infant formula controversy. For these reasons, this campaign stands as an important chapter in the history of the modern consumerism movement.

Consumerism in the Third World

As population growth has slowed in industrialized nations, many companies have looked on the large populations of the developing world as a promising market for continued expansion of sales and profits. This has been particularly true in the food industry, where diet-conscious Americans and Europeans are creating an image of a population that is "fed-up." So, while "lean cuisine" products take increasing amounts of shelf space in American super-markets, product managers for high-calorie, high-fat, high-cholesterol products seek new customers. Some are to be found in developing nations. Indeed, nutritionists point to the irony of populations in industrialized nations facing health problems associated with obesity, while citizens of many developing nations face the problems and consequences of malnutrition.

The fact that there is significant malnutrition in the developing world, and that food companies possess the technology and skill to improve the quantity and quality of food available to a population, intuitively promises an optimistic outcome. The problem is simply one of coordination and resource management. Unfortunately, reality fails to conform to that intuition, and the presence of processed commercial foods has done relatively little to ameliorate chronic malnutrition in the developing nations. Worse still, the promotion and marketing of such products has worsened the state of public health in a number of instances.

Appropriateness and Marketing of Products

Two types of consumer issues arise in the context of selling to the Third World. One group of issues surrounds the appropriateness of the product, as such, in the environment of a Third World nation. There are products, it is argued, that ought not to be permitted for sale and consumption in a developing nation. These range from hazardous goods that are banned in industrialized nations, but that are freely sold in developing nations, to products that are appropriate in the industrialized world but that pose immense risks for Third World populations.

The second category of consumer issues involves marketing concepts, techniques, and approaches that deceive, mislead, and beguile Third World populations into consumption of food products from developed countries. This category focuses on the technology of marketing, ranging from product and market planning, to specific advertising campaigns, to the very assumptions on which market presence and participation is premised. In its most extreme form, the argument is made that the idea of competitive marketing is inappropriate for Third World societies. Criticism of marketing techniques can apply to all products that are sold in the developing world. If a population is unable to discount advertising messages so as not to be misled, it is vulnerable to exploitation in the name of progress, development, or modernism.

Concerns about the appropriateness of what is sold in developing countries, and the means and methods by which these products are promoted for sale, are not transient. They are commanding the attention of international organizations, grassroots consumer groups, and national governments throughout the developing world.

Success Factors

An effective consumer movement has three basic requirements. First there must be an organization of people, institutions, and key actors capable of focusing their energies and collective power toward a single objective. The greater the number of people, organizations, and key actors involved, however, the more difficult effective organization becomes. Maintaining an effective consumer network then, is very much like maintaining a citizen army, with a capability for quick, concentrated action. More importantly, a non-authoritarian decision system requires extensive communication and grass-root support. This exacerbates the organizational needs.

The second requirement for an effective consumer movement is an energizing issue. The concern that draws the people and institutions together must be of the sort that spurs people to action. Moreover, it is important for key actors in vital institutions, such as government agencies, to be energized, either directly by the issue, or indirectly by the enthusiasm of other citizens.

The third requirement is new ideas. The movement's objectives, and the means to achieve them, must not be outdated. Indeed, it is best if these goals represent imaginative, captivating, and provocative ideas. New ideas are especially important to key actors, because they afford those actors the opportunity to create something new on the landscape of political activity. It can be a legacy for a policymaker to have introduced a new idea as a means of resolving an important issue about which many people care. For many public sector officials, that is a genuine mark of success.

Nutrition Policy in Developing Nations

The idea that the nutritional status and practices of the population are an appropriate subject for public policy consideration and intervention is relatively new in the United States, and not widely implemented through legislation or government programs.[2] In the developing nations, however, nutrition policy is often a focus of government social programs. The reasons are fairly straightforward: malnourished people are more susceptible to disease, which causes public health problems and limited the number of people able to participate in the economic development effort of the nation. Extensive research and political consciousness-raising by such international agencies as the World Health Organization (WHO), Food and Agriculture Organization (FAO), and UNICEF have emphasized the intrinsic importance of nutrition in the developing world.

Epidemiological studies have demonstrated that infants and young children are the portion of the population most vulnerable to malnutrition. Moreover, malnutrition among infants and young children drastically increases their susceptibility to diseases such as measles, which can be fatal. Thus, significant malnutrition among infants and young children produces more deaths per thousand than does malnutrition among other age groups. In this general context, then, a number of developing nations have undertaken major campaigns to improve the nutritional status of infants and young children, usually through programs coordinated by the ministry of health.

As in other areas of public policy, the approaches to nutrition policy vary widely. At one extreme, there are comprehensive national food and nutrition plans, such as that in Colombia, which attempt to draw all varieties of nutrition intervention into a coherent plan. The elements of this plan include food production policies; policies directed toward improving and rationalizing the marketing of foodstuffs; a nutrition and media program; programs aimed at improving water supplies, immunizing the public, and achieving better biological absorption of foods; and subsidized food distribution programs.[3] At the other extreme, is highly selective, targeted intervention, which focuses on a particular problem, population segment, or nutritional need (iodized salt, for example). Between the two, of course, lay a variety of incremental approaches in which experience, analogy, and new opportunities coalesce into nutrition intervention programs.

The central themes of recent nutritional policy development in the Third World can be summarized as follows:

protection of highly vulnerable groups through direct supplementation and best-available-alternative feeding options;

use of cost–benefit analysis to identify the best options for increasing food quantity and quality;

encouragement of indigenous food production and consumption.

Each of these themes has a strong, independent current of support among professional nutritionists and health experts. More importantly, these three themes of recent nutrition policy activity have coalesced around the analysis of the nutritional needs and problems of the particular segments of the population most in need of nutritional improvement. Not surprisingly, much attention has been given to the nutritional needs of infants and young children.

Nutrition Policy and Infant Formula

This concern for the nutritional needs and problems of infants and young children is the root of the infant formula controversy. The issue began to develop in the late 1960s as an outgrowth of the professional concern of physicians and other health workers in developing nations who felt that commercial foods were being promoted to people who could neither afford nor properly use them. It was not until Dr. Derrick Jelliffe coined the phrase "commerciogenic malnutrition" to describe this category of nutritional problems in infants, that journalists began to take note of the matter. The early 1970s were a period characterized by increasing journalistic interest and expanding efforts by health professionals to deal with growing numbers of malnourished infants. International organizations such as UNICEF and the Protein-Calorie Advisory Group (PAG) of the United Nations system served as catalysts by convening international meetings and producing papers outlining official positions on the problem. Throughout this period, the international marketing practices of the infant formula industry became a focal point of criticism.

During the mid-1970s, the infant formula controversy became a two-front war. Medical professionals continued to provide clinical research studies, to experiment with programs to improve infant nutrition in developing nations, and to promote awareness of the advantages of breast-feeding. The research and programmatic experience helped build a better understanding of the problem and possible solutions; the proselytizing produced growing awareness, culminating in adoption of a resolution by the International Pediatrics Association in 1975 endorsing breast-feeding as the medically superior method to feed infants. Anticorporate activists, galvanized by a series of publications—including *The Baby Killer*—and films—especially *Bottle Babies*—began a vigorous campaign designed to build public awareness of the issue in the United States and Europe. The rhetoric and the visual impact of starving babies had obvious effects. The industry was placed on the defensive, and its few counter punches—such as Nestlé's defamation suit against the group that republished *The Baby Killer* under the title *Nestlé Kills Babies*—worked to its disadvantage. The hearings on Nestlé's lawsuit in Switzerland became a public forum for airing the charges against the company, and included the testimony of a number of leading medical and health authorities on the health problems of infants in the Third World.

The infant formula controversy became one of the most valuable assets that nutrition policy advocates possessed. The public concern with the plight of malnourished infants, and the intrinsic connections between infant malnutrition and other nutritional and health policy problems, created a much larger constituency than had previously existed. Renewed interest was given to questions of corporate involvement in agriculture in developing nations, the promotion and sale of pharmaceuticals in less-developed countries, and the sale of harmful products such as pesticides and tobacco. The controversy opened up the entire question of the appropriateness of commercial food products in environments where minimum conditions for safe use could not be guaranteed. The uphill battle to build public awareness of what Alan Berg called "The Nutrition Factor" was aided immeasurably by the infant formula campaign.[4]

New Concepts in Consumer Protection

Consumerism campaigns are built on a foundation of many blocks. One of these consists of rhetoric that captures the essence of the issue and crystallizes the positions of the actors. During the infant formula controversy, a number of new ideas emerged as vital pieces of the language and rhetoric of the conflict process.

Demarketing

Throughout the early phases of the infant formula campaign, critics sought a slogan, phrase, or idea that captured the essence of their objectives. In time, a concept drawn from the marketing literaure—demarketing—was chosen to describe the diminution of advertising and promotion, the reduced emphasis on market expansion, and the acceptance by industry of a no-growth future that the campaigners desired. Industry executives railed against the demarketing concept, some arguing that it was anti-capitalist, anti-free enterprise, and anti-American. Such rhetoric notwithstanding, the concept had both a legitimacy in the literature of the field and a conceptual power that unified the case against the industry.

Demarketing speaks to the twin questions of international consumerism: whether a product is an appropriate one for sale in a particular social environment and whether appropriate techniques are being employed to promote the product. Efforts to remove products or change techniques are demarketing actions when the effect is to more effectively harmonize the product, the marketing techniques, and the consumer interest. Today demarketing is an increasingly important concept in discussing the marketing of such products as tobacco, alcohol, pesticides, and other potentially harmful substances. References by consumer activists to demarketing strategies imply a more focused and consistent analysis of the issues of product appropriateness and the propriety of marketing techniques.

The infant formula controversy has also brought a number of new, politically useful concepts to the field of nutrition policy and planning. Following the famous "Kennedy hearings" in the U.S. Senate in 1978, the World Health Organization and UNICEF began preparations for an international meeting of interested parties on all sides of the controversy.[5] The meeting was held in October 1979 in Geneva, Switzerland.

As part of their preparatory work, WHO and UNICEF developed the *Background Paper for Meeting on Infant and Young Child Feeding;* which was a synthesis of expert opinions on a variety of research topics germane to the issue.[6] The report consisted of two extensive papers, one focusing on current knowledge about infant feeding in a scientific and medical sense, the other entitled "Themes for Discussion." The latter, in particular, introduced a number of ideas that have increasing currency in the consumerism debates of the 1980s. Three ideas deserve specific mention:

1. Commercial products must meet a "public purpose";
2. "Legitimate markets" should be defined in advance of product introduction;
3. National and international codes of conduct for the marketing of specific products should be adopted by producers and enforced by governments.

Public Purpose

The *Background Paper* argued that the introduction of any weaning food should be subject to the criterion of public purpose. "Public Purpose implies that before any product is sold or distributed in a country, or to a particular population group, the overall public health and socioeconomic impact of that product has to be assessed; benefits as well as possible dangers have to be identified and evaluated."[7] In countries with severely limited disposable incomes, introducing expensive commercially processed foods is a questionable practice when acceptable indigenous foods are available to lower costs. The *Background Paper* argues forcefully for a standard of real need before such commercial products are introduced and promoted to the public. As the paper makes clear, in nations with severe economic problems, simply expanding the range of products available for the wealthy is not a sufficient rationale for product introduction. Given the usual patterns of income distribution, an expanded array of expensive consumer products available for the wealthy subset of the population simply contributes a further rationale for that segment to accumulate more, and redistribute less, of the nation's wealth. In so doing, the bifurcation of society into two classes—rich and poor—is accentuated, not alleviated by introduction and promotion of goods from developed countries. At the least, the WHO/UNICEF *Background Paper* urges the governments of developing nations to apply new standards of value to commercial requests for permission to sell products in the country. Goods such as infant formula, which are a convenience rather than a necessity, may not meet the standard at all, or only in such a way as to warrant restriction of their sale and distribution to the legitimate market.

Legitimate Market

The idea that products should meet a public purpose leads directly to the definition of the social need that the product will fill. As the *Background Paper* states, "It is not sufficient to argue that the marketing of a product provides consumers with an additional choice or alternative to what are already established practices and available products. . . . [The question is] whether a particular product serves the interest of the country and the community."[8] Some parameters of need must be developed and articulated to justify the introduction of the product.

How might this be done? The answer obviously depends on the product involved and the sociocultural circumstances of the country. But the infant formula issue provides some instructive lessons. First, there has been a long-standing recognition that some babies have an intolerance to milk products (lactose intolerance) and require special formulas, often based on soy derivatives. The size of this sick-baby market, however, has been estimated at less than two to three percent of all infants, and many physicians claim it is less than one percent. Second, there are the children of mothers who are, themselves, malnourished or unable to adequately breast-feed their babies. There is vigorous debate among researchers on this point, but there is a near-consensus that a mildly malnourished mother can adequately breast-feed an infant. More importantly, the cost of upgrading the mother's diet is substantially less than substituting more expensive formula products, which would only help the infant in any event. Third, there are mothers who breast-feed for a time, but because of work or other activities do not continue for a full six months (the time at which weaning can safely occur). Before the babies reach six months, they require a substitute and infant formula is the best fully prepared alternative. Less expensive, but equally adequate alternatives can be prepared for the baby at home, however. Fourth, there are mothers who breast-feed, but because of work or other reasons choose to suplement the baby's diet with formula.

From the standpoint of nutrition policy, the real need diminishes as we proceed from the sick-baby segment to the supplementary-feed segment. Nevertheless, the process of articulating needs in such a way helps clarify who the manufacturer is trying to reach, and at what cost to the country.

Another approach is to begin with the product and ask what conditions are necessary for its safe use and to what extent those conditions exist in a particular market. Infant formula, for example, is a demanding product. It can only be sold in powdered form in the tropical climates of most developing nations, and therefore requires mixing with pure drinking water under sanitary conditions. Water must be boiled, requiring firewood, and the prepared formula must be refrigerated. The mixing instructions must be followed precisely, and any deviation from the ratio of formula to water seriously diminishes the nutrition received by the baby. Because the product is also expensive, requiring as much as seventy-five percent of per capita income for proper feeding in some developing countries, the temptation to overdilute is great and has resulted in cases of infant malnutrition. Given the requirements for safe use, then, a manufacturer or government could undertake an analysis of the risk factors that would define those segments of the population that could safely use the product. This would not prove that the product meets a public purpose, as the WHO/UNICEF *Background Paper* suggested, but it would carefully define the segment of the public that could use the product without harm. The burden would then be on the manufacturer to ensure that the product was not sold to people who, it could be foreseen, would be unable to use it safely.

Is this an unacceptable burden for the manufacturer? Perhaps. But it is no less burdensome for a society to have large numbers of its citizens suffering the consequences of a predictable and foreseeable harm. As the *Background Paper* stated, "For the majority of the population in developing countries, however, the risks are so much greater, that the use of breast milk substitutes, presents a major public health as well as an individual or family problem. . . . These risks are in turn compounded by inadequate healthcare coverage."[9] This approach places the reponsibility on the party best able to manage it, namely, the manufacturer.

Marketing Codes of Conduct

The concepts of public purpose and legitimate market help define whether or not the product is an appropriate one in the environment of the developing nation. If it is not, it is reasonable not to offer the product for sale. If the product is appropriate for a legitimate segment of the population, however, the manufacturer must then deal with a series of issues regarding the marketing practices that are appropriate in reaching that segment. In this context marketing codes of conduct represent an important consumer protection device for Third World nations.

A firm's behavior is a function of many factors in the environment, mediated by the firm's position in the social, economic, and political environment of the nation. The WHO/UNICEF *Background Paper* noted, for example, that "The practices used in marketing breastmilk substitutes vary according to the economic system that prevails a given country, the existence of national policies regarding the marketing of these substitutes, the attitudes of medical and health authorities and the policies and practices of individual companies.[10] The report then specifies practices that may be dangerous in the developing nations:

promotion to medical and health personnel and institutions;

mass media advertising;

persuasive labeling;

distribution of free product samples or feeding accessories;

introductory discount sales and personal contact with mothers by company representatives in maternity wards or at home.

Finally, "insufficient consideration has been given to the end result (i.e. 'performance') of these marketing practices, and the implications of the widespread use of breastmilk substitutes for infant health and for the family and national economy."[11] Clearly, the drafters of the *Background Paper* were speaking of the performance dimensions and secondary effects of marketing activities.

The purpose of codes of conduct is to stabilize competitive practices among companies in the industry, and to eliminate those that have the most serious negative effects on the public. Thus, WHO and UNICEF urge that all promotion of breast milk substitutes to the public should be stopped and that only ethical and factual information necessary for the consideration of product composition should be provided to the medical profession. These two sets of practices—direct consumer advertising and intense courting of health care professions—have been the principal competitive strategies of the manufacturers in the Third World. What WHO and UNICEF sought was nothing less than the elimination of practices that were designed to expand a market that was already too large.

The WHO's experience suggests a number of conclusions about the formulation and implementation of codes of marketing conduct:

1. There is a vast difference between a code of principles and a code that specifies practices. It is a far easier to draft the former than the latter. A code of principles is subject to interpretation; but with a code of specified practices, competitive imagination will undermine the code.

2. Codes of conduct may be mandatory or voluntary, and may be prepared by individual companies, trade associations, national governments, or international agencies. Examples of each type of code have been created during the history of the infant formula controversy.

3. Individual company codes are more effective than trade association codes because they can be consistently implemented and enforced within the organization. Trade association codes tend to be enforced unevenly, unless there are no legal barriers to collaborative enforcement procedures.

4. National government codes are easier to enforce than international codes, but the codes may be weaker because of intense national lobbying.

5. The lack of resources and political commitment is the greatest impediment to effective implementation of codes at the national level.

Each of these points deserves extended discussion that cannot be undertaken here. Let it suffice to say that the infant formula controversy has made clear that codes of conduct can be an important device to raise standards of ethical behavior in an industry, but that the path to an effective code at any level (firm, association, government, international agency) is fraught with pitfalls and traps.

Obviously, no code of conduct can reasonably be effective if its terms are continuously subjected to tortured reasoning and revision. Companies can view marketing codes as mere sops to a world of critics, instruments that are not to be treated seriously. Nonetheless, there are a number of reasons why the governments of developing nations, and the international agencies that are their advocate, will press the development of international codes much further in the next decade. Even the Reagan administration's concern that such codes will be a global straightjacket for U.S. enterprises is unlikely to halt further efforts. As Dr. Umali, Food and Agriculture Organization Regional Director, said when commenting on the reluctance of countries such as the United States to do more in the food and nutrition field, "The 'magic of the marketplace' usually works for those who have the muscle."[12] It is only through collective efforts, like international codes of conduct, to write equitable rules of the game that the poor can find real value, not illusions, in the marketplace.

Conclusion

The drive for effective consumer protection is growing in the developing world. Community groups are increasingly committed to monitoring the behavior and effects of business. They are placing political pressure on national governments for more aggressive consumer protection, and are playing a more prominent role in international forums. The infant formula controversy provides an important illustration of how grassroots concern for consumer interests can be translated into an effective international consumer movement.

International consumerism has two principal concerns: the appropriateness of products offered for sale, and the appropriateness of marketing practices used to promote the sale of products. New concepts are being articulated to translate consumer interests into public policy. Increasingly, commercial products will have to serve a public purpose defined within the framework of national policies. For multinational food companies, the prospects for further market development will be contingent on harmonious integration with national food and nutrition policies. Further, all companies will have to carefully define their legitimate market, more in terms of real public needs and less in terms of simple population size. Simple expansion of consumer choices will prove less and less satisfactory as a rationale for product introduction. Efforts to shape reasonable definitions of the legitimate market appear certain to increase as consumerism thrives in the Third World.

Finally, there will surely be new efforts to develop effective codes of marketing conduct. The most visible result of the infant formula controversy is the WHO/UNICEF code. It is a political document, laden with compromises and concessions to a multitude of interests. But it has institutionalized significant changes in the marketing of breast milk substitute and become a model of the type of effort that international organizations are likely to advocate as conflicts continue between developed world producers and Third World consumers.

These conceptual developments provide important tools for consumer advocates in the Third World. Consumer protection requires ideas, organization, and action. Concepts such as demarketing, public purpose, legitimate markets, and codes of conduct are likely to be the conceptual pillars of the movement in the 1980s. Consumer organizations at the community, national, and international levels are growing. And as the infant formula controversy demonstrates, this coupling of ideas and organization can produce real changes in the marketing of developed world products in Third World markets.

Notes

1. The Nestlé boycott was officially settled in November, 1984. Nestlé's policies are being overseen, in part, by an Audit Commission, chaired by former U.S. Senator and Secretary of State, Edmund S. Muskie.

2. An important exception is the WIC (Women, Infants, Children) Program, which provides nutritional supplements to the mother and baby before and after the birth of a child.

3. Beverly Winikoff, ed., *Nutrition and National Policy.* (Cambridge, Mass.: MIT Press, 1978).

4. Alan Berg, *The Nutrition Factor.* (Washington, D.C.: Brookings Institute, 1973).

5. The hearings represented a "third front" in the campaign, drawing into the fray the U.S. Congress, and ultimately, the Executive Branch. It was at the 1978 hearings that Nestlé's spokesman charged that the consumer boycott of Nestlé in the United States was "an indirect attack on the free world's economic system" and that a "worldwide church organization, with the stated purpose of undermining the free enterprise system, is in the forefront of this activity." U.S. Congress, Senate Committee on Human Resources, Subcommittee on Health and Scientific Research, *Marketing and Promotion and Infant Formula in the Developing Nations, 1978.* 95th Congress, Second Session (May 23 1978).

6. WHO/UNICEF, *Background Paper for Meeting on Infant and Young Child*

Feeding, Parts 1 and 2. (Geneva: World Health Organization, 1979).

7. Ibid., part 2, p. 45.

8. Ibid.

9. Ibid., p. 59.

10. Ibid., p. 61.

11. Ibid.

12. Statement by Dr. D.L. Umali, FAO Regional Representative for Asia and the Pacific, to the Meeting of Subcommittee on Nutrition of the United Nations Administrative Committee on Coordination, Bangkok, Thailand, February 15–19, 1982.

14
Consumerism and International Markets

Esther Peterson

In the publication *Consumerism and Beyond,* published in 1982,[1] I pointed to the tendency of the then relatively new administration to deemphasize domestic consumer protection programs of government. Essentially, I asked the American business community to fill the growing consumer protection void:

> Today when many are very nervous about the withdrawal of consumer programs within government and the withdrawal of funds for the support of consumer programs, we have to look to the business community more than ever before to uphold the progress that has been made. I see it as a tremendous opportunity for business to pick up the ball and carry it and to make innovative changes voluntarily.

In this update of consumer perspective in the 1980s, I will discuss the current posture of the United States toward international consumer protection measures, the face of U.S. consumerism abroad (if you will), and I will relate this aspect of U.S. foreign policy to a U.S. trade deficit that reached $123.3 billion in 1984. I will assume, without bothering to prove it, that there is some relationship between actions taken by the U.S. government in the field of international consumer protection and the openly expressed or informally conveyed policy desires of the American business community. In this discussion, I will refrain from my customary and comfortable habit of relating the actions of the business community to the needs of consumers, showing that business serves its needs for profit by strong and meaningful proconsumer actions and programs. I will instead relate this nation's international consumer protection posture solely to the needs of American business. I will also attempt to avoid any preaching about moral questions raised by official U.S. government actions, tempting though that is.

As most casual readers of the daily newspaper are aware, the United States is the only nation in the United Nations that voted against a resolution for creating an unbiased accurate reference on the legal status of various harmful products that are internationally traded—such a data source could be used, particularly by Third World nations, to protect their populace against unreasonably hazardous products.

Specifically, the United States cast the only dissenting votes against the development and publication of such a hazardous product list in separate actions taken in December 1982 and December 1984. These votes were consistent with an early action taken by the then-embryonic Reagan administration, which abolished an executive order that had been signed by President Carter as a means of domestically regulating the possible shipment of banned or otherwise hazardous U.S. products to foreign nations. In fact, the canceling of the Carter executive order is cited by some as being the stimulus for UN actions on this matter. An Office of Management and Budget (OMB) official, credited with killing the order for President Reagan, said the Carter order was "cumbersome, and it could lead to our products being discriminated against."[2]

Newspapers have also pointed out the singular U.S. opposition to the development, by the United Nations, of voluntary international guidelines for consumer protection. In April 1985, daily papers reported the April 9 vote in the United Nations—finally, after over six years—to approve the voluntary consumer protection code. The United States supported the resolution, but still raised several strong objections to the guidelines. Specifically mentioned in the newspaper stories was the continuing U.S. objection to the elimination, in the guidelines, of the word "unreasonable" as applied to risks or hazards of products, and its objections to the document's references to specific products or industries, such as food products and pharmaceuticals—the very subjects supporters of developing countries deemed the most important.

The U.S. alternate representative to the United Nations, Ambassador Allan L. Keyes, was quoted as saying:

> It would have been fairer and more balanced to omit mention of any specific products or industries particularly when we consider the relative importance of any product varies from country to country.[3]

Hopefully, this will be the last word from the administration in an unsuccessful war against the guidelines. For several years this war has been waged utilizing the traditional U.S. football tactics of "delay of game," "reversal of field," "appeal to the rule book," and finally (when all else failed), "punt." I believe this consistent policy of opposition to general (as opposed to specific) standards on international consumer protection is based on a misperceived notion of American business interests and is related to the apparently growing U.S. trade deficit.

United Nations' efforts to inform importing nations of potentially hazardous products, and its attempt (now successful) to adopt minimum international consumer protection guidelines, have been opposed by various officials in the State Department and the White House, and by assorted administration spear carriers. They would speak to—and presumably for—business, on the grounds that steps aimed especially at protecting consumers in Third World nations introduce policies alien to consumers in Western nations. President Reagan's first Chairman of the Council of Economic Advisers referred to these steps as "alien to consumers in Western nations that thrive on private markets and the principle of competition."[4] His assertions are totally mistaken, since most of the world-wide innovations in the field of consumer protection during this century can be traced to the actions of the fifty states of the United States and the U.S government. It was impossible for the United Nations to draft international consumer protection guidelines that were based on anything else but U.S. experience, practice, and innovation. Indeed, the guidelines are very familiar to U.S. marketers, since they are based on U.S. experience and policy. To what, then, does the reference to "alien policy" apply?

Apparently it refers to the fact that the original draft guidelines contained a provision stating that when new products are introduced, due account should be taken of prevailing local conditions and existing production, distribution, and consumption patterns. The U.S. delegation stated opposition to this provision and it was dropped completely from the final guidelines.

Is the idea of shaping marketing approaches to the norms or particular characteristics of a market completely alien to domestic consumer protection policy? I refer you to an analogous provision in the Federal Trade Commission Act, which defines deception of a consumer audience as "the capacity and tendency to deceive"[5] the consumer audience. Strictly speaking, under our own consumer protection policy, neither intent nor actual proof of damages is required to show deceptive advertising, once capacity and tendency to mislead are found to be present.

Thus, domestic advertisers in the United States must take consumers as they find them—all of their prevailing attitudes, prejudices, and even an occasional stupidity must be taken into account if advertisers are not to risk deceptive advertising abuses of that consumer. Since the incumbent chairman of the Federal Trade Commission has expressed dissatisfaction with that standard, one may assume that the standard is alien to certain beliefs held by certain officeholders within the administration, but it is inaccurate to say that the concept is alien to consumers in Western nations.

It is equally inaccurate to imply that U.S. exporting companies could not consider the prevailing attitudes, mores, and customs of the importing consumer populace when developing advertising and labeling for the exported goods. If we as a nation have problems in developing exporting expertise—and we do—we will find that we face more serious obstacles than complying with consumer protection policies that our own domestic marketers have been complying with for years. I believe a major reason for the opposition to this section of the guidelines was that the wording might limit the ability of the importer to sell products that a country may, for cultural or other reasons, prefer to keep out.

During the seemingly endless wrangling (I confess I use the term "nit-picking") over the UN's hazardous export-product list and consumer protection guidelines, the point was made (more than once on the U.S. side) that UN consumer policy ought not to penalize the few successful U.S. exporting industries. This argument suggests that, since we have some success in exporting pharmaceuticals, pesticides and high-tech items, we would be the nation most hurt by the institution in Third World nations of consumer protection standards that would provide readily accessible information about defects in such products, so that countries could investigate and learn why they were banned and deemed hazardous. In other words, consumer protection for Third World nations would harm what economists call an existing U.S. comparative advantage. This argument implies that support of international consumer protection standards is perhaps un-American, and certainly violates or injures U.S. economic interests, in that we need to grasp tightly our existing market shares in order to redress the current imbalance of trade with other nations—even though it goes against our established policies and practices in the United States.

I cannot believe that our present comparative advantage in certain products depends upon exploiting Third World ignorance regarding hazardous or defective products. Certainly the $123.3 billion trade deficit is not going to be made up by exporting inadequate or second-class products or services. Our leading exporters know that such a practice is the best way to lose their comparative advantage. Redressing the imbalance depends upon our ability to gain a comparative advantage in other goods and services.

Contrary to conventional wisdom, the United States is not suffering from a skyrocketing increase in its imports. Actually, we are importing slightly less than we did in 1980. Our problems as an exporting nation lie principally in the fact that U.S. exports, as a percent of U.S. production, are falling (12.9 to 10 percent since 1980) and we are importing more of the kinds of goods that U.S. industries manufacture.[6] In other words, foreign consumers seem to prefer the quality and price of foreign-manufactured goods over U.S. products.

There seems to be a consensus among the experts that curing our export problems depends upon our ability to address the problem of the price of U.S. goods (which is fundamentally related to the exchange rate of the U.S. dollar versus foreign currencies, and ultimately to budget deficits) and to improve the quality of U.S. goods for export.[7] In short, fundamental domestic economic problems are at the root of our continuing trade imbalances, and these imbalances will be unaffected by increases or diminutions in international consumer protection standards.

Parenthetically, I might add that the pesticide and pharmaceutical industries faced increasingly stringent domestic consumer protection regulation in the United States during the 1960s and 1970s, and yet were able to achieve economic successes. Suggesting that their success abroad depends on a lack of consumer protection does a disservice to both industries. In fact, a policy of acquiescing to high consumer protection standards domestically, while opposing such standards internationally, would create a schizoid personality for U.S. multinational corporations.

In what the economist Robert J. Samuelson refers to as "global matchmaking," U.S. multinational corporations increasingly have been joining their former foreign competitors in joint ventures of various sorts. The General Motors–Toyota joint venture to produce small cars is merely one of many examples of what Samuelson refers to as:

> A dizzying array of private alliances, joint ventures, supplier agreements and technology licenses. This is the face of the future, and alien although it seems, it's probably desirable. These mixed marriages should speed the production of better products and technologies in both countries.[8]

Well, the fact is that those foreign companies and their countries of origin, which support the international consumer protection efforts of the UN, have learned to live with high U.S. consumer protection standards and now increasingly are partners with U.S. multinational companies in proliferating international joint ventures. Business life with our new partners would be difficult, if not impossible, were we and they to exhibit fundamentally conflicting policies towards international consumer protection.

Indeed, the success of increasing joint international business ventures is dependent upon the growing tendency to internationalize consumer protection standards. American business discovered this lesson in the United States during the 1960s and 1970s.

In the history of consumer protection growth in the United States during this century, the American business community was at first opposed to the imposition of federal consumer protection standards. Ostensibly, they preferred the development of state consumer regulations as an alternative. However, when activist states began to enact a multiplicity of differing consumer protection laws and regulations, the American business community supported uniformity through the imposition of federal consumer protection measures—a uniformity that would ultimately decrease business costs. I remember well that when I was Vice President for Consumer Affairs for Giant Food, we had difficulty meeting different standards in different states we served. I am encouraged when I see chief executive officers opening doors to our consumers through consumer awards programs. For the good of both business and consumer, this is a constructive change. Therefore, to oppose uniformity in international consumer protection programs, while our joint-venture partners support it, not only presents problems in the joint-venture family, it is also inconsistent with and apparently ignorant of the lesson that the same companies have learned in the United States. And it is inconsistent with the historical posture of American business towards foreign governmental policies.

For many years American business leaders have decried the disparity of playing rules imposed by foreign governments upon U.S. corporations trying to do business abroad, as opposed to the rules applicable to home-country companies. We have longed for a level playing field that would permit us to compete on equal terms with foreign competitors. Now, as those foreign competitors learn the playing rules under U.S. consumer protection policies and can live with the development of those same policies in Third World nations, the U.S. government's actions suggest that U.S. industry requires one set of playing rules in the United States and a more lenient set of rules in Third World nations. We do need a level playing field and uniformity of playing rules, and the attainment of those goals will hasten our ability to redress current trade imbalances. Opposition to international consumer protection guides and standards reflects a lack of readiness to accept global marketing principles and strategies, and presents the worst kind of sales message abroad. In Bangkok, I was recently asked about Senator Hatch's legislative proposal that would relax existing law in order to permit export of unapproved drugs. As an unofficial representative of my country I was asked: Why are you denying us the very protections that have proved useful in your own country?

Even long-time consumer protection advocates will concede that some product injuries, mistakes, and even tragedies are an inevitable byproduct of the world's increasingly complex technology. Indeed technology, including telecommunications technology, magnifies the effect of such tragedies. While the United States has a history of opposing the elevation of consumer protection standards for Third World nations, the occurrence of the product injuries abroad will inevitably raise charges that there is a cause and effect relationship between the past U.S. business opposition to protecting foreign consumers and the subsequent disaster. I believe this kind of international marketing reputation will ensure our inability to redress trade imbalances. For obvious reasons U.S. business does not project such an image in domestic markets, and should not project such an image abroad. I agree with the view, "Bhopal has tended to say to people that we need to be a little more responsible."[9]

Despite a temporary bipartisan romance with the concepts of regulatory reform and regulatory relief in Washington, D.C., during the early 1980s, no bipartisan coalition has emerged to press for the repeal of the panoply of consumer protection standards created in the 1960s and 1970s. There has been no rollback of consumer protection and environmental legislation in the United States.

Indeed, scandals related to the politicizing of the Environmental Protection Agency, the Occupational Safety and Health Administration, and other agencies have spawned a bipartisan chorus calling for increased social regulation of American practices. The pendulum has, in short, begun to swing back towards vigorous enforcement of consumer, job, and environmental protection in the United States. Friction between the Congress and the White House over delays in regulatory protection imposed by OMB is increasingly evident. Indeed, Republican and Democratic members of Congress complain that the White House is impairing Congress's ability to protect the Constitution by hamstringing Executive Branch regulators in a cost–benefit theology that is not recognized in the statutes created by Congress nor upheld by federal courts.

What the administration has been unable to present to business in the United States under the heading of regulatory reform, it has had no better success in achieving in international forums. In its attempts to gain regulatory reform in the United Nations, the U.S. government has been destroying a long-standing, favorable impression of the United States held by foreign consumers and international consumer organizations.

"Made in the United States," U.S. quality, and U.S. standards of consumer protection used to be an international trademark that guaranteed both site of origin and quality of origin to foreign consumers. The U.S. policy of opposing consumer protections for Third World consumers is destroying that international trademark. The U.S. government should have been using foreign admiration of our consumer protection standards and leveraging foreign inclinations to promote the kind of international consumer protection standards that would enhance our technology advantages. "Made in America" should be a mark of quality, not a warning. The Young Commission (headed by John A. Young, president of Hewlett-Packard Company) has said that the ability of U.S. firms to export goods and services abroad successfully and to outpace imports into this country is dependent upon our ability to leverage our few comparative advantages in the quality of the technology used for the invention and development of commercial products and in the slight advantage represented by the quality of American workmanship. It would make sense to stress these exporting advantages in the development of international consumer protection standards. Instead our posture has been one of completely opposing the development of consumer protection standards in Third World nations.

We may be weary of the problems of Third World nations and more than a little irritated at their use of international forums to oppose the colossus of Uncle Sam. However, Third World nations get 40 percent of U.S. exports, and to alleviate our $123.3 billion trade deficit requires an expansion of our trade to them. While UN votes have sometimes provoked anger and outrage in our citizenry and business community, in a world growing smaller at a dizzying rate, the UN is a tool to do a job that must be done.

In the United States, the American business community did not have to love labor in order to make peace with labor. U.S. business does not have to love the United Nations to participate in rationalizing international consumer protection standards and guides for Third World nations. Since the standards are being asked for by Third World nations, which we need as trading customers, then the standards will come anyway, either in a balkanized form or in a form that capitalizes on our comparative advantages in technology.

Again, assuming that the American business community has some role in influencing or perhaps even shaping the U.S. government's policy towards international consumer protection standards, the business message so far has been radical—alien to sound marketing principles. Our nit-picking of drafts of consumer protection standards and our insistence that no attempt be made to help Third World nations implement standards paint a picture of a mean-spirited Uncle Sam, one who blocks attempts at new protection for Third World consumers and who continues to show a lack of grace in defeat when unable to get his way in the international debate. No doubt the candid recognition by American business people that the Bhopal tragedy requires U.S. industry to stand up and be counted on international consumer protection standards helped to shift what had been outright opposition by the United States government to the consumer protection guides to a final position of grudging support for the final form of the guides—with the reservations noted above.

What have we learned from these public relations disasters for our international marketing hopes? I think the message is: Denying what we enjoy here to Third World nations does not make a coordinated trade policy. As Senator Danforth recently told the National Press Club, we need a "thorough study of what has gone wrong in international trade and what the Administration intends to do about it." The Senate Democratic Committee on Trade recently came to the same conclusion.[11] The position of the United States government on international consumer protection guides and standards is related to the U.S. trade imbalance and is related in the worst possible way.

Notes

1. Paul N. Bloom, ed., *Consumerism and Beyond.* (Cambridge, Mass.: Marketing Science Institute, Report No. 82–102, 1982).

2. "Bhopal Tragedy Rekindles Debate on Hazardous Exports," *The Washington Post,* (Jan. 6, 1985) p. K1.

3. "U.N. Adopts Consumer Protection Code," *The Washington Post* (April 11, 1985), p. E4.

4. *Private Business and Public Policy, International Barriers to Commerce,* Weidenbaum & Fejfor 10th Anniversary. St. Louis, Mo.: Center for the Study of American Business, Washington University, p. 44.

5. Douglas F. Greer, *Business, Government and Society.* (New York: Macmillan, 1983), p. 274.

6. "Slogans Blur Trade Picture," *The Washington Post* (April 8, 1985), p. A26.

7. "We're Being Killed by the Dollar (A Report on the Business Council Meeting at Hot Springs)," *The Washington Post* (May 12, 1985), p. 1.

8. Robert J. Samuelson, "The Value of Global Matchmaking," *Newsweek* (Jan. 14, 1985), p. 63.

9. Ibid.

10. "Economic Weaknesses Seen Hurting U.S. Industry in Global Competition," *The Washington Post* (Feb. 17, 1985), p. E6.

11. "Senate Republicans and Democrats Agree on Trade Talks," *The Washington Post* (April 26, 1985), p. D1.

Part IV
The Response of Business

15
Competing in the Consumerism Industry: Strategies for Success

Paul N. Bloom

T his paper focuses on how marketing can help consumer affairs professionals. I believe that some approaches used today by marketers can be of great service to the consumer affairs profession. These approaches come from a branch of marketing we call social marketing, or the area of marketing concerned with selling ideas and social behaviors. Consumer affairs offices can use some of these approaches in consumer education and other programs to sell ideas and behaviors to targeted consumers. Consumer professionals should be able to compete more successfully in the "consumerism industry" by adopting these approaches.

But before I elaborate on why consumer professionals should all embrace marketing, let me first provide some background on why I have come to believe in marketing's importance to consumer affairs. Specifically, I would like to begin by reviewing a few of the ideas that Stephen Greyser and I have developed about where the consumer movement, or industry, is going over the next few years (Bloom and Greyser 1981a; 1981b).

The Maturing of Consumerism

The research Stephen Greyser and I have conducted over the last few years has led us to propose that consumerism has matured, and that a very different, but still vital, movement will exist for the foreseeable future. Our basic thesis is that the consumer movement has gone through a life cycle, not unlike that of a consumer or industrial product, and that the movement now stands and can be expected to remain in a mature state of this cycle. In the movement's introductory stage, the Procter and Gamble of consumerism, Ralph Nader, began to stimulate demand for consumerism, with the help of just a few other charismatic leaders like Betty Furness and Esther Peterson. The cycle then went through a growth stage, when Nader added some raiders and began successfully selling a wide variety of consumerist products (like new laws, new forms of representation, and new educational programs) in the emerging consumerism industry. Finally, the movement entered a mature stage, when it became more fragmented and diverse, and countless numbers of public and private consumer affairs and consumer protection offices came on the scene to serve the public's demand for consumerism. In essence, the movement has followed a life cycle pattern similar to what we have seen with instant coffees, running shoes, and fast-food outlets.

So like other mature, fragmented industries, the consumerism industry now has all different types of organizations selling all different types of products in all different types of ways to all different types of customers. Competition has evolved among these organizations for money, volunteers, media coverage, and, most importantly, public opinion. Some of the competition, as in any industry, is quite friendly, while some of it is actually hostile. The latter form of competition arises especially when different organizaitons try to sell differing ideas about remedies for consumer problems. Liberal consumer organizations want one thing, while more conservative trade associations or industry groups—who also compete in this industry—want something else.

How long can industries stay in a mature, fragmented state? As long as consumer demand remains strong enough, industries can stay in this condition for quite some time before they enter a decline stage of the life cycle. We believe that the demand for consumerism—or, more precisely, the demand for a better overall deal from the marketplace—remains and will remain strong in the United States. Public opinion polls consistently indicate considerable dissatisfaction among consumers with their situation in the marketplace and sustained support for consumer protection initiatives. The American public has been telling pollsters, at least, that they want consumer protection and that they are even willing to pay good tax dollars to get more of it.

I see these results as being compatible with another important notion in the Bloom-Greyser predictions: that the vitality of consumerism will come less from the activities of the traditional national consumer groups and more from the activities of smaller, grassroots organizations and individual activist consumers. As we have put it, the old spectator consumerism will be gradually replaced by participant consumerism. And, I predict that corporate consumer affairs offices will play a major role in this transformed movement, by serving the needs of the many participants now playing the consumerism game.

A Call for Attention to Marketing

With this research in mind, I believe that most consumer affairs professionals need to think very seriously about how to compete effectively in this transformed consumerism industry. How can a consumer affairs office do a better job of selling ideas, services, and other offerings than competing organizations (both friendly and unfriendly)? As in any mature, fragmented industry, the most successful competitors will be the ones that do the best strategic planning and marketing. In other words, the most successful consumer affairs offices will be the ones that analyze opportunities, develop sound objectives, determine thoughtful marketing strategies, carefully plan and execute those strategies, and, overall, exhibit a farsighted marketing orientation.

But before elaborating on how consumer affairs professionals can use marketing to great advantage, I should clarify exactly what consumer affairs offices sell and to whom they sell. In other words, what are the products and markets?

Consumer affairs offices perform four major functions—correspondence handling (including complaint handling), consumer education, internal advising, and external relations—and are therefore primarily involved with selling ideas to various publics. Many others are involved in selling services, like redress assistance, and some offices are also involved in selling products, such as consumer education materials. But even these activities entail, to a large extent, the selling of ideas. In a sense, consumer affairs offices compete in a war of ideas with numerous other organizations.

In selling ideas, the markets for consumer affairs offices consist primarily of consumers, management personnel in firms and external consumer groups. To consumers, the offices try to sell ideas like:

1. Complain when you have something legitimate to complain about—don't keep silent.
2. Complain to the company's consumer affairs office before you complain to government or media complaint-handling organizations.
3. Use consumer information to help you make better buying decisions.
4. Use products safely.
5. Engage in healthy behaviors—eat nutritiously, exercise regularly, drink in moderation, and so on.

To managers, who tend to feel that consumerists are responsible for a lot of the regulatory red tape they find themselves wrapped up in, consumer affairs offices try to sell ideas like:

1. Use complaint data and other data compiled by the consumer affairs office to guide you in your marketing and management decisions.
2. Modify products, services, advertising appeals, credit policies, and other aspects of the company to be consistent with the desires of consumers and consumer activists.

To consumer groups, consumer affairs offices try to sell ideas like:

1. Cooperate with the company's educational or social service programs.
2. Consider the company's point of view before you decide to attack it publicly on a consumer issue.

And I am sure that many consumer affairs professionals sell ideas that I failed to mention to still other types of markets.

Suggestions from Social Marketing

Selling ideas may be the most difficult form of selling there is. Unlike selling things like vacuum cleaners and cosmetics, it is impossible to readily demonstrate how well an idea cleans or how beautiful it will make someone look. More importantly, people tend to be very resistant to many of the ideas consumer affairs professionals have to sell. Many people don't like to be told that they should eat differently, exercise more, use products more safely, or manage corporations more responsibly.

Fortunately, a few notions from the field of social marketing can help sell ideas more effectively. The social marketing field is concerned with how to sell ideas like getting blood pressure checked, taking hypertension medication regularly, doing breast self-examinations, or limiting consumption of alcoholic beverages. The field has become a reasonably well-defined subdiscipline of marketing—that is, people teach courses on it and books and numerous journal articles have been written about it.

In my opinion, six notions from social marketing have particular relevance to consumer affairs professionals. These are:

1. Segment, target, and differentiate—based on research.
2. Use intermediaries and personal communications.
3. Reduce time costs.
4. Build credibility.
5. Pretest materials.
6. Document results.

These notions do not come solely from the field of social marketing—all marketers have used these ideas. But social marketers have, in my view, found it most important to remember these six notions in running programs similar to those with which consumer affairs people tend to get involved.

In reviewing these six notions, I will primarily be considering about how they can help sell ideas to individual consumers. However, I will also mention how they can help sell ideas to managers and consumer groups.

Segment, Target, and Differentiate

It is a basic marketing tenet that you go after markets with rifles and not shotguns—that trying to sell the same thing in the same way to everyone is foolhardy. Good marketing involves carving up potential markets into homogeneous segments, selecting or targeting the most desirable segments, and developing relatively unique programs for each targeted segment, so that to each segment these programs look different from what competitors are selling. All of this should be done with the guidance of carefully conducted research studies on the characteristics, beliefs, preferences, and so forth of the people in the targeted markets.

This very basic marketing advice is frequently forgotten when ideas are marketed. The marketers of ideas are often convinced that their ideas are so attractive that everyone will accept them once fully exposed to them. Such marketers fail to remember that people vary widely in their inclination to accept a given idea; they overlook the possibility that the idea will sell better if it is packaged, distributed, and promoted in different ways to different groups of people.

The most successful programs for marketing ideas are essentially multiple programs. They use fundamentally different marketing approaches to sell the same basic idea to different segments. For example, men are encouraged to use contraceptives in one way—as in the famous British advertisement showing a pregnant man—and women are encouraged in other ways. Blacks are urged to take steps to detect cancer early with one set of messages and materials, and other segments are urged to do the same with totally different messages and materials. A County Health Improvement Project in Lycoming County, Pennsylvania, urges some community groups to eat better and exercise more with one set of support materials, and it urges other groups with other sets of materials.

The message for consumer affairs professionals is clear. Do not expect to have much of an impact on people's thinking and behavior by approaching them in a uniform manner. Pamphlets, audiovisuals, and other materials should not be designed for everyone. Develop different programs for different target segments.

Use Intermediaries and Personal Communications

Selling ideas often requires the transmission of large amounts of information. And, consistent with the need for multiple approaches, sometimes it is necessary to make this information reasonably individualized. It is therefore often highly desirable to use personal communication to sell ideas. Personal communication is generally more persuasive than media communication: it is harder to say no to someone confronting you personally—no matter what is being said—than to a broadcasted or printed message.

Recognition of the value of personal communication has led social marketers to place great emphasis on locating intermediaries who can pass the word in a personal way to targeted individuals. Most social marketing programs do not have the resources to hire a sales force to do personal selling. The better programs have worked extensively with church groups, community organizations, hospital staffs, and individual healthcare practitioners to assure that personal selling is done. Kits (like a "Helping Smokers Quit Kit"), training sessions, and other support materials are typically provided to intermediaries to help them with their selling task.

The practice of using intermediaries and personal communications has been adopted in a number of consumer affairs programs. Sunbeam, Corning, and General Foods have all worked actively with consumer groups in programs designed to pass the word about the safe use of products and about nutrition. This, by the way, is also a good way to improve relations with consumer groups, making it easier to sell other types of ideas to them in the future.

In addition, consumer affairs offices can serve as intermediaries themselves, providing support for government and nonprofit programs in areas like breast cancer education, high blood pressure education, and seat-belt usage. Consumer affairs professionals can help to pass the word to employees of their companies and to their companies' customers. Such activities can help build a company's credibility with the public—an important task that I will discuss in more detail.

Reduce Time Costs

Social marketers recognize that people are more likely to buy an idea that involves some action if that action is not time consuming to perform. If the cost in terms of time of accepting an idea is too high, then people will simply not act. Thus, social marketers do everything they can to reduce the time costs to their prospective buyers, and they also try to reduce any monetary costs. For example, the use of 800 telephone numbers in programs like the cancer information programs is done to reduce the time and monetary costs of cancer prevention. And various kits and manuals have been designed in other programs, like antismoking compaigns, to make it easier and less time consuming for people to act.

Consumer affairs professionals have, of course, recognized the value of reducing time costs, as demonstrated by the way they have flocked to provide 800 numbers or various "cool" and "hot" lines. A desire to reduce time costs for consumers also seems to be behind developments like Cornings's "Kitchen Survival Kit" and, most recently, General Electric's "Quick Fix" program. This program makes it less time consuming for consumers to get their malfunctioning products fixed promptly and properly, rather than filing a complaint or lawsuit after the malfunction has caused an accident.

The importance of keeping time costs low is of particular importance in complaint-handling activities. If consumer affairs offices want people to complain when they have legitimate complaints—and I think the offices should want this—then it is in everyone's best interests to resolve complaints as quickly a possible. As the research from the consulting firm, TARP (1979) has shown, complainers are more likely to buy the company's products again than noncomplainers. And complainers who have had their complaints resolved quickly are considerably more likely to buy the company's products again than complainers who have had their complaints resolved slowly or not resolved at all.

Build Credibility

Communication researchers have long recognized that messages delivered by high-credibility sources are more persuasive than those delivered by low-credibility sources. Recognition of this principle has led social marketers to try to get highly credible people like doctors, nurses, cured patients, and certain celebrities to serve as communicators or spokespersons.

For consumer affairs professionals this means that they have to do everything possible to build consumers' faith and trust in the company and its consumer affairs officials. If people trust a company, they are more likely to buy what it is selling. People shouldn't think consumer affairs actions are intended to save face or achieve purely public-relations objectives. People should believe that consumer affairs programs are being run because of a deep, sincere interest in consumer welfare.

Giant Food established its credibility in the eyes of consumers by hiring Esther Peterson to run a strong-willed consumer program, and this program has flourished ever since. Giant Food's credibility was built so high that they were able to weather the storm of protest that came when they removed the price-markings from individual items. Other companies like American Express have increased their credibility by engaging in socially responsible ventures like donating to certain charitable causes every time the American Express card is used. Still other companies have built their credibility by setting up consumer panels and by sponsoring major conferences—Corning, Penney's, and Chesebrough-Pond's have pursued this last route.

Pretest Materials

When a lot of creative energy has gone into the development of communications materials—and everyone in the organization is very enthusiastic—it
is very tempting to start using the materials without first pretesting them on
people from the target audiences. This has been a particular problem with
many of the government social marketing programs, on which they have
spent large sums for developing and producing pamphlets and public service
announcements and hardly anything for pretesting whether people compre-
hend and like the messages.

The Department of Health and Human Services, under President Carter,
sought to remedy this problem by setting up a Message Testing Service that
pretested broadcast spots produced by the department. Copy testing procedures used widely in the advertising industry were employed. Among other
things, norms were developed that could be used to indicate whether a spot
was likely to perform better than an average spot. Unfortunately, this program was eliminated under the Reagan administration.

I believe that consumer affairs offices should spend some money pretesting their materials on small samples of people from the targeted audiences.
At the very least, they should have representatives from consumer groups
look over the material before it goes into final production. Such representatives might be able to point out glaring shortcomings or weaknesses before it
is too late to do anything about them.

Document Results

The message here is: evaluate what you are doing. Social marketing programs
that are able to show their sponsors and supporters numbers indicating what
they have accomplished are the programs that seem to keep getting funded.
Evaluation data has also helped these programs fine-tune and redirect their
activities. A good example of a program that has benefited greatly by constantly evaluating itself is the National High Blood Pressure Education Program. By constantly showing Congress and others that the number of hyper-
tension-related deaths has declined steadily since the program began, they
have kept the program's financial support at a strong level. Their evaluation
data also helped guide them several years ago toward a decision to shift from
emphasizing getting blood pressure checked to emphasizing the regular taking of medication.

Evaluations are time consuming, expensive, and, quite frankly, risky for
consumer affairs professionals (or anyone) to do. But I think it is essential
for consumer affairs offices to try to develop numbers that reflect the effectiveness of complaint handling and other activities. I have no magic answers

to how to develop useful measures of effectiveness but TARP (1979) has offered a few suggestions in this area.

I would, however, like to offer one suggestion about self-evaluations: think small! Consumer affairs offices should not try at first to come up with one global index that will provide the bottom line on performance. Instead, they should somehow try to evaluate, using sound methodologies, small segments of their programs. For example, I have seen this successfuly done in the social marketing arena, with a small program set up to have nurses teach women patients breast self-examination. A well-designed experiment indicated great success for the program and the results of the experiment have been extremely useful for formulating other programs.

Conclusion

Effective use of principles from the field of social marketing can help consumer affairs professionals compete more effectively for the hearts and minds of consumers, consumer group leaders, and corporate officials. The application of some relatively straightforward marketing logic can produce substantial results. I believe the most successful consumer affairs programs of the future will be ones that adopt a strong marketing orientation.

References

Bloom, Paul N., and Stephen A. Greyser, 1981a. *Exploring the Future of Consumerism.* (Cambridge, Mass.: Marketing Science Institute, Report no. 81–102, July 1981).

Bloom, Paul N., and Stephen A. Greyser. 1981b. The maturing of consumerism. *Harvard Business Review* 59 (Nov.–Dec.: 130–139).

TARP, Inc. 1979. *Consumer Complaint Handling in America: Final Report.* Washington, D.C.: U.S. Office of Consumer Affairs.

16
Corporate Public Responsibility: A Marketing Opportunity?

Meredith M. Fernstrom

A great deal has been said and written in recent years about the phenomenon of corporate public responsibility, corporate social performance, or corporate citizenship (only a few of the labels by which it has been described). Just what is a company's public responsibility?

Some, like the noted economist Milton Friedman, argue that "the business of business is business," pure and simple. Business serves society by producing jobs and creating products and services; its ultimate goal and objective is the maximization of profit. It answers to no one above its owners or stockholders. Similarly, some observers say that it is enough for companies to obey the laws, to produce safe products, not to pollute the environment, to avoid fraud and deceit, and so on—that compliance with such standards is full evidence of a company's public responsibility.

But is that all there is to it? In today's complex and demanding society, are those the only actions we have a right to expect from the business community? I would suggest that such basic corporate acts as complying with the law, creating jobs, and promoting the goods and services we would like to consume are taken as givens, as the very minimum we expect from business today. Above that minimum level of performance, we have come to demand a great deal more responsibility from the private sector as a corporate citizen of the communities in which it operates.

As one very successful businessman, Ken Dayton, Chairman of Dayton-Hudson Corporation, put it:

> Fundamentally, we believe business exists for only one purpose: *to serve society*. Profit is our reward for serving society well. It is the means and measure of our service, but it is not the end.

This view was echoed by Irving Kristol, noted professor of business at New York University:

> Corporations are not merely economic mechanisms created by legal fiction. . . . They are also institutions rooted in real communities; they have an

implicit obligation to be good citizens of these communities and—most important—it is in their interest to be institutions of good standing in those communities.

There are many economic, political, and social trends that point to the fact that the role of corporations in society is increasing in the 1980s and will continue to do so throughout the remainder of this century.

These trends suggest that U.S. business is becoming a logical inheritor of America's social and cultural conscience. Such trends include, first, the growth of business. Today, the top 500 corporations in the United States employ over 14 million people. Considered as families, this represents a significant portion of the population. Second, social relationships and affiliations in American society have changed in recent years. In 1983, over 17 percent of the total U.S. population made a household move—which translates into 38 million moves. Imagine what effect this trend is having on the sense of belonging to local neighborhoods. At the same time, traditional neighborhood institutions have decreased in membership and influence. For example:

Membership in the Boy Scouts and Girl Scouts decreased for years during the late 1960s and 1970s; only very recently has membership begun to rise again.

Church membership in several major denominations has gone down in the last decade or so, and many religious observers see the influence of organized religion on the wane in the United States.

Membership in trade unions is also slackening.

Finally, the smaller "Mom and Pop" businesses have virtually disappeared from the American landscape; the corner drug store is now the local branch of a huge, standardized national chain.

These and similar trends have had significant effects on the ways we relate to, and communicate with, each other. They have frustrated people's need for involvement and participation in the major aspects of their lives, including social and commercial relations.

With the loss of neighborhoods, the breakdown of local affiliations, the rapid growth of corporations, people are beginning to look to business firms to satisfy at least part of their need for involvement and fulfillment in their lives. People who work for corporations are looking for a sense of belonging, a kinship, in their professional lives; and customers are expecting more from corporations than simply an occasional commercial transaction. While there

may be debate about the appropriateness of corporate philanthropic donations, and while people both in and out of business may continue to formulate new concepts of corporate public responsibility, we all should recognize
that society now expects corporations to play social as well as business roles
in their relations with employees, customers, and the community at large.

This discussion about corporate philanthropy and citizenship becomes
more immediate and topical when we consider the current status of the funding of social and cultural programs in the United States. Cutbacks in government funding for social and cultural causes have created huge shortfalls in
financial support for many worthwhile organizations and programs. This gap
is not narrow; it is on the order of $30–40 billion dollars. According to one
estimate, corporations would need to increase their rate of giving to 15 percent—from their traditional 1 to 2 percent of pretax earnings—to begin to
make up this deficit. Given this fact, it is very important to underscore the
fact that U.S. corporations—even if they were to use all their assets—could
not realistically address the most basic social problems in the country.

So we have a paradox: while corporations alone cannot hope to do the
job required, the basic rationale for corporate philanthropy is that corporations are among the most powerful and wealthy institutions in our society—
so they must do something to help. And we believe that business can do much
more, both conventionally, and especially in new, undiscovered ways. Equally
important, it has been our experience that we can do *well* for our companies
while doing *good* for society.

At American Express, we believe that the pursuit of the proper corporate
objective of making a profit need not be in conflict with—although it is different from—the public interest. We have found that a significant, largely
unexplored overlap exists between corporate interests and public interests;
and we are seeking innovative ways to exploit that commonality. To do this
means viewing our social responsibility not as an afterthought or as an ad-
junct of the business, not as a gesture solely to be given in cash; rather, our
goal is to instill social responsibility as an integral part of every aspect of our
business. Let me describe briefly how American Express carries out this mandate, and give you a few examples of some of our recent projects.

First, I will quickly review our organizational structure for public responsibility. The Office of Public Responsibility is the central coordinating
body for our various policies and programs, but we also rely heavily on a
decentralized approach, encouraging specific attention to these programs in
each of the line units and at the local management level. The Office of Public
Responsibility includes the Consumer Affairs Office, which provides consumer information and serves as the in-house consumer advocate; and the
Executive Consumer Relations Unit, which handles consumer inquiries and
complaints received in the executive offices.

The office also coordinates our two Public Responsibility Committees: a committee of the board of directors and one of senior management, representing all parts of the company. Together, these committees develop our public responsibility policies and oversee their implementation in areas such as: the advancement of women and minority employees, minority business development, the protection of customer and employee privacy, employee volunteerism, our policy on South Africa, and similar issues in which the public interest intersects with or is affected by our business practices.

Another major component of our public responsibility program is the American Express Foundation, through which we provide a sizeable amount of financial support to a variety of philanthropic organizations around the world. In 1984, our grants budget totaled approximately $8.5 million; in 1985, it is $11 million. These funds are allocated more or less equally among organizations or projects in the areas of health and welfare, education, arts and humanities, and civic and community service. In the area of health and welfare, for example, approximately 15 percent of our total grants budget goes to the United Way. (This is, of course, over and above the personal contributions of our employees.) We also allocate a significant portion of the foundation's funds to grants in major U.S. cities and foreign countries, so that local management can respond to local community needs.

But we believe we have much more than just cash to give. We are also sharing our employees' time—through numerous employee volunteer activities—and our executives' expertise through various forms of technical assistance. For example, one of our subsidiaries, Shearson Lehman/American Express, provided a grant to the Agency for Child Development in New York, to help launch a pilot day-care project for nonsubsidized families. More important than the grant, however, was the management advice our executive provided to the agency in legal, tax, accounting, and marketing skills. The goal of the project is to expand the availability of licensed day care, while also training entrepreneurs how to establish day-care businesses.

We also frequently provide "in-kind" services to nonprofit organizations when contributions are not available or appropriate. This type of service includes the use of some of our facilities for community group meetings, donations of used equipment, or contributions of graphic arts services. For instance, our audiovisual department produced a promotional film for the Burden Center for the Aging in New York, which the center will use for its fund-raising efforts.

Finally, we tap our creative marketing expertise to promote philanthropic causes and leverage support from other sources. For example, in the "cause-related marketing" program of the American Express Travel-Related Services Company, a small sum is donated to a selected cause each time one of our products is purchased or used. In late 1983, we contributed $1.7 million to the restoration of the Statue of Liberty through a national cause-related marketing campaign. We also helped bring a number of foreign athletes to the

1984 Olympics through similar campaigns in Mexico, Japan, and other countries. The cause-related program has been implemented in dozens of U.S. cities and in countries around the world.

Through such programs, we have demonstrated how our company can do well by doing good. For example, during the Statue of Liberty campaign, we experienced a 45 percent increase in the number of new card members and a 28 percent increase in card usage over the same period the previous year.

Many other companies are seeing similar benefits from implementing aggressive, strategic public responsibility programs tied to their marketing objectives. Control Data is a notable example of how fulfilling society's needs can represent profitable business opportunities. During the last fifteen years, Control Data has moved six new plants to inner-city locations, employing more than 1,500 workers, with the intention of developing new markets in these communities. It also joined with twelve other Minneapolis–St.Paul firms in organizing "City Venture Corporation," a for-profit planning and development service to encourage small businesses to locate in the inner city. Control Data created a housing renovation business that refurbishes and resells run down inner-city dwellings for small down payments and low interest rates.

Numerous other companies are finding ways to address social problems with both cash and noncash assistance. Here are just a few examples:

Some California banks handle the accounting for some nonprofit institutions, even if they don't keep their funds in those banks.

An insurance company based in Washington, D.C., has donated money and expertise to untangle local voter lists.

A gas and electric company in Kansas, working with the Red Cross, established a program that allows customers to add a dollar to their monthly bills to help defray costs for the elderly.

A Baltimore radio station bought a diner, and with the help of private donations, is converting it into a teaching restaurant for high school students.

Aetna Life & Casualty has an aggressive minority banking program, in which it deposits $6 million in below-market CDs with 60 minority-owned banks across the country and through which it makes $156 million of Treasury tax and loan payments annually.

General Mills offers the use of its telephone bank to nonprofit organizations for fund-raising purposes.

Safeway Stores donates all edible but unsalable food items to local food banks, and also prints promotional messages for nonprofit groups on their grocery bags.

Target Stores has a nationwide program with Goodwill Industries in which it donates unsalable or returned merchandise and vendor samples in over sixty-five cities. Target and Dayton-Hudson Corporation host "senior citizen shopping nights," in which they provide transportation, free entertainment, and a discount on all purchases.

These are just a few of the many creative ways that companies are addressing community needs, and at the same time meeting their own business objectives. A *Wall Street Journal* editorial spoke precisely about this need for creative approaches to public responsibility:

> Where business can contribute most is in thinking about social problems in practical, entrepreneurial get-the-job-done ways. About how to make money by setting up plants in inner cities. Or how to improve vocational training in local school systems. Or how to lower the cost of transportation and housing and healthcare. Or how to share financial expertise and knowledge of economic opportunities with local governments. . . . Many businessmen already do these things and those that do them well usually find it makes good business sense to do so.[1]

It is clear that no corporation, regardless of its size, can exist today as a purely economic entity. Corporations affect—and are affected by—their employees, customers, shareholders, and the physical and social environment in which they operate. The most fundamental tenet of good corporate citizenship is providing quality prooucts, fair prices and integrity of service, before and after the sale. Building on this foundation, business has an enormous opportunity to contribute to human development and social well-being among its diverse constituencies. And best of all, in this game everybody's a winner.

Note

1. "Limits of Voluntarism," *Wall Street Journal* (Feb. 9, 1984).

Index

Italic numbers refer to pages of reference entries.

Future, consumerism in evolving, 3–15;
business response to, 13–14;
consumer response to projected
conditions, 6–7; environment and,
19–20; historical relativism and,
18–19; likely areas of activity, 21–
22; local organization activity and,
7–13; "malarial economy" and, xiv,
4–6; marketing mix and, 20–21;
marketplace and, 6; predictions for
1990s, 17–22

Gardner, J., 24
Gaski, J.F., 78, *82*
Gelb, B., 103, *111*
Gender: activism and, 92; attitudes
toward business and, 80
General Electric Company, 197
General Foods, 196
General Mills, 205
General Motors-Toyota joint venture,
183
Gerbner, G., 102, *111*
Giant Food, 197
"Good life," pursuit of, 9
Goodwill Industries, 206
Government: marketing, 153–164;
response to scarcity issues, 43–44;
special services issues for, 52–54,
55. *See also* Public policies
Government Accounting Office (GAO),
156
Grabicke, K., 87, *95*
Graduated-payment mortgage plans,
157
Grassroot organizations, effectiveness
of, 68–69. *See also* Local
organization activity
Great Britain, 143, 145
Greer, D.F., 187*n*.5
Greyser, S.A., xv, *xviii*, 31, *35*, 56*n*.1,
57*n*.28, 61, 68, 70, 73, 85, *95*, 123,
127, 162, *163*, 191, 192, *199*
Grievances, 91, 158–159
Griffith, B.C., 105, 108, 109, *110*
Gross, L., 102, *111*

Habicht, E.R., Jr., 33, *35*
Handler, J.F., 29, 34*n*.6, *36*
Harrell, G.D., 82*n*.2, *83*

Harrington, M., *111*
Harris, L., 56*n*.1, 62–64, 65, 70, 73,
81, *83*
Hatch, Senator, 184
Hayflick, L., 105, 111
Hazardous product list, U.N., 179–
181, 182
Health care issues, 21, 39, 45–46, 106–
107; insurance, 107–108
Heard, right to be, 38, 39, 158–159,
160
Hearing impairments in the elderly, 106
Hennon, C.B., 99, 102, *111*
Herrmann, R.O., 61, 73, 85–87, 91, *95*
Hispanic consumers, 114–117
Historical relativism, 18–19
Hodges, L., 124, 128
Holsworth, R.D., 27, *36*
Horowitz, I.L., 30, *36*
Household: composition, changes in, 8;
production, shift to, 9–10
Housing and Urban Development,
Department of, 157
Housing Inspection Department,
Boston, 160
Howard, 99
Hustad, T.P., 75, 81, *83*

Ideology, 28–30
Immunity, sovereign, 161
Inactive group, 89–93
Income: activism and, 92–93; attitudes
toward consumerism and, 65;
changes in relative, 41; increased
focus on, 10–12; instability of the
disadvantaged consumer's, 115–
116; maldistribution of, 4–5; per
capita real vs. median real
household, 5–6
Induced scarcity, 42, 44
Infant formula controversy, 166, 169–
176
Inflation, 4, 41, 119
"Infomercials," 145, 149
Information: commercialization of,
139–143; dealing with abundance
of choice and, 45, 46; demand for
improved consumer, 7; elderly
consumers' use of, 105; generated
through regulation, 39–40;

About the Contributors

Alan R. Andreasen is visiting professor at the Graduate School of Management at UCLA. His early work on consumerism and disadvantaged consumers resulted in the book *The Disadvantaged Consumer*. More recently, he has focused on issues of consumer satisfaction/dissatisfaction and federal regulation.

George T. Baker III is director of the Center on Aging at the University of Maryland, College Park, one of the largest educational research programs in this country. His primary biomedical research activities have involved molecular-genetic alterations in a non-mammalian system, but his diversity of activities and general knowledge of the fields concerned with aging have led to his involvement in this area as well. He holds numerous committee positions, in both the private and public sector, directly related to the quality of life of the elderly. In particular, he has been involved in programs dealing with the older worker, and more recently, with the area of technology and aging.

Ben M. Enis is a professor in the Marketing Department at the University of Southern California. He has written several books, including *Marketing Principles, The Marketing Research Process, and Personal Selling*. In addition, he has contributed a number of research papers to such publications as *Journal of Marketing, Journal of Marketing Research, Journal of Advertising Research, Journal of Retailing, California Management Review,* and *Business Horizons*. He serves on the Editorial Review Board of the *Journal of Marketing*. Dr. Enis has been a consultant to organizations in functional services, retailing, building materials distribution, healthcare, consumer goods manufacturing, publishing, and government.

Michael J. Etzel is professor of marketing at the University of Notre Dame. He has a BBA from the University of Portland, MBA from Kent State University, and DBA from the University of Colorado. Professor Etzel has published in the *Journal of Marketing Research, Journal of Marketing, Journal of Consumer Research,* and *Journal of Retailing,* among others. His primary area of research interest is consumer decision making.

Meredith M. Fernstrom is Senior Vice President—Public Responsibility, of American Express Company, where she oversees a variety of policies and programs to ensure the company is responsive to the needs of its customers, employees, and communities. Ms. Fernstrom joined American Express in 1980 as Vice President—Consumer Affairs. She served as Director of Consumer Affairs in the U.S. Department of Commerce from 1976 to 1980, where she was also a member of the White House Consumer Affairs Council. Ms. Fernstrom is president of the International Society of Consumer Affairs Professionals in Business and is a director of the National Consumer League, the Metropolitan New York Better Business Bureau, and the International Consumer Credit Association. She served a three-year appointment to the Consumer Advisory Council of the Federal Reserve System.

John F. Gaski is assistant professor of marketing at the University of Notre Dame. His degrees include a BBA and MBA from Notre Dame, and an MS and a PhD from the University of Wisconsin at Madison. Dr. Gaski's primary research interests are power and conflict in channels of distribution, and the social impact of marketing. His research has been published in the *Journal of Marketing,* the *Journal of Marketing Research, Business Horizons, Psychology and Marketing, Social Behavior and Personality,* and *The Journal of European Economic History,* as well as in proceedings of the American Marketing Association and the Association for Consumer Research.

Philip A. Harding is vice president, Office of Social and Policy Research, CBS/Broadcast Group. Prior to joining CBS, he was with the research department of the National Association of Broadcasters and before that held advertising and marketing research positions with Dancer-Fitzgerald-Sample, Inc. Since 1973, he has been the CBS Trustee of Marketing Science Institute, an independent center for research in marketing. In 1984, he was named chairman of the institute's Executive and Research Policy Committee. Mr. Harding is also department editor of *Public Opinion Quarterly* and a member of the editorial boards of the *Journal of Advertising Research* and *Psychology & Marketing.* He holds a BA in psychology from Lehigh University and an MA in social psychology from Rutgers University.

Robert O. Herrmann is professor of agricultural economics at The Pennsylvania State University. He has collaborated with Dr. Warland on a number of studies of the consumer movement and food choice behavior. His other professional interests include the improvement of consumer education programs.

Mary Gardiner Jones is the president of the Consumer Interest Research Institute, a nonprofit organization devoted to the analysis of public policy issues from the consumer perspective. A practicing lawyer, Ms. Jones has also served as a Federal Trade Commissioner, a professor of law and business at the University of Illinois, and a Vice President of Consumer Affairs at Western Union Telegraph Corporation. Ms. Jones is a trustee of Wellesley College, and a board member of several public policy institutes and of two major American corporations.

Edward J. Metzen is professor and chair of family and consumer economics at the University of Missouri, Columbia. He has been involved in a variety of professional and organizational activities in the consumer movement since the 1950s. His experiences and service include ten years as executive director of the American Council on Consumer Interests (ACCI), as well as president and board member of ACCI; steering committee for the Consumer Federation of America; founder of the Missouri Association of Consumers; education advisory committee for Consumers Union; policy and editorial boards for several journals; board of directors of the American Home Economics Association, and chair of the Family Economics—Home Management Section of AHEA.

Robert Cameron Mitchell, a sociologist, is a senior fellow at Resources for the Future, a Washington-based nonprofit research organization specializing in resource, energy, and environmental issues. Dr. Mitchell has conducted extensive studies of environmental public opinion and the environmental movement, the results of which have appeared in journal articles and book chapters. More recently he has been developing ways to use survey research to measure the benefits of water pollution and risk reduction improvements for benefit/cost analysis.

Dan E. Moore is associate professor of rural sociology at The Pennsylvania State University. He has a long-standing interest in citizen participation at the state and local level. Currently he is involved in a study of the effectiveness of the transfer of agricultural technology by the agricultural technology delivery system.

Esther Peterson is a well-known name in the consumerism movement. She spearheaded Giant Food's consumerism thrust and was adviser to the President on consumer affairs during 1976–1980. She is now the representative working for the National Consumers' League.

James E. Post is professor at the School of Management at Boston University. He is interested in international consumerism and a respected expert in the Nestlé infant formula controversy.

Lee E. Preston is a professor and director at the Center for Business and Public Policy at the University of Maryland. He was a staff economist with the Council of Economic Advisors during the Kennedy administration, and has been a consultant to private firms and public agencies on a wide range of business and policy issues. Dr. Preston's publications include: Private Management and Public Policy (with James E. Post, Prentice-Hall, 1975); "Corporate Social Accounting-Reporting for the Physical Environment" (With Meinolf Dierkes), *Accounting, Organization and Society;* and "Analyzing Corporate Social Performance:Methods and Results," *Journal of Contemporary Business.*

Stewart Lee Richardson, Jr. is a professor and G. Maxwell Armor Eminent Scholar in the Department of Marketing at the University of Baltimore.

Darlene Brannigan Smith is a PhD candidate in marketing and an instructor at the University of Maryland. She received her BS and MBA degrees from the University of Baltimore. Ms. Smith has published papers in the *Proceedings of the Association for Consumer Research and Industrial Marketing Management.* Her primary interests are in the area of public policy and consumer behavior. Current research activities include an empirical examination of the Federal Trade Commission's Advertising Substantiation Program.

Rex H. Warland is professor of rural sociology, Department of Agricultural Economics and Rural Sociology at The Pennsylvania State University. In addition to his research on the American consumer movement, his recent projects include developing a model to explain food behavior and an investigation of the use of nonadditive models in sociological research.

Dean L. Yarwood is a professor of political science at the University of Missouri at Columbia. He is the editor of *The National Administrative System: Selected Readings* and has contributed articles to several professional journals. His recent articles have appeared in such journals as *Administration and Society, Judicature, Policy Studies Journal,* and the *Public Administration Review.*

About the Editors

Paul N. Bloom is professor of business administration at the University of North Carolina at Chapel Hill. He has written extensively on consumerism and related subjects and serves as the editor of the series *Advances in Marketing and Public Policy,* published by JAI Press. He spent the 1980–81 year as Visiting Research Professor at the Marketing Science Institute and taught at the University of Maryland for ten years. He holds a PhD in marketing from Northwestern University, an MBA from The Wharton School of the University of Pennsylvania, and a BS from Lehigh University.

Ruth Belk Smith is an assistant professor of marketing at the University of Baltimore. She has researched the elderly consumer for the past five years, publishing a number of papers and articles on the subject and coordinating several special sessions on elderly consumers at national academic conventions.